Britain and the American Revolution

Edited by
H.T. DICKINSON

Longman
London and New York

Addison Wesley Longman Limited
Edinburgh Gate,
Harlow, Essex CM20 2JE,
United Kingdom
and Associated Companies throughout the world.

*Published in the United States of America
by Addison Wesley Longman, New York.*

© Addison Wesley Longman Limited 1998

First published 1998

ISBN 0–582–31861–0 CSD
ISBN 0–582–31839–4 PPR

Visit Addison Wesley Longman on the world wide web
at http://www.awl-he.com

British Library Cataloguing in Publication Data

A catalogue entry for this title is available from the British Library

Library of Congress Cataloging-in-Publication Data

Set by 35 in 10/12pt Baskerville
Produced by Addison Wesley Longman Singapore (Pte) Ltd.,
Printed in Singapore

Contents

Preface

This collection of essays offers readers a more detailed and rounded single-volume study of Britain and the American Revolution than is at present available. In marked contrast to the numerous studies of America during the revolutionary decades, there are surprisingly few single-volume works on this subject and those that are available generally either end in 1776 with the American Declaration of Independence or focus on the War of Independence between 1775 and 1783. Only two books attempt to cover the whole period. The oldest is Ian Christie's *Crisis of Empire* (1966). It covers the years from 1775 in less than fourteen pages, and is less than half the length of the present study. Keith Perry's *British Politics and the American Revolution* (1990) is as short, is not based on any original research and even ignores some of the major secondary sources. It is very limited in its approach, being essentially a narrative account of the actions of successive British administrations, and it is erratic and error-prone. The present book, on the other hand, explores in greater depth than most others not merely the colonial policy of the British government and the war against the rebellious colonies, but the ideological debate, the British critics of government policy in and out of parliament, the diplomatic situation, the impact of the American crisis on Ireland, and the consequences of the loss of the American colonies.

I have long been interested in Britain and the American Revolution and taught the subject many years ago, but other tasks and interests prevented me devoting sufficient research time to publish on the subject. Sabbatical leave and the great privilege of being appointed as the Douglas Southall Freeman visiting professor at the University of Richmond, Virginia, in 1997, has allowed me time to do some serious research on Britain and the American Revolution. I am very grateful to those who endowed this professorship and to Professor John Gordon, chair of the History Department at Richmond, and all his staff and colleagues there, as well as those students who took my course at Richmond, for making my stay there so enjoyable and fruitful. It is enormously stimulating to work in the academic environment of the United States and the American Revolution is an endlessly fascinating topic.

For many years now I have been advised on the research of American historians working on the colonial side of the American crisis by my colleague Dr Alan Day. Another colleague, Dr Frances Dow, has read with great care the drafts of my work throughout my many years at Edinburgh University, has improved all that I have written, and has had a major impact on all I have done.

While I am responsible for two chapters in this collection and for planning the whole volume, I have been extremely fortunate in the quality of my fellow contributors. They are all major and very busy scholars, but they were ready to accept my suggestions about the shape of their contributions and they all submitted their essays on time – a rare event for such collaborative ventures. Andrew MacLennan in the Academic Department at Addison Wesley Longman offered encouragement at the right time and showed faith in this volume. I can only hope this was justified.

Harry Dickinson
Edinburgh University

List of Abbreviations

Add. MSS	Additional Manuscripts
AHR	*American Historical Review*
BJECS	*British Journal of Eighteenth-Century Studies*
BL	British Library
Burke's Corr.	Thomas W. Copeland et al., eds, *The Correspondence of Edmund Burke* 10 vols (Cambridge, 1958–70)
Burke's Writings and Speeches	Paul Langford et al., eds, *The Writings and Speeches of Edmund Burke* 9 vols (Oxford, 1981–98)
Corr. of George III	Sir John Fortescue, ed., *Correspondence of King George the Third from 1760 to December 1783* 6 vols (London, 1927–8)
EcHR	*Economic History Review*
EHR	*English Historical Review*
HJ	*Historical Journal*
HLQ	*Huntington Library Quarterly*
HMC	Historical Manuscripts Commission
JAH	*Journal of American History*
JBS	*Journal of British Studies*
JICH	*Journal of Imperial and Commonwealth History*
JMH	*Journal of Modern History*
NLI	National Library of Ireland
Parliamentary History	William Cobbett, ed., *The Parliamentary History of England . . . to the Year 1803* 36 vols (London, 1806–20)
PH	*Parliamentary History*
P&P	*Past and Present*
PRO	Public Record Office
PSQ	*Political Science Quarterly*
TRHS	*Transactions of the Royal Historical Society*
WMQ	*William and Mary Quarterly*

List of Contributors

JAMES E. BRADLEY graduated as a history major at Pasadena College before going on to a BD at Fuller Seminary and a PhD at the University of Southern California. He has been teaching at Fuller Seminary in Pasadena for more than twenty years, and has been a full professor since 1990. He is at present the Geoffrey W. Bromiley Professor of Church History. He is the author of *Popular Politics and the American Revolution in England: Petitions, the Crown, and Public Opinion; Religion, Revolution, and English Radicalism: Nonconformity in Eighteenth-Century Politics and Society; Church History: An Introduction to Research, Reference Works, and Methods* (with Richard Muller); and articles in learned journals. He is currently working on a book on religion in the English Enlightenment.

JOHN A. CANNON, CBE, is Emeritus Professor of Modern History at the University of Newcastle upon Tyne. He graduated from Cambridge University and gained his PhD at Bristol University, where he taught for many years before going to Newcastle as professor. He is the author of *The Fox–North Coalition: Crisis of the Constitution, 1782–4; Parliamentary Reform 1640–1832; Aristocratic Century: The Peerage of Eighteenth-century England; Samuel Johnson and the Politics of Hanoverian England;* editor of *The Letters of Junius; The Historian at Work; The Whig Ascendancy; The Blackwell Dictionary of Historians; The Oxford Illustrated History of the British Monarchy;* and *The Oxford Companion to British History;* and a contributor of numerous essays to books and journals.

STEPHEN CONWAY graduated from the University of Leeds and then studied under the supervision of Ian Christie and gained his PhD at University College London, where he is now a Reader in the History Department. He is the editor of several volumes of *The Correspondence of Jeremy Bentham* and the author of *The War of American Independence 1775–1783*, as well as of articles on different aspects of the American conflict in various learned journals. He is in the final stages of a book exploring the impact of the war – political, economic, social and cultural – on Britain and Ireland.

JOHN W. DERRY retired in 1998 as Professor of Modern British History at the University of Newcastle upon Tyne, where he had taught for twenty-eight years. A Cambridge graduate, he was previously a Research Fellow of Emmanuel College, Cambridge, a Lecturer at the London School of Economics, and a Fellow and Director of Studies at Downing College, Cambridge. He has published widely on major themes connected with British history in the eighteenth and early nineteenth centuries. His books include: *The Regency Crisis and the Whigs; William Pitt; Charles James Fox; Castlereagh; English Politics and the American Revolution; Politics in the Age of Fox, Pitt and Liverpool;* and *Charles, Earl Grey.*

HARRY T. DICKINSON is a former student at Durham and Newcastle universities. He has taught at Edinburgh University since 1966 and has been Richard Lodge Professor of British History since 1980. He has also been a Concurrent Professor of Nanjing University, China, since 1987. He is the author of *Bolingbroke; Walpole and the Whig Supremacy; Liberty and Property in Eighteenth-Century Britain; British Radicalism and the French Revolution 1789–1815; Caricatures and the Constitution 1760–1832;* and *The Politics of the People in Eighteenth-Century Britain;* the editor of *The Correspondence of Sir James Clavering; Politics and Literature in the Eighteenth Century; The Political Works of Thomas Spence;* and *Britain and the French Revolution 1789–1815;* the editor of the journal *History,* since 1993; and a contributor of essays to many books and journals.

KEITH MASON was educated at Oxford University, received his doctorate at the Johns Hopkins University, Baltimore and is now Lecturer in American History at the University of Liverpool. He was recently a New World Comparative Studies Fellow at the John Carter Brown Library, Brown University. He has contributed articles on the socio-political history of British North America and the Caribbean to several journals, including the *Journal of Southern History* and the *Virginia Magazine of History and Biography.* He is currently engaged on two books: *The American Revolution* and *Slavery and Emancipation in North America, the British West Indies, and Haiti.*

FRANK O'GORMAN studied at Leeds and Cambridge universities and has taught at Manchester University for more than thirty years. He has held a Personal Chair there since 1992. He is the author of *The Whig Party and the French Revolution; Edmund Burke: His Political Philosophy; The Rise of Party in England; The Emergence of the British Two-Party System, 1760–1832; British Conservatism: from Burke to Thatcher; Voters, Patrons and Parties: The Unreformed Electorate of Hanoverian England, 1734–1832*; and *The Long Eighteenth-Century: British Political and Social History, 1688–1832*; and he has contributed a large number of essays and reviews to learned journals and periodicals.

HAMISH M. SCOTT was educated at the University of Edinburgh and the London School of Economics. He has taught at the universities of Birmingham and St Andrews, where he is at present a Senior Lecturer in Modern History. He is the author of *The Rise of the Great Powers 1648–1815* (with Derek McKay) and *British Foreign Policy in the Age of the American Revolution*; the editor of *Enlightened Absolutism: Reform and Reformers in Later Eighteenth-century Europe; The European Nobilities in the Seventeenth and Eighteenth Centuries* (2 vols); and *Royal and Republican Sovereignty in Early Modern Europe: Essays in Memory of Ragnhild Hatton* (with Robert Oresko and G.C. Gibbs); and has contributed numerous articles to learned journals. He has recently completed *The Emergence of the Eastern Powers: Prussia, Russia and the Reorientation of European Diplomacy 1756–75*; and he is the general editor of 'Cambridge Studies in Early Modern History' and Addison Wesley Longman's 'Modern Wars in Perspective'.

NEIL L. YORK earned his doctorate at the University of California, Santa Barbara and is at present Professor of History and Director of the American Studies program at Brigham Young University, Provo in Utah. He is the author of *Mechanical Metamorphosis: Technological Change in Revolutionary America* and *Neither Kingdom Nor Nation: The Irish Quest for Constitutional Rights, 1698–1800*; and the editor of *Towards a More Perfect Union: Six Essays on the Constitution* and *Maxims for a Patriot: Josiah Quincy, Junior, and His Commonplace Book*. He has recently completed a book on the infamous arsonist, 'John the Painter', and he is currently studying failed federal solutions to the American crisis, 1774–5.

Introduction

H.T. DICKINSON

The American Revolution was the first great modern revolution and it has arguably been the most permanent, successful and widely admired, if not the most profound and destructive. It certainly led in time to the oldest surviving written constitution in the world, to a remarkably successful liberal political regime, to the most dynamic economy and to the strongest nation state on earth. Not surprisingly, such a major event, which led directly to the founding of the new United States of America, has received the attention of a host of American historians concerned to understand its causes, course and immediate consequences. With regard to the causes of the revolution, the problem has been to explain why the British colonists in North America reacted so swiftly, consistently and effectively to British policies which fell well short of the oppressive measures that usually provoke a colonial people to rebellion. Historians have had to dig below the surface of political events – such as the Stamp Act, the Townshend duties and even the coercive legislation of 1774 – in order to understand why the American colonists came to see these relatively limited infringements on their lives and liberties as a profound constitutional challenge that merited a Declaration of Independence and a long war to secure that independence. Why did the colonists have such a tender regard for their liberties, why were they so afraid of arbitrary power, and why did they interpret such modest tax burdens as an assault on their constitutional rights? To answer such questions, historians (Americans in particular) have stressed the internal tensions within the colonies, have explored the economic, social and especially the political advances made by these dynamic colonies in the century after the Glorious Revolution of 1688, and have examined the religious, ideological and material

1

reasons for colonial resentment against British imperial policies and agents in the American colonies.

In contrast, far fewer historians (even British historians) have explored in depth the motives and deeper justifications for the imperial policies that were pursued by successive British governments and were widely supported in parliament and the nation at large. This, in part, may be because the British case ended in defeat. But it is also because more British historians have been interested in purely internal British affairs – the aims of George III, the succession of short-lived administrations in the 1760s, the career of John Wilkes and the nature of the emerging radical movement – than in Britain's imperial policies in North America. Even when the British side in the dispute with the American colonies has been explored in depth – as in Peter Thomas's fine volumes[1] – the British case has been explained primarily as a problem in practical politics rather than as an issue about motivation, argument and justification. Apart from the volumes by Thomas, there are only a handful of other modern works by British historians that focus directly on Britain's relations with the American colonies. Like Thomas's works, their explorations of British actions usually end with the American Declaration of Independence in 1776. Those historians who have examined the topic beyond 1776 have mainly started and finished with the War of Independence. Here too, we can find many more works written by American historians on the military campaigns fought by the rebellious colonists in North America. Even more American historians have devoted their efforts to the making and ratification of the new Federal Constitution after the War of Independence and to the ideological debates that these efforts engendered. By contrast, no British historian has made any detailed study of the consequences for Britain of its defeat in the war for America.

The nine chapters in this book cannot hope to do full justice to all aspects of Britain's involvement with the American colonies during the crisis of the American Revolution and they cannot be expected to redress the historiographical balance when such a heavy preponderance of work on the revolution has focused on events and attitudes in the colonies. They do, however, seek to explore the most important aspects of Britain's involvement in the American crisis. They seek to explain why the British–colonial link was unsatisfactory

Unless otherwise stated, the place of publication of all books cited in the notes is London.
    1. Peter D.G. Thomas, *British Politics and the Stamp Act Crisis* (Oxford, 1975), *The Townshend Duties Crisis* (Oxford, 1987) and *Tea Party to Independence* (Oxford, 1991).

by the beginning of the 1760s; why the British perception of that relationship was different from that of the colonists; why successive British administrations and majorities in parliament supported policies that proved fatal to British power in the colonies; what sympathy or support there was for the American case in Britain; why Britain's diplomatic, military and naval efforts proved inadequate to the task of forcing the colonies to submit to British policies; and how the loss of the colonies influenced developments in Britain in general and Ireland in particular.

British attitudes to the colonies

The American Revolution has often been explained as a brave and justified colonial defence of American liberties in response to a determined and insistent British effort to impose its imperial authority on the colonies. While there is clearly much truth in this approach, it is often based on the claim that before Britain adopted such aggressive policies in the 1760s the relationship between Britain and the American colonies had been stable, harmonious and mutually beneficial in almost every respect. In other words, many historians, in adopting this approach, have tended to accept the judgement of those American colonists who protested that they were loyal and obedient British subjects until they were driven first to protest, then to resist, and finally to rebel, because of the determined efforts of successive British administrations to destroy their liberties and to undermine a satisfactory status quo. From this perspective, there would have been no American crisis in the 1760s and 1770s if only Britain had refrained from introducing and seeking to enforce measures that the colonists found so damaging to their interests. Historians who have been influenced by this approach do not deny that the colonists would have secured their independence at some future date, but, they maintain, if it had not been for the unwise and unjust measures adopted by the British government at this time, the American colonies would probably have gained their independence much later and by peaceful means through the slow erosion of British power and influence and the gradual growth of a distinctive political and social culture in the colonies. The problem with this interpretation of the American crisis is that it implies that all the colonial demands were reasonable and just, and that Britain could have solved the crisis by abandoning its oppressive and unconstitutional policies. All of these suppositions have been challenged by some American historians[2] and they are all further undermined by the chapters by Mason, Derry and Dickinson below.

Relations between Britain and the American colonies were not as stable, beneficial, harmonious and acceptable to both sides as has often been supposed before Britain appeared to destroy this status quo by its legislative innovations of the early 1760s. Rather, the situation in both Britain and the American colonies throughout the earlier eighteenth century was fluid and unstable, and the constitutional relationship between Britain and the colonies was shifting and ill-defined. It was Britain's determined efforts to stabilize what it perceived as an unsatisfactory relationship, rather than its efforts to destroy a harmonious status quo, that provoked a crisis in its relations with the American colonies. As Keith Mason clearly demonstrates in Chapter 1, the American colonies experienced rapid and profound change on almost all fronts – demographic, economic, social and political – from the late seventeenth century onwards.[3] These developments enabled the colonies to develop political institutions of considerable strength, confidence and sophistication. By the mid-eighteenth century the colonial assemblies had become the principal vehicles through which the provincial elites could exert their authority and the colonists could protect their rights and privileges. Like the Westminster parliament, the colonial assemblies held two crucial levers of power: the right to vote on taxes and expenditure, and the right to initiate legislation. The colonial assemblies were also more representative of the inhabitants of the colonies in general because a higher proportion of adult males there could vote than was the case in Britain. The colonial assemblies therefore had the means and the moral authority to place effective limits on the power of the crown's agents and officials in the colonies. During the American crisis, whereas Britain insisted that these legislatures were subordinate to the Westminster parliament, the colonists proceeded to develop powerful and persuasive arguments which stressed that the colonial assemblies were the only legitimate representatives of their rights and interests. In the

2. See, for example, Robert W. Tucker and David C. Hendrickson, *The Fall of the First British Empire: Origins of the War of American Independence* (Baltimore, MD, 1982), pp. 67–73; and Jack P. Greene, *Peripheries and Center: Constitutional Developments in the Extended Polities of the British Empire and the United States, 1607–1788* (Athens, GA, 1986), chs 3–5.

3. See also Jack P. Greene, 'An uneasy connection: an analysis of the preconditions of the American Revolution' in Stephen G. Kurtz and James H. Hutson, eds, *Essays on the American Revolution* (Chapel Hill, NC, 1973), pp. 32–80.

end they were prepared to declare their independence rather than accept that the British parliament could tax and legislate for the colonies.[4]

For its part, Britain too had experienced rapid change after the Glorious Revolution of 1688 as it developed a new constitution (based on a much stronger and more active parliament), improved its economy, increased its overseas trade and maritime strength, and established a large, world-wide empire. By the end of the Seven Years War in 1763 Britain possessed a vast global empire; in North America alone, she had colonies stretching from Canada to Florida and from the Atlantic seaboard to the Mississippi river. And yet, as Keith Mason also makes clear, Britain's actual power and imperial authority in North America were surprisingly weak. Royal governors could do little without the financial support and goodwill of the colonial assemblies. Imperial authority rested in essence on the consent of the colonists. The British army was scattered across a vast tract of territory and it was too small to perform all the defence tasks required of it; it was certainly inadequate to impose British policies on the colonies by force of arms. The Royal Navy too was too small and overstretched even to prevent widespread smuggling by the colonists and its warships could obviously exercise very little influence inland.

Britain had gone to war with France in the mid-1750s in order to defend its very considerable commercial and strategic stake in North America. The vast new possessions she had secured during the Seven Years War offered the prospect of immense commercial and strategic benefits in the long run, but, in the short term, they imposed huge military and financial burdens on shoulders already overloaded by the efforts of the recent fighting. Britain's reasonable desire to reduce these burdens, by restricting American colonial expansion into the new territories to the west and by requiring the colonists to bear some of the financial burden of imperial defence, raised the whole question of what constitutional authority and what legitimate power Britain possessed in the colonies. Recent experiences had taught British ministers that their imperial authority in the colonies rested on very shaky foundations and that the crown's agents and officials in the colonies lacked the finances, influence and force needed to bolster their local authority.

4. Jack P. Greene, 'Competing authorities: the debate over parliamentary imperial jurisdiction, 1763–1776' *PH* 14 (1995), pp. 47–63; and Richard R. Johnson, '"Parliamentary egotisms": the clash of legislatures in the making of the American Revolution' *JAH* 74 (1987), pp. 338–62.

The explanation for British weakness in the colonies was due in part to the recent growth in the power and influence of the colonial assemblies, but it was also due to the absence of an accepted constitutional relationship that clearly defined the rights of the colonies and the authority of the imperial power. During the earlier eighteenth century the British policy of 'salutary neglect' – of very little interference in the internal affairs of the American colonies – had allowed the colonists to develop their own political institutions to such an extent that they came to regard their legislative assemblies as the local equivalents of the Westminster parliament and as the principal guarantor of their rights, liberties and property. 'Salutary neglect' enabled these assemblies to become established by custom and sanctioned by accepted usage. In Britain, meanwhile, the Westminster parliament had greatly expanded its own role in the political life of the nation and the political elite there had become steadily more attached to the constitutional doctrine that ultimate sovereignty lay with the king-in-parliament.[5] Few men of influence in Britain doubted that parliament's sovereign authority extended over the American colonies and, so long as this authority was restricted to the regulation of Atlantic trade and the control of the colonies' external relations, few colonists challenged this perception. They did not yet perceive that parliament was a threat to their own legislative institutions. Thus, in the earlier eighteenth century, both the colonies and Britain were developing distinctive notions of the power and authority of their respective legislatures without clearly defining the precise constitutional relationship between the Westminster parliament and the colonial legislatures.

By the late 1740s, however, British ministers and officials were becoming very conscious of the immense commercial and strategic value of the American colonies and, moreover, of Britain's inability to control the internal affairs of the colonies. They responded, as Keith Mason shows below, by promoting a new and reasonably systematic campaign to bring the colonies under closer supervision by attempting to reduce their autonomy and to remodel their constitutions. These efforts were not pursued with sufficient vigour at this time to become effective, though they did provoke colonial resentment and suspicion.[6] During the Seven Years War British ministers and crown agents in the colonies witnessed further encroachments on royal authority by the colonial assemblies and

---

5. H.T. Dickinson, 'The eighteenth-century debate on the sovereignty of parliament' *TRHS* 5th series, 26 (1976), pp. 189–210.

6. Greene, *Peripheries and Center*, ch. 3.

lamented what they regarded as the inadequate colonial response to demands for men and money to fight the French. The colonists, for their part, resented and resisted the impositions that the British military attempted to impose upon them.[7] When Britain defeated the French and acquired new colonial possessions, British ministers were even more convinced that the colonies ought to bear a fair share of the imperial burden, whereas the colonists saw even less need for the British army now that French forces had been removed from the continent.

This conviction led the British government to embark on a policy of interfering in the internal affairs of the colonies and imposing internal taxes on the colonies in order to help defray a portion of the costs of imperial defence. As my own chapter and that by John Derry make clear, British ministers thought these policies were entirely fair and reasonable, and the overwhelming majority of peers and MPs were convinced that parliament possessed the constitutional authority to pass such measures. They were genuinely surprised at the scale of the resentment that their actions provoked in the American colonies. There were various reasons for this surprise. Few British ministers or politicians had any deep understanding of the real situation in the colonies and most made little effort to repair their ignorance. This was partly because they were preoccupied with political events in Britain and distracted by ministerial instability and popular protest movements there. The difficult political problems they had to face at home meant that the colonial situation was rather low down their list of priorities. William Bollen reported in 1759 that he found many British officials 'either wholly strangers to the nature of the colonies (one of the chief of them having frankly told me he was shamefully ignorant of them) or under some prejudice concerning them'.[8]

Those in Britain who did have first-hand or detailed knowledge of the colonies were often either critical of the colonists or had little influence on the government's American policy. Many of the British civil, military and naval officers who had served in the American colonies, particularly during the Seven Years War, returned to Britain with a jaundiced view of the American colonists. They criticized the colonists for profiteering during the war (even to the extent of trading with the enemy), for seeming incapable of burying their

7. Alan Rogers, *Empire and Liberty: American Resistance to British Authority 1755–1763* (Berkeley, 1974), pp. 124–34.

8. Quoted in Michael G. Kammen, *A Rope of Sand: The Colonial Agents, British Politics and the American Revolution* (Ithaca, NY, 1968), p. 92.

mutual antagonism and rivalry, and for failing to provide sufficient
men and money to bolster the British military effort against France.
Many British regular soldiers viewed the colonists with condescension
bordering on contempt: as selfish, grasping and even unpatriotic.
To them the colonists wanted all the benefits of the imperial link
with Britain, but were unwilling to bear any of the burdens.[9] Within
parliament about forty to fifty MPs had personal knowledge of or a
direct interest in the American colonies, but very few of these men
showed any great sympathy with the colonies.[10] Within the British
government there were experts on colonial affairs, particularly in
the Board of Trade and Plantations, but some of these experts
shared the military's prejudice against the colonists and favoured a
policy of tighter imperial control over them. John Pownall, the
permanent secretary to the Board of Trade, who had seen service
with the board since 1741 and who was a brother of Thomas Pownall,
former governor of Massachusetts, had the greatest influence over
the government's American policy in the 1760s, but he was not a
great friend of the colonies. Indeed, Benjamin Franklin wrote of
him in December 1766: 'America has rarely, for many years past,
had a friend among them [the Board of Trade]. The Standing
Secretary seems to have a strong bias against us, and to infect them
one after another as they come to it.'[11] Even if British officials were
expert and well disposed to the American colonies, they found
it difficult to influence government policy because there was no
coherent machinery of empire and those subministers with the
greatest knowledge often lacked significant political leverage.[12]

To confound matters even further the colonists lacked direct
representation in parliament and could only endeavour to lobby
ministers and MPs in their efforts to have the colonial case heard at
Westminster. The colonies had come to recognize the need to lobby
at Westminster, but the agents they employed were unable to deflect the British government from pursuing and parliament from
supporting the imperial policies of the 1760s and early 1770s. Each
colony had its official representative in London by the 1760s, but
sometimes the same man acted for more than one colony, and
sometimes colonies had more than one agent. By the time of the
Stamp Act crisis there were eighteen colonial agents in London.
The agents' room for manoeuvre was circumscribed by the written

9. Douglas Edward Leach, *Roots of Conflict: British Armed Forces and Colonial Americans, 1677–1763* (Chapel Hill, NC, 1986), pp. 76–166.

10. Thomas, *Stamp Act Crisis*, p. 31.   11. Quoted in ibid., p. 26.

12. See ibid., ch. 2; and F.B. Wickwire, *British Subministers and Colonial America
1763–1783* (Princeton, NJ, 1966).

instructions they received from the colonies and they were also often handicapped by a lack of instructions, by instructions which were vague or arrived too late, or by instructions which were too rigid or too inflammatory to be followed. The colonial agents were rarely well paid, were not always of the highest calibre, and often worked for the colonies only part-time. They were usually lawyers, merchants or minor politicians. A few were Americans, with considerable first-hand knowledge of the colonies, but most were British. The most able were astute and did their best to put the views and interests of the colonies before ministers, MPs and even the reading public. A handful sat in the House of Commons, but most could only act as petitioners to parliament. While they had some influence on minor aspects of government policy, they failed to deflect ministers from the fatal decision to tax the colonies or to alert parliament to the real dangers of seeking to exert its sovereign authority over the colonies. Moreover, as the American crisis increased in seriousness, their political influence withered away.[13]

British pro-Americans

As Frank O'Gorman's chapter below makes very clear, there was no major or effective force in parliament that fully understood or endorsed the colonial position during the American crisis. While the supporters of Rockingham and Chatham opposed specific government measures and strove for reconciliation with the colonies, they either could not renounce the doctrine of parliament's sovereign authority over the colonies or could not accept that the colonial assemblies had the same authority in all matters as the Westminster parliament. This evident and widespread support in parliament for British sovereignty over the colonies has led many historians to conclude that this attitude was shared by the British people at large. Peter Thomas, for example, has claimed: 'There was no fund of goodwill in Britain towards the colonies, and an almost universal belief in Britain's right to exercise full sovereignty over them through Parliament.'[14] James Bradley's chapter below, however, offers a serious challenge to this conclusion. He argues convincingly that there was very considerable public unease at the government's support for coercive legislation and for armed intervention in the colonies. It is possible to go even further. Well before the outbreak of armed resistance in the colonies and the prospect of war, there is evidence

13. Kammen, *Rope of Sand, passim.*   14. Thomas, *Stamp Act Crisis*, p. 32.

of some sympathy for the American cause among elements in British society outside the political elite.

Outside parliament the most active sympathizers with the American cause were found among the emerging radical groups in London and other large cities, many of whom were merchants, tradesmen, professional men and Dissenters. A number of merchants trading with the American colonies sympathized with the colonists and organized petitions and protests against government efforts to tax the colonies. They played a major role in persuading parliament to repeal the Stamp Act in 1765, a decision that was very popular in many British ports and manufacturing towns.[15] Petitions against the Townshend duties also led to the repeal of most of these; the tea duty was only retained as a symbol of parliament's right to tax the colonies.[16] More active still were a number of Americans living in Britain, including Arthur Lee, William Lee and Stephen Sayre in London, Benjamin Rush in Liverpool and Henry Cruger in Bristol. Arthur Lee became prominent in radical circles in London, wrote pamphlets and newspaper articles in support of the American cause and persuaded the London radicals to include the government's American policy among their list of grievances in 1769.[17] These Americans were closely linked with the burgeoning radical movement that grew up around the charismatic John Wilkes from the late 1760s. Wilkes himself gave consistent support to the American cause and their grievances were regularly mentioned in the petitions and protests of his supporters. When he eventually took his seat in parliament in 1774 he spoke out against the coercive legislation of that year and thereafter he regularly condemned the war against the American colonies.[18]

Even more important in developing and disseminating a wide range of arguments in support of the American cause were a number of Rational Dissenters and men engaged in the publishing trade. These were men who had been educated in the Real Whig or Commonwealthman tradition,[19] who were committed to the campaign for greater religious toleration, and who all adopted a pro-American

15. Bryce E. Withrow, *A Biographical Study of Barlow Trecothick 1720–1775* (Emporia, KS, 1992), pp. 11–30; Paul Langford, *The First Rockingham Administration 1765–1766* (Oxford, 1973), pp. 109–14, 119–24; Thomas, *Stamp Act Crisis*, pp. 145–9, 216–21, 248.

16. Thomas, *Townshend Duties Crisis*, pp. 123–4, 132, 143.

17. Paul Langford, 'London and the American revolution' in John Stevenson, ed., *London in the Age of Reform* (Oxford, 1977), pp. 55–78; and John Sainsbury, *Disaffected Patriots: London Supporters of Revolutionary America* (Kingston and Montreal, 1987).

18. Peter D.G. Thomas, *John Wilkes, a Friend to Liberty* (Oxford, 1996).

19. Caroline Robbins, *The Eighteenth-Century Commonwealthman* (Cambridge, MA, 1959).

stance. They included Richard Price, Joseph Priestley, John Cartwright, John Jebb and James Burgh. The British press propagated the views of all of these men as well as much other pro-American material. Seventy-five of the main colonial pamphlets on the American crisis, including works by Otis, Dulany, Dickinson, Jefferson and John Adams, were reprinted in London, as well as the proceedings of the Stamp Act Congress and the Continental Congress. Over 1000 separate pamphlets on the American cause, written by British authors, were also published between 1764 and 1784 and a significant number of them were pro-American. A pro-American stance was also adopted by many leading newspapers, including the *Political Register*, the *London Chronicle* and the *London Evening Post* in the capital and the *Kentish Gazette*, the *Leeds Mercury*, the *Bath Journal* and the *Birmingham and Stafford Chronicle* in the provinces. In 1776 a virulently republican magazine, *The Crisis*, circulated in the provinces until it was suppressed by the authorities.[20] Most of the pro-Americans in Britain had been brought up in the same ideological tradition as the American patriots in the colonies.[21] This shared ideological heritage taught them to be fearful of arbitrary power, suspicious of the executive, concerned about the corruption of the constitution and vigilant in the defence of liberty. British radicals and American patriots were alike convinced that George III and his ministers had embarked on a coordinated campaign to undermine the constitution and subvert the liberties of the subject.[22] British radicals could point to the abuse of general warrants, attempts to muzzle the press, troop violence against crowds of demonstrators, and the refusal of parliament to accept the clear and repeated verdict of the voters in support of John Wilkes in the Middlesex elections of 1768–9. A newspaper report in 1769 claimed: 'the cause of liberty in England and America is one common cause . . . The attacks on both have been made and carried on by the same set of men, with the same views, and with the same illegal violence.'[23]

20. James E. Bradley, *Religion, Revolution and English Radicalism* (Cambridge, 1990), pp. 1–46, 91–158; John Seed, 'Gentlemen Dissenters: the social and political meanings of political Dissent in the 1770s and 1780s' *HJ* 28 (1985), pp. 299–325; C.C. Bonwick, 'English Dissenters and the American Revolution' in H.C. Allen and Roger Thompson, eds, *Contrast and Connection* (1976), pp. 88–112; Isaac Kramnick, *Republicanism and Bourgeois Radicalism* (1990), chs 2, 7; and Colin Bonwick, *English Radicals and the American Revolution* (Chapel Hill, NC, 1977), chs 1–3.

21. Bernard Bailyn, *The Ideological Origins of the American Revolution* (Cambridge, MA, 1967).

22. H.T. Dickinson, *Liberty and Property: Political Ideology in Eighteenth-Century Britain* (1977), pp. 163–92; and John Brewer, *Party Ideology and Popular Politics at the Accession of George III* (Cambridge, 1976), pp. 77–95.

23. *Political Register* 4 (1769), p. 176.

There is a wealth of evidence to demonstrate that there was British support for every constitutional principle raised by the American colonists in their disputes with the British government. There was very considerable support for the American claim that they could not be taxed without their consent. This was widely regarded on both sides of the Atlantic as one of the fundamental rights guaranteed by the British constitution.[24] John Wilkes condemned any 'attempt to take their money from them without their consent, contrary to the common rights of all mankind, and those great and fundamental principles of the English constitution, for which Hampden bled'.[25] Many commentators believed that the colonists could be taxed only by their own assemblies, in which they were directly represented. The American claim of 'no taxation without representation' was widely accepted by British radicals. Moreover, while the constitutional notion of parliamentary sovereignty was fast becoming an orthodoxy within parliament, many Britons outside parliament held an older view of the constitution similar to that held by most American colonists. They insisted that parliament's authority could be restrained by fundamental law, the law of nature, the law of God, and the needs of the people. British radicals such as Price and Cartwright even stressed the sovereign authority of the people.[26]

Britain's defeat in North America

Over thirty years ago an American historian observed: 'The War of Independence has two sides. . . . for numberless books have been written about how the war was won, but far fewer about how it was lost. The victors wanted to celebrate their victory, the defeated to ignore their defeat.'[27] Piers Mackesy's fine study of the war from the British side did appear the same year that this observation was made, and a small number of works by British historians have appeared since then,[28] but it remains true that the war has been

24. James Burgh, *Political Disquisitions* 3 vols (1774), ii, pp. 274, 310, 328.
25. *London Magazine* 44 (1775), p. 565.
26. Richard Price, *Observations on the Nature of Civil Liberty* 7th edn (1776), pp. 15–16; and John Cartwright, *American Independence: The Interest and Glory of Great Britain* (1774), p. 9.
27. William B. Willcox, *Portrait of a General: Sir Henry Clinton in the War of Independence* (New York, 1964), p. vii.
28. Piers Mackesy, *The War for America* (1964; 2nd edn 1993); Christopher Hibbert, *Redcoats and Rebels: The War for America, 1770–1781* (1990); Jeremy Black, *The War for*

far more a preoccupation of American than of British historians. Often starting from the unfounded position that American success against Britain was a surprising and astonishing achievement, American historians have not only described and analysed every major engagement and minor skirmish, but have paid great attention to how the war affected American political, social and economic life.[29] American historians have endeavoured to explain how the former colonists managed to raise, maintain and deploy a significant Continental Army, how they successfully used irregular forces, how they secured the support of several European states, and how they isolated and intimidated those loyalists who wished to retain the connection with Britain. In contrast, British historians have so far largely neglected the impact of the war on British society.[30] When they have devoted their scholarly endeavours to the war, they have tended to concentrate on the overall strategy adopted by the British government and commanders rather than on the land campaigns in America, and they have looked almost as much at the war with France and Spain in the wider world as at the war with the Americans in North America. Indeed, it remains a curious fact that nearly all the major works on the British commanders operating in North America have been written by American rather than by British scholars.[31] The concentration of British historians on the government's grand strategy and on the wider war with France and Spain is justified since defeat was largely due to strategic failings and to the fact that a huge British effort had to be made against these traditional

---

America (Stroud, 1991); Stephen Conway, *The War of American Independence 1775–1783* (1995); and William Seymour, *The Price of Folly: British Blunders in the War of American Independence* (1995). See also Eric Robson, *The American Revolution 1763–1783* (1955).

29. See, in particular, Don Higginbotham, *The War of American Independence: Military Attitudes, Policies, and Practice* (New York, 1971); John Shy, *A People Numerous and Armed: Reflections on the Military Struggle for American Independence* (1976; rev. edn, Ann Arbor, MI, 1990); and Charles Royster, *A Revolutionary People at War: The Continental Army and American Character, 1775–1783* (Chapel Hill, NC, 1980).

30. Stephen Conway plans a monograph to fill this gap. He has already made a start with 'Britain and the impact of the American war, 1775–1783' *War in History* 2 (1995), pp. 127–50; 'Locality, metropolis and nation: the impact of the military camps in England during the American war' *History* 82 (1997), pp. 547–62; and 'The politics of British military and naval mobilization, 1775–83' *EHR* 112 (1997), pp. 1179–201.

31. John R. Alden, *General Gage in America* (Baton Rouge, LA, 1948); Troy Anderson, *The Command of the Howe Brothers during the American Revolution* (1936); Ira D. Gruber, *The Howe Brothers and the American Revolution* (New York, 1972); Richard J. Hargrove, *General John Burgoyne* (Newark, DE, 1983); Franklin and Mary Wickwire, *Cornwallis: The American Adventure* (Boston, 1970); and Willcox, *Portrait of a General.*

enemies in the non-American theatres of the war. It was, after all, as the chapters by Hamish Scott and Stephen Conway below make very clear, the diplomatic isolation of Britain after 1763 and the conversion of the American War into a vast global struggle that largely explain Britain's loss of the American colonies. Given the enormous problems facing Britain once several European powers had joined the conflict on the American side, the efforts of the British government and of Britain's naval and military forces were not as poor as has sometimes been portrayed. Britain did send and sustain for several years the largest military force it had ever sent such a vast distance from home, as well as performing quite well against France and Spain in many parts of the globe. The colonies were certainly lost, but it is not easy to see how they could have been retained; and absolute disaster was clearly avoided. The war eventually became such an enormous test of Britain's financial, human and material resources that victory became unattainable and, as Conway concludes, Britain did really rather well to restrict her losses and to prevent France emerging in triumph from the war. Even Britain's decline as a great power proved more apparent than real. In retrospect, the American War appears almost unwinnable: the Vietnam War has taught us all that even a superpower with the most sophisticated weaponry and means of communication cannot guarantee victory against a much more primitive military power when the latter wins the war for the hearts and minds of the indigenous population.

It is a mistake, however, to believe that what happened in the American War was in fact inevitable. The Americans had to make an enormous effort to build up an army from scratch and to sustain forces in the field against a professional British army that kept inflicting serious damage on these forces. It is also difficult to see how the Americans could have decisively defeated the British army in the field without French support and Britain did manage to hold on to New York, Savannah and Charleston until they were handed over to the Americans at the very end of the war. Moreover, it is possible to imagine three ways in which the British might have denied success to the rebellious colonies. Britain might have adopted a 'seaboard strategy' of holding on to several major ports and towns close to the sea and imposing a tight naval blockade in order to ruin American overseas trade and prevent any supplies and succour reaching the rebels until the cost of continuing the rebellion proved too expensive and the colonists sought a reconciliation. In the very early stages of the war Britain might have adopted a second, different strategy of a ruthless campaign of devastation and destruction that enforced a tight naval blockade, sought out and destroyed Washington's Continental Army, burned towns, treated the rebels harshly, and inflicted such losses on the rebels that their cause would quickly collapse. Once the European powers entered the war, however, its nature and scale inevitably changed. Britain's reduced chance of success then depended on seeking to pursue a third strategy of securing absolute mastery of the seas so that valuable French and Spanish colonies could be captured and the French could not send or sustain a significant army in North America. This might then have allowed Britain to win control of the southern colonies, where potential loyalist support was greater and rebel forces were weaker. The aim should have been to gain firm control of at least one colony, restore a loyal civil government and then expand control and government in a steady operation behind the advancing regular forces. This might just have secured ultimate victory or more likely have forced the American rebels to accept that only some of the American colonies could secure their independence.

Britain failed however to adopt any clear, coordinated strategy. The first strategy was not adopted because it would have surrendered control of vast areas to the rebels and put almost all loyalists at their mercy; it might have denied the rebels victory without ensuring complete success for Britain. The British were too determined to crush the rebellion and too confident of their military superiority over what they regarded as an indisciplined rabble to fight a defensive war from the outset. The second strategy of terrorizing the Americans into submission by devastating the country was never adopted because the British government and commanders were not sufficiently committed to all-out war in the early stages of the conflict. The British government always hoped to effect a political reconciliation and was reluctant at first to pursue a costly and ruthless strategy, while British commanders in the field underestimated the rebels' will and ability to fight regular actions and could not decide on a single strategy about how best to fight the war. Despite the bloody nature of some of the fighting and the indiscipline of some troops, the British forces did not pursue an aggressive, all-out war of destruction to inflict maximum human and material damage on their opponents. Such a strategy would in any case have almost certainly lost the war for the hearts and minds of the Americans and ensured another rebellion in the near future. The third chance of success, despite enormous efforts at sea and across the world, never occurred because Britain simply lacked the resources to ensure complete command of the seas. Yorktown was in many ways a naval rather than a military disaster. In the southern colonies the British also failed to recruit sufficient loyalists or to organize them into forces which could hold substantial tracts of territory without the support of regular troops.

In the end, however, it is idle for an historian to play the role of an armchair general. Britain made a very commendable effort to win the war, was not disgraced and lost the struggle for America for many obvious reasons. None of the generals leading the British forces in North America was a truly great commander, though they were all experienced, brave and competent soldiers. General Gage failed to provide adequate defences around Boston and adopted the wrong tactics at Bunker Hill. Burgoyne rashly plunged on to disaster at Saratoga in 1777 when outnumbered and unsupported. Howe failed to crush Washington in 1776 or to coordinate operations with Burgoyne in 1777. Clinton was too cautious and offered Cornwallis inadequate support in the southern campaign in 1780–1, while Cornwallis tried to accomplish too much with too small a force in 1781. In pitched battles British officers and men generally performed well. Unfortunately, much of the war was not fought in the manner of European engagements: Britain was fighting Washington's professional army, but also trying to subdue a people in arms. The British strategy of holding on to ports and urban centres, while necessary to give the army secure bases and to keep it supplied from home, tied down a large proportion of the available forces and forced the British to defend these fixed targets. This strategy meant that the regular British forces (and the German mercenaries serving with them) failed to sustain the loyalists, especially in the south in the early stages of the war, and allowed too many of them to be intimidated by rebel militia and irregulars. It was difficult to rally enough loyalists in the face of rebel reprisals. The loyalists themselves often wanted revenge rather than reconciliation and disagreed with British efforts to be lenient to rebels in order to persuade them to change sides. The British army either had to hold down limited territory in order to protect the local loyalists or chase after the rebels and leave the loyalists vulnerable to short, sharp attacks from the rebel militia and irregulars. The British use of Indian warriors on the frontiers and the half-hearted efforts to enlist the support of black slaves probably did more to anger and alienate than militarily to inconvenience the rebels.

Far more serious were the enormous physical and material obstacles facing the British in North America. The country was vast, with only a few limited major centres of population. The British army could capture major towns, but not force the rebels to capitulate as there was no vital strategic centre that the Americans could not afford to lose. Indeed, the Americans always had the option of retreating into the vast hinterland. Beyond their own camps the British could exercise no control and could frequently gather no accurate military intelligence. The terrain was extraordinarily difficult for a professional European army trying to carry its supplies with it; the troops had to struggle with mountains, woods, wilderness, rivers with few bridges or fords, and with a climate which could be hot and humid or bitterly cold, while constantly facing the prospect of ambush and attacks by small, mobile rebel forces. The British had to bring in military supplies and reinforcements over 3000 miles by sea; a task that became increasingly difficult as French and Spanish efforts made the logistical problems so enormously difficult. Vast resources were diverted to other areas of conflict and there were not enough troops, transports and warships to keep up a huge military effort in North America, while temporary loss of control of the sea always threatened the British with complete disaster. The problems of transportation, communications and supply in an age of sailing ships were simply beyond Britain's capacity. Finally, Britain never had an army of the size needed to guarantee success in North America. The army operating there was rarely much over 30,000 strong and this force was scattered over a vast area from Canada to Florida. There were never enough troops for all the tasks the army needed to perform: to hold down all the major towns that were captured, to provide protection for loyalists and neutrals from attacks by irregular forces, and to keep a significant mobile force in the field to seek out and destroy Washington's Continental Army. Most serious of all, the British army was never in a strong enough position to hold enough territory to win the hearts and minds of the many neutral Americans, who increasingly came to accept that British authority had collapsed and the rebels could provide them with more protection and a more secure form of government. On the other hand, the American rebels had a virtually armed population from which to draw reinforcements. Britain rightly feared invasion and it also had to devote significant resources to defending more important strategic areas such as the West Indies. After 1777 it could never commit all its resources to the war in North America. In the end, Britain lacked the will to continue deploying vast resources in a desperate and costly struggle that appeared endless and unwinnable. The American rebels had everything to gain by victory and everything to lose by defeat: this stiffened their resolve enormously. The British parliament and people, after a huge effort, were unwilling to pay the heavy price of continued warfare.

Radical lessons from America

Military defeat was an enormous, if temporary, blow to Britain's status and morale. As Neil York argues below Britain's military problems had a significant effect on its relations with its first and nearest colony, Ireland. Although Irish patriots had long campaigned for a greater measure of legislative independence for the Dublin parliament, their efforts would probably not have been successful as early as 1782 but for Britain's losing struggle with the American colonies and its recognition that it could not afford a prolonged and damaging dispute with the Irish patriots. Major political concessions were therefore necessary. On the other hand, as John Cannon demonstrates below, the consequences for Britain itself of the loss of the American colonies did not prove as disastrous as had been widely anticipated. Both short-term and long-term consequences can be detected, but they were not as profound or as damaging as had been expected or forecast. As Cannon concedes, however, failure in the American War did encourage a revival of the extra-parliamentary movement for economic and parliamentary reform in Britain. Though this movement failed to force any significant concession from crown or parliament, it can be argued that the American crisis had a significant impact on the ideology and confidence of British radicalism.[32]

The shift from a Country to a radical ideology in Britain began to occur in the 1760s and a major influence on this transformation was the intense debate generated by the American cry of 'no taxation without representation'. Before the American crisis most British critics of the prevailing political order were content to advocate a redistribution of parliamentary seats to the larger counties and more populous towns, and more frequent general elections. The American patriots however started a prolonged debate about who could vote and whether all taxpayers needed to be directly represented in the legislature. The American arguments were clear, direct and rational, and they had a profound impact on advanced

32. Brewer, *Party Ideology*, pp. 201–16; Bonwick, *English Radicals and the American Revolution*, chs 6–9; Colin C. Bonwick, 'Contemporary implications of the American Revolution for English radicalism' *The Maryland Historian* 7 (1976), pp. 33–58; and Arthur Sheps, 'The American Revolution and the transformation of English republicanism' *Historical Reflections/Réflections Historiques* 2 (1975), pp. 3–8.

thinkers in Britain. British radicals soon concluded that all men paid taxes and so all men should possess the right to vote. John Cartwright, a pro-American radical, was the first to advocate the vote for all adult males in 1776 and, by 1780, the advanced radicals of the Westminster Committee of the Association movement had accepted the legitimacy of the demand for universal male suffrage.[33] A second major shift in radical ideology in Britain emerged from the colonists' debates on the nature and location of sovereignty. The Americans started by discussing the limits placed on parliament by fundamental laws and the law of nature, but they graduated to a belief in the sovereign people. Their arguments were quickly picked up by British radicals, who led an important shift away from appeals to the historic rights of Englishmen to the natural and inalienable rights of all men. Richard Price, for example, claimed: 'If omnipotence can, with any sense, be ascribed to a legislature, it must be lodged where all legislative authority originates; that is, in the PEOPLE. For their sake is government instituted; and their's is the only real omnipotence.'[34]

The Americans also taught British radicals that ancient virtues could be recovered and new constitutions could be established. During their successful contest with Britain the Americans appeared to have recovered and revitalized their civic virtue and were using it to promote the general welfare of the people in their new republic. Once the Americans began to develop their new constitutions at state and federal level, British radicals were excited by the fresh paradigm and the many new examples they provided. The Americans were making new experiments in politics from which others could learn. They rejected monarchy, aristocracy and all hereditary political rights and they sought to establish cheap, honest and peaceful government. Forms of government were subordinated to written constitutions ratified by the people, and the rights of the citizens were safeguarded by a more extensive bill of rights and a wider franchise than in Britain. The Americans also deliberately rejected a state church, opposed religious tests for admission to political office, and allowed a considerable measure of religious toleration. What impressed British radicals even more was the fact that these major political changes were achieved without creating social instability or economic upheaval. They demonstrated that radical political reforms were not a sure recipe for anarchy, mob rule

33. John Cartwright, *Take Your Choice!* (1776), p. 22; and *The Report of the Sub-Committee of Westminster* (1780), pp. 3–8.
34. Price, *Observations on the Nature of Civil Liberty*, pp. 15–16.

and economic collapse. A move towards democracy did not automatically bring social disorder or social levelling. For the British in particular the Americans showed that the good parts of the British constitution could be retained, while the corrupt parts were removed. The American Revolution therefore was admired by British radicals because it established political models worth copying and constitutional ideals worth emulating. Richard Price praised this 'revolution in favour of universal liberty which has taken place in America, a revolution which opens up a new prospect in human affairs, and begins a new era in the history of mankind'.[35]

35. Price, *Observations on the Importance of the American Revolution* (1785) in Bernard Peach, ed., *Richard Price and the Ethical Foundations of the American Revolution* (Durham, NC, 1979), p. 182.

CHAPTER ONE

Britain and the Administration of the American Colonies

KEITH MASON

The closing years of the Seven Years War (1756–63) saw Britain's imperial star at its zenith. An impressive run of successes at home and abroad culminated in the Treaty of Paris of 1763, which ratified British possession of a vast new global empire. In North America alone, according to its terms, Britain formally acquired not only Canada, but all the French colonies east of the Mississippi river together with Spanish Florida. These acquisitions were greeted with joy both in the metropolis and in Britain's North American colonies. Benjamin Franklin, for instance, was convinced that the peace was 'the most advantageous for the British nation . . . of any your annals have recorded'. With the acquisition of Canada, in particular, a glorious destiny seemed to await the inhabitants of the newly expanded British empire regardless of which side of the Atlantic they resided. '[A]ll the Country from St. Laurence to Missis[s]ip[p]i', Franklin declared, 'will in another Century be fill'd with British People; Britain itself will become vastly more populous by the immense Increase of its Commerce; the Atlantic Sea will be cover'd with your Trading Ships; and your naval Power thence continually increasing, will extend your Influence round the whole Globe, and awe the World!' These reflections even led him to claim that 'the Foundations of the future Grandeur and Stability of the British Empire' now lay in America.[1]

Franklin's boast was soon to sound rather hollow, however, for British military success brought in its wake a host of thorny administrative problems that were as much a product of the recent conflict as his optimism. How, for example, should the imperial government

1. Quoted in Esmond Wright, *Franklin of Philadelphia* (Cambridge, MA, 1986), p. 123.

handle the defence and government of its newly acquired possessions? What provisions should the authorities make for the settlement of western lands? How could they contain an unprecedented
national debt of almost £140 million and still shoulder their new
responsibilities? And the trickiest problem of all, as it happened:
what contribution should the colonies make to all of this? Taken
by themselves, these issues were potentially explosive. Their impact
was significantly greater, however, because they fuelled festering re-
sentments on both sides of the Atlantic over the imperial–colonial
relationship. In fact, by gaining Canada, the government ironically
set in motion a train of events that would end twenty years later
with the loss of the rest of British North America. Through an examination of the earlier course of imperial–colonial relations as well as
an analysis of the impact that the Seven Years War had upon their
dynamics, this chapter explores the reasons why the high hopes
expressed by Franklin and others evaporated so quickly.

Early political and commercial relationships

The relationship between Britain and its North American colonies
had oscillated since the establishment of the first permanent English
settlement at Jamestown, Virginia in 1607.[2] Laissez-faire initially characterized government policy and early outposts in the Chesapeake
and New England regions had been granted considerable *de facto*
autonomy. From 1675 to the early 1720s, however, the imperial
authorities made sporadic and ultimately ineffective attempts to
tighten the bonds that tied the colonies to the metropolis. A period
of accommodation and relaxation, termed the era of 'salutary neglect', followed from the mid-1720s until 1748. Then, immediately
prior to the Seven Years War, reform was once again high on the
agenda under the direction of Lord Halifax, president of the Board
of Trade. While the exigencies of the renewed conflict with France
in the mid-1750s brought a temporary halt to his efforts, the drive
was ultimately renewed and expanded in the early 1760s. A recurrent
cycle of neglect and intervention therefore characterized metropolitan

2. The following account of the different phases of the imperial-colonial relationship is based on Jack P. Greene, 'Metropolis and colonies: changing patterns of
constitutional conflict in the early modern British empire, 1607–1763' in his *Negotiated Authorities: Essays in Colonial Political and Constitutional History* (Charlottesville,
VA, 1994), pp. 43–77. Also, see William A. Speck, 'The international and imperial
context' in Jack P. Greene and Jack R. Pole, eds, *Colonial British America: Essays in the
New History of the Early Modern Era* (Baltimore, MD, 1984), pp. 384–407.

policy towards the American colonies, with, perhaps predictably, imperial-colonial relations at their best during the former periods and their most troubled during the latter.

Colonial ventures had, initially, owed little to the mother country's direction or involvement. As Edmund Burke asserted in 1757: 'Nothing of an enlarged and legislative spirit appears in the planning of *our* colonies.'[3] Instead, individuals, joint-stock companies or corporate and proprietary groups took the lead in establishing English outposts in locales as diverse as Virginia, Massachusetts and the Carolinas. In return, they secured a range of legal, political and economic privileges under their charters and other founding documents. Theoretically, of course, the crown remained the ultimate source of authority in America and charter rights and even land titles derived from royal grants. But Charles I's efforts to exercise supervision through his privy council tended to founder because domestic distractions made it hard to perfect either a consistent colonial policy or effective mechanisms of imperial control. In this context, the rare initiatives that were launched – such as the attempt in 1637 to rein in Puritan Massachusetts by forcing it to return its charter – were doomed to failure.[4]

By the mid-seventeenth century, however, official concern grew over the pernicious consequences of continuing, by default, with a laissez-faire policy. During the English Revolution metropolitan leaders became increasingly anxious that colonial freedom might ultimately degenerate into destructive economic competition among the American settlements or between them and the mother country. Some even feared that the American colonies might eventually take advantage of their charter privileges to establish their autonomy or possibly become allies of England's main commercial rivals, the Dutch. In response to these concerns, tighter regulation was advocated. This drive led to the passage of the Navigation Ordinance in 1651, the first substantive effort to define the economic relationship between England and the colonies. The ordinance excluded nearly all foreign shipping from the colonial trade. It required that all goods imported into England or the colonies must arrive on English ships manned predominantly by English sailors, with colonial vessels and crews qualifying as such. The aim was clearly to create a self-contained economic system that spanned the Atlantic,

---

3. Quoted in Greene, 'Metropolis and colonies', p. 43.
4. For developments under Charles I, see Robert M. Bliss, *Revolution and Empire: English Politics and the American Colonies in the Seventeenth Century* (Manchester, 1990), pp. 17–44.

whilst strengthening England's naval might and increasing customs revenues.[5]

The Stuart Restoration in 1660 saw continuity rather than change in commercial policy. Building on the earlier ordinance, further Navigation Acts were passed in 1660, 1663 and 1673. Together they supplied an enduring rationale for the colonial system: to serve the economic interests of the mother country. Enforcing these measures in distant settlements across the Atlantic proved difficult, however. Proprietors like Lord Baltimore of Maryland or charter colonies such as Rhode Island ignored and, in many cases, openly flouted the acts because of the privileges granted them earlier. The unsettled nature of the post-Restoration machinery of colonial administration did not help matters. Although in July 1660 responsibility for trade and plantations was entrusted to a single, small committee of the privy council, this merely marked the beginning of a succession of bodies that were active from 1660 to 1674. The most important of these was the Council of Plantations established in 1670 along lines suggested by Lord Ashley (later Earl of Shaftesbury) and John Locke. The council called for the systematic collection of information about the colonies and for oversight of their proceedings to ensure that they were adhering both to trade regulations and to their own charters. Like its predecessors, however, the council remained simply an advisory body and only survived until 1674.[6]

During this period it became increasingly apparent to the metropolitan authorities that attempts to impose stricter control and greater uniformity on the colonies would invariably fail unless a clearer lead came from England. In the half-century after 1675, this conclusion spawned a faltering effort to reform the political relationship between England and the colonies that fell into two phases. The first ran from the mid-1670s until the Glorious Revolution of

5. The classic account of the making of the Navigation Acts is Charles M. Andrews, *The Colonial Period of American History* 4 vols (New Haven, CT, 1964), iv. For an essay that plays down the importance of mercantilist thought, see Speck, 'The international and imperial context'. Speck draws on the debate over the work of Stephen S. Webb, which emphasizes the importance of military rather than commercial considerations in the development of English colonial policy. See Webb's *The Governors-General: The English Army and the Definition of Empire, 1569–1681* (Chapel Hill, NC, 1979); and 'The data and theory of Restoration empire' *WMQ* 3rd series, 43 (1986), pp. 431–59. For a critique, see Richard R. Johnson, 'The imperial Webb: the thesis of garrison government in early America considered' in ibid., pp. 408–30.

6. For developments after the Restoration, see Andrews, *Colonial Period*, iii and iv; Bliss, *Revolution and Empire*, esp. pp. 103–218; and J.M. Sosin, *English America and the Restoration Monarchy of Charles II: Transatlantic Politics, Commerce and Kinship* (Lincoln, NE, 1981).

1688, and the second from the establishment of the Board of Trade in 1696 until the early 1720s. During both periods, however, the same underlying policy objective was pursued. Essentially, as Jack P. Greene has claimed, it involved 'substituting for the traditional contractual arrangement in which both colonists and crown had been bound by certain mutual obligations set down in the charters a new relationship in which the authority of the crown would be unlimited and pre-eminent, if also benign and just'.[7]

The first phase began with the creation in 1675 of a new instrument of central direction, the Lords Commissioners of Trade and Plantations, a standing committee of the privy council. Holding executive and policy-making powers, the Lords injected a more consistent and vigorous approach to the administration of the American settlements. Receiving encouragement from both Charles II and his brother, James, they also benefited from the growing continuity in personnel provided by the divergent personalities of James himself, the Earl of Shaftesbury, William Blathwayt and Edward Randolph.[8] Commercial considerations – namely the enforcement of the Navigation Acts – occupied the authorities in the first instance. Earlier in 1673 the operation of the customs service was extended to America for the first time, and officials for Maryland, the Carolinas and Virginia were swiftly appointed. In 1678 a collector was even chosen for New England.[9] Meanwhile, the Lords Commissioners worked to create the conditions under which the Navigation Acts would be obeyed. This invariably led to discussion of the political as well as the commercial relationship between the metropolis and the colonies. The Lords advocated strengthening executive authority in the existing royal colonies. To this end, they tried to subject the governors themselves to closer scrutiny. Not only were these colonial executives to submit regular reports to London, they also received more specific instructions in return. Even more important, however, the Lords Commissioners attempted to curtail the powers of the elected colonial legislative assemblies. Originating in the governors' financial dependence upon them, the assemblies' writ was beginning to extend over many aspects of

7. Greene, 'Metropolis and colonies', pp. 46–7.
8. For assessments of these individuals, see K.H.D. Haley, *Shaftesbury* (Oxford, 1968); Stephen S. Webb, 'William Blathwayt, imperial fixer: from Popish plot to Glorious Revolution' *WMQ* 3rd series, 25 (1968), pp. 3–21; and Michael G. Hall, *Edward Randolph and the American Colonies* (Chapel Hill, NC, 1960).
9. For the operation of the customs service, see Thomas C. Barrow, *Trade and Empire: The British Customs Service in Colonial America, 1660–1775* (Cambridge, MA, 1967).

colonial government. To reverse this trend, the Lords tried to persuade the colonial legislatures to grant a permanent revenue covering the salaries of the governor and other royal officials. The Lords' programme was not confined to the existing royal colonies. They also sought a ban on the creation of any more charter or proprietary settlements and aimed at transferring the existing ones to direct crown control. Under their direction, the New Hampshire towns were divorced from Massachusetts Bay in 1679 and made a royal colony. Although Pennsylvania was founded under proprietary auspices in 1681, the Lords Commissioners ensured that William Penn was subjected to tighter controls than his predecessors. They also resorted to the courts to attack the charters of private colonies – a policy that met with immediate success with the annulment of Massachusetts Bay's in 1684.

The Lords Commissioners' programme culminated with the creation of the Dominion of New England in 1686. This created a unified government for the northern colonies, including New York, under a single royal governor and council. In a radical move, no provision was made for a representative assembly. The dominion was a sign of things to come. Ultimately, the crown intended similar administrative reforms for the middle and southern colonies in the interests of a more efficient enforcement of commercial regulations, a more ordered system of defence, and more effective central control from London. With the Glorious Revolution and the overthrow of James II, however, this era of administrative reform was brought to an abrupt halt.[10]

The second phase was launched a few years later under William and Mary. In 1696 two developments helped create the underpinnings of a coherent colonial system. First, a new Navigation Act confirmed the existing restrictions on colonial trade, but added certain provisions designed to tighten their implementation: a special oath taken by governors to enforce the acts, the use by customs officers of 'writs of assistance' (general search warrants that did not have to specify location), and the trial of accused offenders in Admiralty Courts where the outcome was determined by government-appointed judges. Second, a new department was created – the Board of Trade – in place of the old Lords of Trade and Plantations.[11]

10. See David S. Lovejoy, *The Glorious Revolution in America* (New York, 1974); and J.M. Sosin, *English America and the Revolution of 1688: Royal Administration and the Structure of Provincial Government* (Lincoln, NE, 1982).
11. On the early history of the Board of Trade, see Ian K. Steele, *Politics of Colonial Policy: The Board of Trade in Colonial Administration, 1696–1720* (Oxford, 1968).

The board, which continued to function throughout the remainder of the colonial period, was primarily concerned with advice and policy-making. But during its early years it worked vigorously towards subjecting the American settlements to more efficient metropolitan control. Commercial regulation and defence remained the board's central priorities. By 1700 it had launched a campaign against illegal trade and piracy in American waters. The board also sought to establish a military union of the three northern royal colonies – Massachusetts, New Hampshire and New York – under the command of a single governor.

Resistance to the union and on-going breaches of the Navigation Acts convinced the board that it had to go further along the road of administrative reform. Another attempt was made to bring the private colonies under direct crown supervision. In this effort, it had a potential advantage denied to the Lords of Trade and Plantations. In the wake of the Glorious Revolution, the board could work through parliament. A bill placing the private colonies on the same footing as their royal counterparts was actually introduced in the House of Lords during 1701, but was not passed. As a result, the only concrete result of this initiative was the crown's resumption of New Jersey in 1702.

The failure of the board's renewed attack on colonial charters is important because of what it portended. First, the campaign demonstrated that the board was on rather shaky ground when moving from the conduct of routine business to policy formulation and implementation. Second, it showed that the government did not really regard colonial reform as a high priority. The king's ministers gave parliament little time to discuss North American affairs and the legislature itself seemed to lack an active interest in them. Third, even this limited campaign provoked a fierce colonial reaction. Colonial agents in England, led by William Penn and other nonconformists, mounted a vigorous defence of their charters. This demonstrated that the board had to combat not only government apathy, but contending colonial interests with access to ministers, politicians and other men of influence.[12]

Following its attack on the charters, the Board of Trade's authority gradually waned. The departure in 1707 of William Blathwayt, a

---

12. For this dimension of the imperial–colonial relationship, see Alison G. Olson, *Anglo-American Politics, 1660–1775: The Relationship between Parties in England and Colonial America* (Oxford, 1973); *idem, Making the Empire Work: London and American Interest Groups, 1690–1790* (Cambridge, MA, 1992); and her 'The Board of Trade and London-American interest groups in the eighteenth century' *JICH* 8 (1980), pp. 33–50.

prominent imperial reformer, was a clear sign of its diminishing status, as were its own increasing complaints about its powerlessness. Even during this disheartening period the board continued to address its routine business. Instructions were formulated to governors, advice was forthcoming on appointments, and petitions from the colonies were received. On issues of policy, however, it remained stymied. The board's pleas urging the crown to assume more direct power over its transatlantic possessions continued to fall on deaf ears until the appointment of Lord Halifax in 1748.[13]

With the board's initiatives running into the sand, the period from *c.*1720 to 1748 has been termed the era of 'salutary neglect'. Interest in major reforms of colonial government certainly waned during the long ministry of Sir Robert Walpole. The nation was at peace; revenue from customs was increasing as transatlantic trade boomed; and government ministers were intent on using American offices as an extension of their patronage networks. Still, some historians have questioned the appropriateness of the traditional epithet. Arguing that the British authorities continued to take an active interest in colonial affairs after Walpole's appointment, James Henretta has discerned a further period of intervention between the mid-1720s and the mid-1730s – a decade that saw the resumption of the Carolinas by the crown in 1725, the establishment of Georgia in 1732, and the passage of the Hat and Molasses Acts. It was only when the Duke of Newcastle took control of colonial affairs that the government began to neglect them. Even then, in Henretta's view, the neglect was hardly salutary. On the contrary, he concludes that: 'Newcastle failed to make a single positive contribution to the functioning of the colonial system . . . His was an era devoid of achievement and vision, a period of culpable mismanagement and negligence which led directly to many of the intractable problems of the next generation.'[14]

Colonial political culture and economic growth

What was the relationship, then, between the so-called era of 'salutary neglect' and the events that followed? The key point to grasp is

13. Steele, *Politics of Colonial Policy*, pp. 85–172.

14. James A. Henretta, *'Salutary Neglect': Colonial Administration under the Duke of Newcastle* (Princeton, NJ, 1972), p. 269. For a different perspective on Newcastle, albeit for a later period, consult Richard Middleton, 'The Duke of Newcastle and the conduct of patronage during the Seven Years War' *BJECS* 12 (1989), pp. 175–86.

that the stability and harmony that accompanied this relaxation of metropolitan policy were deceptive. Beneath the surface calm, pressures were building. The imperial–colonial relationship – always 'an uneasy connection' – was becoming increasingly strained.[15] In North America the colonies took advantage of their freedom to develop their own dynamic political culture. In the process, as Jack P. Greene claims, they acquired 'virtually all the conditions necessary for self-governing states'.[16] By the middle of the century, for example, indigenous ruling elites were providing skilled and experienced political leadership. These groups had emerged in older colonies like Virginia as early as the late seventeenth century. Even among new provinces such as New Jersey, Pennsylvania and the Carolinas, however, rapid growth and social differentiation accelerated the process of elite development, so that they too spawned a recognizable cadre of leaders by the early eighteenth century. As time progressed, these elites consolidated their position by absorbing social climbers, whilst simultaneously emphasizing the importance of inherited wealth, social standing and lineage. Though occasionally facing challenges from below during periods of crisis, these ruling groups normally expected to receive deference. Certainly they were sufficiently confident of their ability to maintain social control to call for popular support amid the imperial crisis of the 1760s and 1770s.[17] Equally important for the future, as Bernard Bailyn has shown, the intellectual environment of this colonial gentry was germinating the seeds of a republican ideology which was to flourish during the American Revolution.[18]

These elites exercised their authority through the dense web of representative institutions that flourished in all the colonies at local and provincial levels. With origins in the early years of settlement, these bodies grew in strength and confidence during the eighteenth century. The process was most marked in the case of the most important of these institutions – the elected lower houses of

15. Jack P. Greene, 'An uneasy connection: an analysis of the preconditions of the American Revolution' in Stephen G. Kurtz and James H. Hutson, eds, *Essays on the American Revolution* (Chapel Hill, NC, 1973), pp. 32–80.

16. Ibid., p. 35.

17. On elite development and its effect on colonial politics, see Jack P. Greene, 'The growth of political stability: an interpretation of political development in the Anglo-American colonies', in John Parker and Carol Urness, eds, *The American Revolution: A Heritage of Change* (Minneapolis, 1975). For a contrasting view of the course of political change in the colonies, see Bernard Bailyn, *The Origins of American Politics* (New York, 1968).

18. Bernard Bailyn, *The Ideological Origins of the American Revolution* (Cambridge, MA, 1967).

assembly, the principal vehicles through which the provincial elites exerted their authority. They had haphazardly and unevenly extended their rights in the seventeenth century, despite the imperial authorities' occasional attempts to rein them in. The Glorious Revolution, however, encouraged their members to push for even greater powers consonant with the importance they attached to representative institutions as the chief guardians of individual liberties.

By the mid-eighteenth century the colonial assemblies, like the Westminster parliament, held two crucial levers. First, they had the power of the purse in their right to vote on taxes and expenditures. Second, they possessed the power to initiate legislation, not merely the right to act on executive proposals. The assemblies exploited these powers to extend their range further. Governors were restrained by the legislatures' control of salaries, which were voted annually and sometimes not at all. Because they controlled finance, the assemblies demanded and often got the right to name tax collectors and treasurers. They subsequently stretched this claim to cover other officers such as public printers and the supervisors of public works. By specifying how appropriations should be spent they even played an important role in areas like military affairs and Indian relations. All through the eighteenth century, then, the assemblies expanded their reach, passing laws and setting precedents the overall significance of which neither they nor the imperial authorities fully recognized. Once established, however, they became fixed principles, part of the colonial 'constitution'. In the event of the imperial authorities challenging this settlement, disputes were highly likely.[19]

Another significant characteristic of colonial politics, at least by contemporary standards, was its broad popular base. There were certainly property restrictions on the franchise based on the notion that only men who held a 'stake in society' could vote responsibly. These varied from colony to colony. At the more inclusive end of the spectrum a 40/-freehold or a small amount of land was usually sufficient to confer voting rights across New England. By contrast, New York called for a freehold of $40 and South Carolina eventually demanded ownership of 100 acres of land or the payment of annual taxes of 10/-. Everywhere in British North America, however, property holding was widespread and, as a result, a large proportion of the population could vote. Most estimates suggest that voting rights were conferred on 50 to 80 per cent of white

19. For the rise of the colonial assemblies, see Jack P. Greene's classic study, *The Quest for Power: The Lower Houses of Assembly in the Southern Royal Colonies, 1689–1776* (Chapel Hill, NC, 1963).

adult male colonists, a figure that set the colonies on a different trajectory from Britain.[20] Two other features of colonial political culture were important. First, below the assemblies, town meetings in the northern colonies and counties and parishes in the south provided vital representative government at the local level. This acted both as a proving ground for future provincial leaders and as an opportunity for lesser property holders to gain some practical political experience. In the Chesapeake colonies of Virginia and Maryland, for example, small planters did not simply vote: they also participated in a wide variety of local offices.[21] Second, a relatively open press meant that political ideas and opinions were disseminated widely across the social spectrum, providing a further aid to popular mobilization at local and provincial levels.[22]

These political developments took place against the backcloth of a remarkable demographic and territorial expansion. Fuelled by both natural increase and immigration, the colonial population was growing rapidly. From about 50,000 in 1650, the number of settlers reached 250,000 in 1700 and then rose to over a million by 1750. As pressure on land developed, pioneers pushed into the interior regions of all colonies from New Hampshire to Georgia, increasing the area under cultivation. As a result of this expansion, the colonial economy expanded at a rate three or four times faster than that of Great Britain over the seventy-five years before American independence. Whereas colonial production was diminutive on a comparative basis in 1650, by 1775 the mainland settlements had developed an economy nearly two-fifths the size of Great Britain's.[23] Moreover, growth was not just extensive; by the mid-eighteenth century the colonies were entering an era of intensive

20. Robert E. Brown, *Middle-Class Democracy and the Revolution in Massachusetts, 1691–1780* (Ithaca, NY, 1955); Jack R. Pole, *Political Representation in England and the Origins of the American Republic* (1966); and Robert J. Dinkin, *Voting in Provincial America: A Study of Elections in the Thirteen Colonies, 1689–1776* (Westport, CT, 1977).

21. For a useful introduction to this subject, see the essays in Bruce C. Daniels, ed., *Power and Status: Office Holding in Colonial America* (Middletown, CT, 1986). Also, David W. Jordan, *Foundations of Representative Government in Maryland, 1632–1715* (Cambridge, 1987).

22. Charles E. Clark, *The Public Print: The Newspaper in Anglo-American Culture, 1665–1740* (Oxford, 1994).

23. The best introduction to early American economic history is John J. McCusker and Russell Menard, *The Economy of British North America, 1607–1789* (Chapel Hill, NC, 1985). See also, Gary M. Walton and James Shepherd, *The Economic Rise of Early America* (Cambridge, 1979) and Edwin J. Perkins, *The Economy of Colonial America* 2nd edn (New York, 1988).

development.[24] They were no longer tenuous outposts on a distant continent. Per capita incomes for members of free, white households in British North America were higher than those in England on the eve of the revolution. This burgeoning economy helped mitigate social tensions and gave the mainland settlements the potential for independence. Hence the colonies were blossoming by the mid-eighteenth century. Growing in stature, they already possessed many of the features characteristic of self-governing polities – acknowledged and experienced elites, strong governing institutions at provincial level, and a growing competence, stability and regularity in their internal affairs. Moreover, a wide franchise, broad participation in local government, an open and accessible press, and a widespread suspicion of centralization gave colonial political culture a distinctive character. With a robust economy underpinning these developments, the colonies' potential was obvious. The key question was whether it was to be fulfilled inside or outside the confines of the British empire.

British authority in the colonies

While the colonies grew stronger during the mid-eighteenth century, British imperial power in North America remained surprisingly weak. The Board of Trade, the principal central government agency in Britain with authority over colonial affairs, had only advisory powers. It struggled – and usually failed – to gain support for its efforts to develop a more efficient administrative system. Often blown off-course by the conflicting demands of powerful interest groups, it had few resources and limited manpower. Just keeping abreast of the changing conditions across the Atlantic was a problem.[25] Until a system of packet boats was established in 1755, there was not even a reliable channel for official correspondence between Britain and its American colonies.

In the course of the eighteenth century other administrative agencies and offices became involved in aspects of colonial government, but this merely created overlapping jurisdictions and clashes of interest.[26] The most important of these was the secretary of state

24. 'The gifts of peace: social and economic expansion and development in the periodization of the early American past, 1713–1763' in Greene, *Negotiated Authorities*, p. 130.
25. Ian K. Steele, *The English Atlantic, 1675–1740: An Exploration of Communication and Community* (Oxford, 1986), esp. pp. 211–78.
26. For a useful, short overview, see Ian K. Steele, 'Metropolitan administration of the colonies, 1696–1775' in Jack P. Greene and Jack R. Pole, eds, *The Blackwell*

for the Southern Department. He was the senior royal executive officer who reported to the cabinet and the privy council concerning the colonies and issued any orders that resulted in the monarch's name. Also, royal governors were responsible to him for defence and military matters. As the secretary also handled Mediterranean affairs and relations with France and Spain, however, he was often too busy to give sustained attention to the colonies. In addition, staffs of subordinate bodies under the Treasury were responsible for the gathering of various royal and imperial revenues in America and, in part, for the enforcement of the laws of trade. Its Board of Customs Commissioners supervised collectors and comptrollers of customs in North American ports, as well as overseeing the naval officers who were the official recorders of ship movements. The problems of finance also gave the Treasury itself an important voice at times in the shaping of policy. The Admiralty played its part as well. It provided convoys for the colonial trades and Royal Navy patrols to protect the North American coast and to stem violations of the navigation laws. With several bodies therefore having an interest in colonial affairs, as the Board of Trade complained, 'no one office is thro'ly informed of all matters relating to the Plantations'.[27] A complex and rickety bureaucratic structure lacked the ability to obtain support for its policies at home or to enforce them in the American settlements.

The key figure within the colonies themselves was the governor, who headed the local administration and acted as the link between the province and the metropolis. His formal powers were considerable. He could determine when and where the assembly met; prorogue or dissolve it at his pleasure; and refuse to sign its bills. The governor also nominated the members of his council, which functioned both as the upper house of the legislature and the highest court of appeal in the colony. With respect to the judiciary, the governor still normally held the prerogative of creating courts and of naming and dismissing judges. Finally, as chief executive he could appoint and remove officials, command the militia and naval forces, and grant pardons.

Eighteenth-century governors were, on the whole, men of some skill and ability who compared favourably with leading metropolitan

---

Encyclopedia of the American Revolution (Oxford, 1991), pp. 9–16. Also, Michael Kammen, *Empire and Interest: The American Colonies and the Politics of Mercantilism* (New York, 1970); Leonard W. Labaree, *Royal Government in America: A Study of the British Colonial System before 1783* (New Haven, CT, 1930); and F.B. Wickwire, *British Subministers and Colonial America, 1763–1783* (Princeton, NJ, 1966).

27. Quoted in Barrow, *Trade and Empire*, p. 108.

office-holders. Many had had previous experience of the colonies and displayed energy and enterprise whilst in post. Despite these qualities and their extensive theoretical powers, the governors faced grave problems.[28] The representative assemblies were gaining in strength through their control of the power of the purse and often the colonial executive felt he had no choice but to accede to their demands. After all, the governors had almost no armed forces at their disposal to buttress their authority if it came to the crunch. Before large contingents of British troops arrived at the beginning of the Seven Years War, there were no more than a few regular soldiers in any colony on more than a temporary basis. The governors also lacked the informal ability to build a following tied to them by the distribution of offices or employment. They never had much patronage at their disposal and, especially during the era of 'salutary neglect', what little they had was being nibbled away by the colonial assemblies on the one hand and the metropolitan authorities on the other.[29] In reality, then, British power in the colonies rested on potentially shaky foundations by the mid-eighteenth century and the authorities were unable to rely on either force or influence to bolster their position.

The growing dynamism of the colonies and the continued shortcomings of British administration exacerbated tensions within the imperial–colonial relationship which, in turn, greatly heightened the potential for transatlantic misunderstanding. There was an obvious gulf between the metropolitan authorities' perception of the colonies on the one hand and their actual condition on the other. Put simply, the American settlements were outgrowing the traditional constraints of the imperial–colonial relationship and ideally that required some imaginative adjustment in official thinking. This shift appeared to have been made during the era of 'salutary neglect' when an informal accommodation between the metropolis and the colonies had seemingly been reached – one that permitted the latter a degree of *de facto* self-government and economic freedom. The problem was that this accommodation was entirely opportunistic: the British authorities had not abandoned their underlying assumption that the colonies remained mere dependencies. Indeed, by helping to stem overt colonial challenges to the status quo, it actually

28. On the contrast between the scope of the governors' formal powers and their limited influence, see Bailyn, *Origins of American Politics*; and William A. Speck, *British America, 1607–1776* (Brighton, 1985), esp. pp. 32–4.

29. Greene, *Quest for Power*; *idem*, 'Uneasy connection'; and Henretta, '*Salutary Neglect*'.

buttressed the conventional view and helped convince the British political nation that the American settlements were firmly in hand. Another tension within the imperial–colonial relationship was between divergent conceptions of where authority lay within the empire. Stemming from their belief in a unitary state, the British were convinced that sovereignty rested with the centre. The colonists, by contrast, were equally persuaded that power must be shared with the periphery: otherwise their provincial assemblies and their rights would count for nothing. Given this almost unbridgeable divide, why did the settlers remain within the empire for so long? A partial answer lay, of course, in the benefits they derived from the imperial connection in spheres like defence and trade. Far more important, however, were the still-powerful, if intangible, bonds of allegiance and affection that tied the colonies tightly to the parent state. In fact, as Greene points out, the strength of these ties actually increased through the middle decades of the eighteenth century because of the colonies' growing involvement with Britain, the desire of colonial elites to reproduce 'British' society in North America, and the resulting Anglicization of colonial life.[30]

These bonds could not bind the colonies to Britain under all circumstances, however. The settlers' attachment to the metropolis, though strong, was hedged with conditions. Essentially Britain was not to violate the informal and, of course, unwritten colonial 'constitution'. Its most obvious and explicit element was the desire that the imperial government should not undermine the integrity of the elected lower houses of assembly and other institutions and symbols of self-government. Another was that the colonists would enjoy a degree of economic independence commensurate with the free pursuit of their own interests. Finally, the metropolitan authorities were not to undermine their personal autonomy by taking steps that would reduce them to virtual slavery. Other conditions also fed into the equation. The colonists wanted Britain to act as a virtuous yardstick by which they could measure their own achievements and they expected continued protection and encouragement.

This cluster of settler expectations sat uneasily alongside the metropolitan authorities' conception of the imperial–colonial relationship. The gulf between them was, in Greene's words, the 'essential

30. Greene, 'Uneasy connection', pp. 47–52. See also Timothy H. Breen, 'An empire of goods: the Anglicization of colonial America, 1690–1776' *JBS* 25 (1986), pp. 467–99. The term 'Anglicization' originally comes from John M. Murrin, 'Anglicizing an American colony: the transformation of provincial Massachusetts', unpub. PhD diss. (Yale University, 1966).

precondition that gave the British Empire a latent potential for revolution through the middle decades of the eighteenth century'.[31] Still, these discrepancies required clearer definition and exploration before they actually became capable of causing the empire's disintegration. What began this process was the British authorities' decision to abandon the policy of accommodation characteristic of the era of 'salutary neglect' and bring the colonies under tighter control. This decision was taken, not suddenly in 1763, and not even in 1759, as Bernard Knollenberg has argued,[32] but gradually in the decade beginning in 1748 as Greene has shown.[33] Nor did it mark any sharp ideological break with the past. It merely represented another attempt to implement the traditional aims of English colonial policy. Conditions had changed, however, since the days of the Stuarts or the Glorious Revolution. The colonies were now much more mature and correspondingly less dependent upon Britain, and the attempt immediately followed a period during which the imperial government appeared to have abandoned most of its earlier goals. This meant that, whatever underlying continuity existed between post- and pre-1748 policy, there was a profound discontinuity in its effect on imperial–colonial relations.

Efforts at tighter control

What accounts for this change in the tone and direction of British policy? The most important factor was undoubtedly the increase in the colonies' value to Britain – a product of their extraordinary territorial, demographic and economic growth. In fact, the mainland settlements became the fastest-growing part of the empire before 1750 and accounted for a significant proportion of the total volume of British overseas trade. The value to Britain of American and West Indian commerce increased more than 120 per cent, from £1,855,000 per annum at the beginning of the century to £4,105,000 per annum at mid-century. The commercial tie with North America was therefore making an increasingly significant contribution to the British economy.[34] But while this was a source

31. Greene, 'Uneasy connection', p. 62.
32. See Bernhard Knollenberg, *Origins of the American Revolution: 1759–1766* (1960).
33. See Greene, 'Uneasy connection', pp. 32–80.
34. Alison G. Olson, 'The changing socio-economic and strategic importance of the colonies to the empire' in Greene and Pole, eds, *Blackwell Encyclopedia of the American Revolution*, p. 20.

of pride, it also generated anxiety within the metropolitan establishment. What if the colonies sought greater economic independence and became Britain's rival rather than partner? Or, what if France or Spain seized the North American settlements? Both these concerns prompted renewed interest in the colonies and their administration during the late 1740s.

Two other considerations also played an important role in the timing of the shift in metropolitan policy. The first was the re-establishment of domestic political stability under Henry Pelham in 1747 following several years of factional in-fighting. With international peace also returning the following year with the end of the War of the Austrian Succession, Britain's political leaders were free once again to turn their attention to the colonies. An even more important consideration that helped determine the timing of this policy shift and heightened the growing anxiety that animated it was the simultaneous outbreak of a series of serious political and social disturbances in many of the colonies.[35] New Jersey was racked by land riots, while serious factional disputes in New Hampshire, North Carolina and New York took their toll. This shook the authorities' confidence that the empire was firmly in their grasp. Instead, it seemed disintegration loomed during the late 1740s and early 1750s. The growing realization in Britain of the colonies' value and the accompanying fear of the long-term implications of their rapid expansion, on the one hand, and the re-establishment of metropolitan political stability and the shattering of the imperial illusion of control, on the other, explains the reorientation of British policy in the late 1740s.

Under George Dunk, Earl of Halifax, the Board of Trade once again took the lead in the effort to shore up imperial power in the colonies. Beginning in 1748, the board first sought to define the problems facing it and to work out a system of priorities for dealing with them. As on earlier occasions, it gave precedence to the problem of defending the colonies against New France. Its preferred solution this time was to turn frontier Nova Scotia into a fully-fledged British settlement. To this end, that colony was both strengthened and subsidized. The board's other major initiative was less successful, however. An attack on colonial currencies foundered when a bill to stop further paper money issues, introduced in parliament in March 1749, was not enacted.

---

35. For a case study, see Thomas L. Purvis, 'Origins and patterns of agrarian unrest in New Jersey, 1735–1754' *WMQ* 3rd series, 39 (1982), pp. 600–27.

Halifax and his colleagues also turned their attention to the colonies' internal governance. The board's initial approach to these problems was almost entirely piecemeal and *ad hoc*. But its actions all tended in the same general direction: towards stronger executive control. The board insisted that royal governors keep to their instructions from the crown and censured those who assented to laws in violation of those orders. With colonial assemblies simply refusing to accept executive intervention, however, the only effect of the board's initiative was to increase colonial instability. The governors' position was made even more precarious by the board's inability to back them up when challenged. Overwhelmed by the sheer volume of business, it either put them off or ignored their pleas. Except for the Nova Scotia settlement and the Currency Act of 1751, therefore, the board had little to show for its efforts by early 1752. Not one of the underlying problems it had inherited had been resolved. In fact, the board's aggressive behaviour towards the governors was making a bad situation worse and metropolitan control over the colonies seemed even more tenuous at the beginning of 1752 than it had four years earlier.

Frustration reigned on both sides of the Atlantic. Governors believed that they could not rely on the board to support their efforts and its endless delays drove them to despair. Halifax was equally disenchanted and, in response, he pushed hard to have himself appointed as a separate secretary of state with broad jurisdiction over the colonies. Although this effort failed, he finally secured enlarged powers for the board in early 1752. It received exclusive authority over the appointment of all governors, councillors, attorneys-general and secretaries in the colonies, who were now directly responsible to it.

The extension of the board's powers inaugurated a second phase in its effort to halt the decline in metropolitan authority across the Atlantic. This period, lasting until the outbreak of the Seven Years War in 1756, was one of renewed activity – and ultimate failure. Armed with its new powers, the board embarked upon an even more vigorous campaign to bring the colonies under closer metropolitan control. It tried to secure more up-to-date information on the colonies by insisting that governors provide new answers to the standard queries hitherto required only irregularly and send home all public papers promptly. To speed this process, it set up the packet boat system in 1755. The board also continued to insist that governors adhere strictly to their instructions. One of the underlying goals here was to check the powers of the lower houses of assembly over areas like establishing new constituencies, apportioning representatives, settling accounts and appointing local officers. The board reviewed colonial laws carefully and insisted on the inclusion of clauses suspending operation until explicit metropolitan approval had been granted. It also recommended unsuccessfully that the assemblies convert all earlier legislation into a clear body of statute law that could be cleansed of improper measures by metropolitan authorities. Finally, to stem the lower houses' financial powers, the board revived the idea of a civil list funded from permanent revenues.

In addition to challenging the colonial assemblies, the board pursued several other policies aimed at strengthening imperial authority. After 1752 it tried to reform provincial court systems and alter judicial tenure from good behaviour to royal pleasure. The board also endeavoured to prevent the emission of any further legal-tender paper currency by extending the reach of the Currency Act of 1751 beyond New England. Finally, it attempted to extend its jurisdiction over the remaining private colonies by demanding that Rhode Island and Connecticut transmit their laws to London, and by pressurizing the proprietors of Pennsylvania and Maryland to curtail the authority of their lower houses.[36]

These metropolitan initiatives ran into stiff opposition from across the Atlantic, as the lower houses and other powerful colonial interests refused to accept them. Assemblies up and down the Atlantic seaboard resisted every effort to diminish their authority, claiming that they were an attack upon their established constitutions and a violation of their rights. Confronted with this opposition, there was little the Board of Trade could do. Despite some limited gains, Halifax was painfully aware by 1756 that his principal strategic goals remained unfulfilled. Significant in its own right, his failure also helped shape the contours of the ensuing imperial crisis. The fate of Halifax's reforms persuaded the British political establishment that the drive to establish effective metropolitan control required a comprehensive and sweeping programme of reform, not just the often piecemeal solutions that had been attempted between 1748 and 1756. Also, many were now convinced that only direct parliamentary intervention stood any chance of bringing the recalcitrant colonists to heel, inviting a direct clash between rival legislatures.[37]

36. Greene, 'Uneasy connection', pp. 69–73.
37. For this dimension of the conflict, see R.R. Johnson, ' "Parliamentary egotisms": the clash of legislatures in the making of the American Revolution' *JAH* 74 (1987), pp. 338–62.

The Seven Years War

Although the Seven Years War forced the temporary shelving of the imperial reform programme, the conflict itself only intensified the impulses that had lain behind it.[38] It enhanced pre-existing fears of loss of control over and potential rivalry from the colonies, and deepened suspicion that the settlers harboured secret desires for independence.[39] Throughout the war, the colonial assemblies exploited the government's need for defence requisitions to wrest even more authority away from the executive; colonial merchants flagrantly violated the Navigation Acts, even trading with the French and Spanish Caribbean; and many lower houses refused to come forward with men and material for the war effort.[40] Actions such as these left many members of the British political establishment feeling bitter and hostile towards the colonists and ever more determined to put them in their place. They regarded repeated refusals to comply with royal requisitions and other instances of opposition to imperial regulations as evidence of extreme ingratitude that should not go unpunished.

As soon as British and colonial forces had defeated French forces, metropolitan officials, as Bernhard Knollenberg has shown, undertook a fresh series of restrictive measures during 1759 to 1764 to bolster their authority.[41] The impulse behind these measures was not new, however. They merely represented a renewal and an extension of Halifax's earlier reform programme. But they were an extension within a significantly different – and far more fragile – context. Whereas the Seven Years War had heightened the fears of the imperial authorities, it had boosted the self-confidence of the colonists even further. They had found the conflict a liberating and fulfilling experience. The settlers' substantial contribution, as they saw it, to the war effort prompted a surge of British patriotism among them and created heightened expectations for a larger role

38. For the impact of the Seven Years War, see John M. Murrin, 'The French and Indian War, the American Revolution, and the counterfactual hypothesis: reflections on Lawrence Henry Gipson and John Shy' *Reviews in American History* 1 (1973), pp. 307–18; and Jack P. Greene, 'The Seven Years War and the American Revolution: the causal relationship reconsidered' *JICH* 8 (1980), pp. 85–105.

39. For the history of this sentiment, see J.M. Bumsted, ' "Things in the womb of time": ideas of American independence, 1633–1763' *WMQ* 3rd series, 31 (1974), pp. 533–64.

40. Alan Rogers, *Empire and Liberty: American Resistance to British Authority, 1755–1763* (Berkeley, 1974), esp. pp. 90–120.

41. Knollenberg, *Origins of the American Revolution*.

within the empire, a role that would finally raise their status to near equality with the metropolis. Assemblies, for example, had enjoyed additional responsibilities which made them increasingly impatient of tight imperial control, especially over issues like paper money and the need for suspending clauses. Suddenly, in Richard Middleton's words, it seemed that 'the umbilical cord of maternal union was threatening to become a noose'.[42] At the same time the colonists were also beginning to look beyond the horizons of their own provinces. In fighting alongside soldiers from other parts of North America, the war had demonstrated to them that they had much in common with their neighbours. Another embryonic identity was beginning to emerge alongside their 'Britishness'.

As well as changing expectations in potentially dangerous ways, the war also altered the very structure of the imperial-colonial relationship. Britain now had to defend newly conquered territories that included 60,000 French Canadians, 3000 Spanish subjects in Florida, and perhaps 150,000 western Indians. Given that these peoples were not well disposed to live under the authority of George III, a standing army was imperative in order to maintain order.[43] This was an important innovation in itself, but so was the expense required. During the war many British officers and officials had been impressed by the apparent wealth of the American settlers. It therefore seemed only fair that they should pay for part of the overall cost of both the conflict and the ensuing peace. The colonists, after all, were among the principal beneficiaries of Britain's massive war efforts against France.

These considerations led the government in London to conclude that imperial reform was essential. As Henry Fox wrote in 1763: 'the settlement of American affairs has become the greatest and most necessary of all schemes'.[44] Halifax's efforts at rationalization and centralization had to be renewed. This reasoning was encapsulated in Thomas Pownall's *The Administration of the Colonies*.[45] In this pamphlet, the former governor of Massachusetts argued for a single department to handle American business so that authority was no longer diffused among several metropolitan agencies. Otherwise, Pownall suggested, the colonies would drift out of British

42. Richard Middleton, *Colonial America: A History, 1585–1776* 2nd edn (Oxford, 1996), p. 440.

43. On the subsequent role of the standing army, see John Shy, *Towards Lexington: The Role of the British Army in the Coming of the Revolution* (Princeton, NJ, 1965).

44. Quoted in Richard Simmons, *The American Colonies: From Settlement to Independence* (New York, 1981), p. 294.

45. Thomas Pownall, *The Administration of the Colonies* (1764).

control altogether. Other administrators and politicians agreed and, equally important, urged that the authority of parliament be brought to bear on the settlers. Hence, by removing their competitors and thus making it less necessary to placate the colonists, the British victory left metropolitan authorities with a much freer hand to go ahead with a further round of imperial reform. Moreover, for the first time during and after the war, the British had large numbers of royal troops in the colonies. By giving them renewed confidence in their ability to suppress potential opposition, the presence of these troops made officials bolder in their handling of the colonies than they had been earlier.

The colonists naturally saw matters rather differently. They ascribed the recent military success in large part to their own exertions. Moreover, as Lawrence H. Gipson has argued, the expulsion of the French and Spanish from eastern North America removed the need for the last absolutely essential protective element the British had to offer the mainland colonies – defence against European rivals. Now the settlers were freer than ever before to pursue their own destiny, wherever that might take them.[46] The acquisition of vast lands in the west prompted visionaries like Franklin to dream of an empire stretching from the Atlantic to the Pacific. More prosaically, colonial adventurers could see large profits or new lives in their exploitation. The ending of the war also unleashed a strong desire for greater freedom in commercial matters. While most colonists basically accepted the British mercantilist system, some did feel annoyed at the restrictions it imposed. They were irritated, for example, by the customs service's continued use of writs of assistance. This system was challenged in the Massachusetts' courts during 1761 by the lawyer James Otis Jr., and his arguments were a sign of things to come as the colonists grew tired of government actions that seemed increasingly arbitrary.[47]

The colonists' sense of liberation was tinged with anxiety, however. Dark clouds seemed to hover over them, all stemming from the imperial tie. First, there was the continued presence of the British army. Its quartering and recruiting practices had persuaded many that it threatened civil liberties. Such actions, exacerbated by traditional fears of standing armies, lent credence to the notion that this force was really intended for the subjection of the colonial

---

46. Lawrence H. Gipson, 'The American Revolution as an aftermath of the great war for empire, 1754–1763' *PSQ* 65 (1950), pp. 86–104.

47. On Otis, see John J. Waters Jr., *The Otis Family in Provincial and Revolutionary Massachusetts* (Chapel Hill, NC, 1968).

population.[48] A second cause for suspicion, especially in New England, was the activities of the Anglican church. Rumours abounded that the appointment of a bishop for North America was under consideration, sparking fears that this was the initial step towards the creation of an established church. This was a prospect that raised the spectre of religious persecution.[49] A final reason for distrust of Britain was the widespread feeling among many educated colonists that metropolitan corruption threatened their liberty. Classical empires had fallen because of their corrosive effects on public morality. With the parliamentary opposition constantly denouncing the government as venal, the threat seemed to exist in Britain as well. With the colonists perceiving liberty as fragile and under constant threat from power and corruption, the stakes were potentially very high indeed in the post-war empire.[50]

The optimism and joy accompanying the end of the Seven Years War proved shallow and ephemeral. That conflict had, in reality, injected a new volatility into the imperial–colonial relationship. With attitudes changing on both sides of the Atlantic, the 'uneasy connection' was about to be rent asunder. The colonists had emerged from the war with enhanced self-confidence, less need for British protection, and understandable fears about the metropolitan authorities' intentions. British officials, by contrast, were now determined to implement long-standing plans for administrative reform, probably through the vehicle of parliament. And, if challenged, they believed that they had an army in North America to enforce their will. Seen in the context of recent developments, then, both British actions in the 1760s and the colonial reaction to them were predictable. The result was the fatal undermining of the delicate balance between central and peripheral interests crucial to the successful functioning of an extended polity like the British empire.[51]

48. Rogers, *Empire and Liberty*, esp. pp. 37–89.
49. On the religious dimension to the imperial crisis, see Carl Bridenbaugh, *Mitre and Sceptre: Transatlantic Faiths, Ideas, Personalities, and Politics, 1689–1775* (New York, 1962); Alan Heimert, *Religion and the American Mind from the Great Awakening to the Revolution* (Cambridge, MA, 1966); and Patricia U. Bonomi, *Under the Cope of Heaven: Religion, Society, and Politics in Colonial America* (New York, 1986), esp. pp. 187–216.
50. For these fears and the way that they play themselves out in the ensuing imperial crisis, see Bailyn, *Ideological Origins*.
51. 'Negotiated authorities: the problem of governance in the extended polities of the early modern Atlantic world,' in Jack P. Greene, *Negotiated Authorities*, p. 24.

CHAPTER TWO

Government Policy and the American Crisis 1760–1776

JOHN DERRY

The loss of the Thirteen Colonies in North America was the greatest humiliation inflicted upon the British state in the eighteenth century. It was not, therefore, surprising that disaster in America should be seen as the culmination of misguided and foolish policies embarked upon by a succession of British governments.[1] Americans came to believe that there was a sinister intention behind British policy, that taxation was merely the symptom of a deep-laid plot to deprive them of their liberties, and many British radicals, eager to discern a conspiracy which threatened liberty on both sides of the Atlantic, associated struggles over the freedom of the press and the rights of electors with a comparable assault upon American liberties. There were elements of continuity in the policies of British governments – chiefly an anxiety to raise revenue in America to offset the costs of the Seven Years War and the maintenance of British garrisons in the colonies – but there were also significant differences between the ways in which successive British ministries approached the crisis in America. There was much misunderstanding, a great deal of wishful thinking and an inability to grasp that the Americans often preferred their own interpretations of traditional liberties to those which were commonly accepted in Britain, but there was no grand conspiracy. Ironically, British politicians believed that what they were seeking to achieve in America was essential for the defence of

1. For a recent reiteration of the traditional critique of British politicians see Paul Johnson, *A History of the American People* (1977), pp. 106–16. Other studies providing a more sympathetic introduction to the policies of successive British governments during the American crisis include: Ian R. Christie, *Crisis of Empire* 2nd edn (1974); John Derry, *English Politics and the American Revolution* (1976); Keith Perry, *British Politics and the American Revolution* (1990); Peter D.G. Thomas, *British Politics and the Stamp Act Crisis* (Oxford, 1975); *idem, The Townshend Duties Crisis* (Oxford, 1987); and *idem, Tea Party to Independence* (Oxford, 1991).

the constitution, the preservation of imperial harmony and the security of the empire against foreign foes. Tom Paine warned the Americans that tyranny like hell was not easily conquered. Much of what British governments did was more reminiscent of an attempt to prove that the way to hell was paved with good intentions.

Fundamental to the behaviour of British politicians throughout the American dispute was their belief in the sovereignty of the British parliament. Among major politicians only Chatham was prepared to limit the sovereignty of parliament and devolve to the colonial assemblies the right and the duty of granting supplies to the crown. The majority of his contemporaries, including many who flattered themselves that they were friends of America, were convinced that in law the British parliament's supremacy was absolute. It was the British parliament which had the responsibility of legislating for the empire as a whole and the awesome task of controlling trade in the interests of the empire. Even when some came to doubt the wisdom or the practicability of raising revenue by means of internal taxation in the Thirteen Colonies they could not bring themselves to renounce the sovereignty of parliament. The assertion of parliament's rights was the chief preoccupation of British politicians. They had no desire to affirm the prerogatives of the crown: had their approach been more imaginative they might have stumbled upon the crown as a means of easing tension and resolving controversy, but in a story which was rich in paradox George III had no wish to assert royal prerogatives in the colonial context, seeing his public duty as the vindication of parliament's rights throughout all territories owing allegiance to the British crown.

The costs of empire

At the end of the Seven Years War no one anticipated a crisis in America. Although the Peace of Paris was widely and often irresponsibly criticized it was a good peace for Britain. But the cost of victory had been immense and the financial burden of winning the war compelled British politicians to tackle problems of taxation and the cost of defence in the American colonies. The apparent removal of the French threat with the acquisition of Quebec made it understandable that British ministers believed that they could no longer ignore problems which had never been coherently addressed. In 1763 the British national debt stood at £132,716,000. British politicians were convinced that the British taxpayer had shouldered the main expense of paying for the war. It was generally believed that the American colonists had not paid their fair share. In fact, the response of the individual colonies to the challenge of the war had varied, but there was no doubt that the majority of British MPs were convinced that the colonial assemblies had failed to grant adequate supplies to the crown. And if the cost of the Seven Years War was an inescapable feature of any review of the political prospect, anxieties about future financial expenditure in the colonies were bound to be a recurrent obsession with governments desperately trying to match income with expenditure.

No consideration of public costs in North America could be divorced from the Indian question. The outbreak of Pontiac's rebellion in 1763 was a vivid reminder of the complexity and sensitivity of the Indian problem. For the British, conflict with the Indians was best avoided. For the Americans, confrontation with the Indians seemed an inescapable accompaniment of colonial development. Although it was premature to talk of 'manifest destiny' many Americans believed that it was only natural that the interior of the continent should be explored and settled. The frontier tradition has often been romanticized but it was already a feature of colonial life. Westward expansion would inevitably mean conflict with the Indians and in 1763 the British government sought to prevent trouble by issuing a proclamation banning expansion west of the Allegheny mountains. Many Americans were angered by this attempt to set a definite limit to the western frontier. They believed that the British had little grasp of the realities of life in the colonies, arguing that ministers in distant London were too sympathetic to the Indians and too sensitive on the issue of treaty obligations to the Indian tribes. The attempt to restrict westward settlement seemed a judicious precaution to the British. To the Americans it confirmed their suspicions of British lack of perception and of the British desire to maintain garrisons in the colonies. The Americans believed that they could deal with the Indian threat expeditiously themselves, without relying on British regular troops, whose competence in Indian fighting they questioned. And since the French threat was no longer ominous the colonists suspected that the British wished to maintain troops in the colonies for the purpose of policing them rather than defending them. A distrust of standing armies had long been manifest in Britain, and this inherited prejudice had already taken on a greater intensity within the American colonies.

Similarly, British governments were bound to approach issues of imperial trade in a different spirit from that of the Americans.

There is now considerable scepticism about whether doctrines of mercantilism had ever been consistently applied throughout the British empire, but there was a widespread belief in Britain that imperial commerce should in some sense be controlled by Britain in the interests of the empire as a whole, and there is no doubt that British merchants and manufacturers resented anything which looked like competition from the American colonies. Although practice never fully matched theory, most British politicians believed that the British parliament had a duty, first to ensure that British economic and commercial interests were secured, and second to try to balance the competing interests of the various colonies in such a way as to benefit the entire empire. Broadly speaking, British governments were aware of four main lobbies in this connection: first, the domestic commercial interest; second, the West Indian planters; third, the East India Company; and finally, the American colonists. It was no easy task to devise policies which would satisfy these competing interests. Inevitably the domestic pressure group was usually the most effective in influencing government policy – this was certainly true in the discussions which led to the repeal of the Stamp Act – but the conduct of British governments was often construed in a sinister sense by Americans who believed that politicians in London were always more willing to accede to pressures from the East Indian or West Indian lobbies than to defer to colonial agents and other spokesmen for American opinion in London. Sadly, the majority of British politicians failed to appreciate American sensibilities in this context, and they were frequently surprised by the intensity with which the Americans reacted to policies which from the British perspective seemed to be reasonable and characterized by compromise rather than – as the Americans often claimed – arrogance and aggression.

A further complication in matters of trade was the British attitude towards the prevalence of smuggling in North America. Smuggling was the inevitable accompaniment both in Britain and America to the levying of customs and excise duties on popular items of commerce at excessively high rates. While the British saw attempts to control smuggling as the inescapable responsibility of any administration which was seeking to encourage legitimate trade, the Americans regarded them as evidence of the British willingness to subordinate American concerns to those of other interest groups which were solicitous in winning the ear of British governments.

Another source of distrust was the necessity for British governments to respond to the demands of the political situation in

Britain. In an era when conventions for the conduct of cabinet government were ambiguous, when the party system was inchoate, and when no ministry could survive without the goodwill of the independent country gentlemen in the House of Commons, British governments frequently had to give precedence to priorities which were dear to the hearts of backbenchers rather than to those cherished by the Americans. Only in retrospect may the American dispute be seen as the dominant controversy in the 1760s and 1770s. For many British MPs the American colonies were on the periphery of politics. At various times policy in America took second place to questions such as winning parliamentary approval for the Peace of Paris; the ongoing conflict between the House of Commons and John Wilkes, whether over the freedom of the press, parliamentary privilege or the Middlesex elections; the Regency crisis of 1765; the difficulty of finding a stable ministry in the 1760s; the Falkland Islands dispute in 1770 and 1771; the Royal Marriages Act of 1772; as well as recurrent crises in the affairs of the East India Company – one of which was to have a decisive impact upon the American question. Even when British ministers flattered themselves that they were grappling with the American problem it was rarely as significant for them as it inevitably was for Americans, whether they were radical or loyalist by conviction.

Raising revenue: George Grenville and the Stamp Act

Nevertheless, it was an initiative taken by a British government which ignited the controversy. George Grenville's determination to tax the Americans was at the heart of the dispute. Grenville was a man of ability, with long experience in the House of Commons and administrative experience as secretary to the navy and secretary of state. He was a fearsome debater, tenacious in argument and relentless in defending his point of view. But he had long been overshadowed in politics by his brother Lord Temple and even more so by his brother-in-law, William Pitt the Elder. When he became First Lord of the Treasury in 1763 he was eager to make his mark. He hated inefficiency and longed to bring order and system to the management of financial and colonial affairs. He was sensitive to any suspicion of a slight, distrusted the influence of Bute with the king, and was often stiff and formal in his dealings with his colleagues. George III found him impossibly pedantic and insufferably tiresome, complaining that when Grenville had wearied him for two hours he looked at his watch to see if he might tire him an hour more. Grenville eventually lost office because of his mishandling of the Regency Bill in 1765 and his ill-judged efforts to impose his will on the king in the sensitive matter of household appointments. He did not lose power because of his conduct of American policy. But his dealings with the Americans were instances of how an application to public business could lead a well-intentioned politician into crucial misjudgements. Grenville had no wish to antagonize the Americans; indeed, it is a measure of his lack of imagination that he flattered himself that he had taken all necessary soundings to make his policy acceptable on both sides of the Atlantic.[2]

It was once said that Grenville went astray because unlike many of his predecessors he took the trouble to read despatches from America. This is misleading. Grenville was preoccupied with Britain's financial problems. He wanted the colonists to pay their fair share of the costs of empire. If the Americans claimed the privileges of freeborn subjects of the British crown, he believed that they must accept the duties incumbent upon them. It was wholly in character that Grenville carefully looked at precedent before deciding what to do. Although the Stamp Act of 1765 was the most notorious of Grenville's measures it was only part of what Grenville believed legitimate in order to deal with colonial problems in a comprehensive manner. He sought to control the issue of paper money in the American colonies by means of a Currency Act passed in 1764 and he carried a Quartering Act which authorized the billeting of British troops in the colonies and which required the colonists to supply necessary provisions for the soldiers. This act was bitterly unpopular in America, where parallels came to be drawn with James II and his standing army and even the means by which Louis XIV had suppressed the French Protestants. In 1764 parliament also passed a Sugar Act amending the Molasses Act of 1733. The duty on foreign-produced molasses was reduced to 3d. a gallon – half the rate which had been in operation since 1733. The duty on foreign sugar was increased from 5/- a hundredweight to 27/-, and the importation of rum into the American colonies was banned. Linens, indigo, coffee, pimento and foreign wines carried heavy duties. The intention was to combine the defence of the West Indian

2. For Grenville's motives and conduct see Thomas, *Stamp Act Crisis*, chs 1–7; Philip Lawson, *George Grenville: A Political Life* (Oxford, 1984); and John L. Bullion, *A Great and Necessary Measure: George Grenville and the Genesis of the Stamp Act 1763–1765* (Columbia, MO, 1982).

economy with the stimulation of the American distilling industry. Grenville argued that the Molasses Act provided a valid precedent for what he had done, but while he certainly wanted to direct and encourage various types of colonial trade he hoped to raise revenue as well, possibly as much as £45,000 a year. The Americans were quick to see that the British intended to apply the Sugar Act as strictly as they could, but whatever misgivings the Americans had they had to admit that the act could be seen as being primarily concerned with imperial commerce. Once the Sugar Act seemed to be accepted in the colonies Grenville was convinced that it was right to push on with the Stamp Act.

Here he was even more certain that precedent was on his side, pointing to the Post Office Act of 1711 as well as to the Molasses Act as evidence that British governments had legislated for the purpose of raising internal revenue. He failed to see – and his blindness was shared by many contemporaries, including Benjamin Franklin – that because the Stamp Act was clearly directed towards the levying of internal revenue in America, rather than the control of trade, it would provoke a storm of protest in the colonies. From the British point of view the Stamp Act seemed unexceptionable. Asking the Americans to pay stamp duties on legal documents, bills of sale, newspapers, playing cards and the like was doing little more than bringing them into line with current British practice. Grenville asserted that no fair-minded person could regard the stamp duties as burdensome. They were preferable to any alternative, such as a tax on negro servants.

Grenville gave the colonists a year in which they could make suggestions for other means of raising revenue or propose amendments to the Stamp Bill to make the collection of the duties simpler and more amenable. Grenville's motives for doing so are still a matter of debate. Possibly he thought that the failure of the Americans to come forward with viable proposals of their own would make them accept the stamp duties as unavoidable, or he may have been seeking to earn a reputation for open-mindedness while remaining convinced that his stamp tax would prove to be the only feasible option. He was aware that there had been several occasions in the past when stamp duties had been considered, though had he been wise he might well have remembered that it had been thought best not to proceed with such schemes. In New York and Massachusetts the colonists were already paying stamp duties levied by their colonial assemblies. Grenville, like most British politicians, ignored the most significant aspect of these taxes, that they had been imposed by the colonists' own representatives, and debate was to rage, not so much over the scale of the stamp duties – though the Americans found it convenient to claim that they were grievous and vexatious – but over the fact that they had been imposed by the British parliament in which the colonists were not represented. Grenville insisted that all revenue raised by the Stamp Act would be spent in America for the benefit, at least as he saw it, of the Americans, and in order to avert charges that he was about to deluge the colonies with swarms of tax-farmers from Britain he stated that American officials would be responsible for the collection of the duties. Since he estimated that the Stamp Act would fail to raise enough money to pay for the upkeep of British garrisons in America he recognized that Britain would still have to bear two-thirds of the costs involved in defending the colonists.

Grenville was taken aback by the intensity of American opposition to the Stamp Act. It was hard for British politicians to conceive of the reasons for American hatred of the Stamp Act. They were ignorant of the situation in the colonies, failing to understand that America was already a more vibrant and less hierarchical society than that of eighteenth-century Britain. From the British point of view it seemed that the Americans were resorting to hysterical and ill-founded pretexts for refusing to make a reasonable contribution to the costs of imperial defence. Even at this stage of the controversy few British politicians had any real grasp of the American standpoint. It was easy to assume that American radicals were an unrepresentative minority, and that a policy of firmness would quickly rally majority opinion, which was assumed to be loyalist and eager for peace and tranquillity.

Some of the arguments put forward by the Americans were taken at their face value when they seemed to confirm British assumptions and prejudices. When Daniel Dulany argued that most Americans accepted the validity of external duties, for the control of trade, while rejecting internal taxes for the purpose of revenue, it was convenient to believe that most Americans agreed with him. Some British commentators were less happy with the American rejection of virtual representation, with which the British had sought to make the sovereignty of the British parliament more acceptable in America. On both sides of the controversy arguments were used with a greater regard for the tactics of debate than for the realities of the situation. Charles Townshend had no doubt that the distinction between external duties and internal taxes was intellectually fraudulent, a mere trick to avoid accepting legitimate authority. He was also convinced that if the Americans put forward such a distinction it might prove convenient to take it with apparent seriousness in order to exploit it in the interests of Britain.

Conciliation, and further conflict

Grenville fell from power before the Stamp Act crisis was resolved. For the rest of his life he defended what he had done, arguing that his political conduct had been intelligent and wholly justifiable. The Rockingham ministry had to face the storm which had erupted in America over the Stamp Act. They brought to the American dispute no distinctive insights and certainly no previously worked-out policy. Like most British politicians Rockingham and his colleagues were astonished and appalled by the riots, demonstrations and trade boycotts which broke out in America. Rockingham was aware of his political vulnerability. The death of the Duke of Cumberland weakened the ministry in its dealings with the king, and it was evident that whatever the rights and wrongs of the question many British merchants, worried by disruptions of trade and rising unemployment, found it convenient to blame the Stamp Act for a worsening economic situation. The ministers knew that if they followed a conciliatory line over the Stamp Act they would face sustained denunciations from Grenville. It was also apparent that Pitt was throwing his considerable prestige behind the colonists in their struggle against the Stamp Act. In debate Pitt talked of rejoicing that the Americans had resisted, denied the relevance of the argument of virtual representation, made much of the distinction between taxation for the purposes of revenue and taxation for the control of trade, and called for the repeal of the Stamp Act. George III, meanwhile, was deeply uneasy about any concessions which compromised the sovereignty of parliament or which yielded to violence or sedition. The king's preference was for the amendment rather than the repeal of the Stamp Act. While the Rockinghamites were eager to damp down disorder in America they did not wish to seem pusillanimous in their attitude to riot and unrest. They were sensitive, too, about the desire of many MPs to see due restitution made in the colonies to the victims of arson, violence and intimidation. And they knew that they could not ignore opinions about the American dispute voiced by the West Indian and East Indian lobbies, whose anxieties about imperial trade meant that they had no desire to see the government act in such a way as to give advantages to disgruntled and disaffected Americans.

The Rockinghamites advanced cautiously and tortuously towards implementing a policy which would restore tranquillity in America while reassuring the commercial interest in Britain that its well-being was not being sacrificed to political expediency in dealing with the colonists. It was convenient for the Rockinghamites to claim that they were primarily concerned with restoring the normal patterns of trade and that the sufferings of British merchants and manufacturers were uppermost in their minds. They knew that they could not ignore the determination of the overwhelming majority of the House of Commons to uphold the sovereignty of the British parliament, come what may. Arguably, the conflicting pressures of domestic politics, coupled with their own vulnerability, carried more weight with the ministers than any concern for the Americans, but in March 1766 the ministry succeeded in putting together a policy which seemed to satisfy, at least in the short term, the expectations of most interested parties. They repealed the Stamp Act, citing as their main justification for doing so the need to restore normal commerce, while passing a Declaratory Act, which affirmed in un-compromising language the legislative supremacy of the British parliament throughout the British empire, in all cases whatsoever. In matters of constitutional principle no concessions were made to the Americans.[3]

The repeal of the Stamp Act was intended to win back American goodwill by removing the main cause of complaint. The policy was defensible and commendable, but it provided no long-term answer to the vexed questions of colonial administration. All the Rockinghamites did was to try to restore the situation as it had existed before Grenville's Stamp Act. This reflected Edmund Burke's ideas on the American dispute. Burke believed that in strict constitutional law parliament had the right to tax the Americans, but he maintained that there were circumstances in which it would be foolish and misguided for the British to exercise such a right. Antagonizing the Americans risked sacrificing the ties of affection, which were the truest bonds of empire, to the demands of revenue, and doing so would prove misguided and foolish. It was wise to refrain from asserting a right, even though it was technically correct to do so. This approach represented that magnanimity in politics which Burke

3. The American policies of the Rockingham ministry are analysed in Thomas, *Stamp Act Crisis*, chs 11–13; Paul Langford, *The First Rockingham Administration 1765–1766* (Oxford, 1973), esp. ch. 4; and Frank O'Gorman, *The Rise of Party: The Rockingham Whigs 1760–1782* (1975), ch. 6.

regarded as the highest wisdom. In reality it meant applying a sophisticated and intelligent expediency to the demands of the hour, but it was not a solution to the colonial problem. The Rockinghamites made other concessions to colonial opinion, reducing the molasses duty to a penny and establishing free ports in Jamaica and Dominica. They sought to ensure that due recompense was paid to those who had suffered at the hands of American rioters. All this fell short of a comprehensive policy for a reform of colonial administration, and when the ministry fell in July 1766 as the result of internal dissensions all that they had achieved so far as the Americans were concerned was the removal of the most obvious source of contention.

The appointment of Pitt as prime minister ought to have reassured those who were eager for conciliation with the colonists. George III had now outgrown his youthful distrust of Pitt, and the king hoped that he had found the stable ministry which had eluded him for so long. Pitt disliked the Declaratory Act: he had wanted to delete the phrase 'in all cases whatsoever' from it. Unlike the majority of his colleagues he believed that there were limits to the sovereignty of the British parliament. Parliament had the right to control trade, to levy customs duties, to apply the Navigation Acts, to billet soldiers, to do everything, in short, which was necessary for securing the empire and defending British interests throughout the world. But Pitt conceded that supplies to the crown should be voted by the Americans in their own assemblies. The right of approving taxation could belong only to their own representatives. In this sense, Pitt took seriously the distinction which many Americans had exploited tactically – that between internal and external taxation. But Pitt remained an imperialist. He wanted to strengthen the British empire as it had emerged from the Seven Years War and his policy in America was intended to secure the ties of empire. Conciliation and a recognition of American liberties were seen by Pitt as the best means of safeguarding British interests in North America.

Yet the Chatham administration proved disastrous in the American context. Pitt's decision to go to the Lords as Earl of Chatham was a mistake. His great strength had been in the House of Commons, where his powerful rhetoric and imposing personality could sway opinion. More serious still was his nervous breakdown, which meant that the ministry was directed by the Duke of Grafton, whose control over his colleagues was uncertain and who could never rival Chatham in his ability to master events. Instead of pursuing policies of conciliation in America the ministry reopened the dispute in a manner which led to an escalation of the conflict and a radicalization of American opinion.[4]

Charles Townshend has often been depicted as the irresponsible and malevolent genius of the American dispute. Brilliant, resourceful, eager for applause and impatient of restraint, he took the ministry into renewed confrontation in America. But Townshend did not act alone. The ministers were still anxious to raise revenue in the colonies and an additional preoccupation emerged to supplement the long-standing concern for the maintenance of British garrisons. In several of the American colonies there were bitter disputes over the appointment and payment of governors and judges. The more radical members of the colonial assemblies wanted to use the power of the purse to control the executive and the judiciary more effectively. Many of the governors and colonial administrators, on the other hand, were looking for ways of escaping from the control of the assemblies, arguing that this was necessary for more responsible administration and more objective dispensation of justice. The British government sympathized with the colonial governors and sought the means of paying governors' salaries from taxation raised by the British parliament. Townshend believed – and it would appear that his colleagues agreed with him – that it would be possible to do so by exploiting the distinction between taxation for the purposes of revenue and taxation for the control of trade to which many Americans had referred during the controversy over the Stamp Act. Townshend argued that by levying a series of customs duties he would be able to raise sufficient money to pay the salaries of governors, judges and other colonial officials. If the Americans really believed in the distinction between the two types of taxation they could hardly object. He thought that the distinction was nonsense, but by taking the Americans at their word he would be able to achieve what he wanted without repeating the mistakes which Grenville had made with his Stamp Act. In 1767 customs duties were imposed on tea, paints, glass, paper and lead.

While Townshend deceived himself and his colleagues into thinking that he had found an unobjectionable means of raising revenue in the colonies, his ruse was quickly exposed as fallacious. Those

---

4. The fullest treatments of the Chatham ministry are in John Brooke, *The Chatham Administration 1766–68* (1956) and Thomas, *Townshend Duties Crisis*, esp. chs 1–8. For Townshend see Peter D.G. Thomas, 'Charles Townshend and American taxation in 1767' *EHR* 83 (1968), pp. 33–51; Cornelius P. Forster, *The Uncontrolled Chancellor: Charles Townshend and his American Policy* (Providence, RI, 1978); and L.B. Namier and John Brooke, *Charles Townshend* (1964).

Americans who had accepted the distinction between internal and external taxation denied that Townshend was genuinely accepting the distinction. Others went on, given Townshend's lack of scruple, to reject the validity of the original distinction. More seriously still, Townshend had involved the wrangle over taxation with colonial disputes over the payment of civil officials and the power of the colonial assemblies in such a manner as to heighten American suspicions about the good faith of the British government in the ongoing debate over patterns of government and modes of representation in the colonies. He had wanted the revenue to be used to pay the salaries of governors, judges and other royal officials in order to make them independent of the colonial assemblies. The British assertion of parliamentary sovereignty had seemed bad enough when it was used to endorse the Stamp Act, but now it implied duplicity in the raising of revenue, bad faith in the control of imperial trade, and sinister intent towards the practice of representative government in British North America.

The Boston Tea Party and the Intolerable Acts

The British government was once more taken aback by the vehemence of American opposition to Townshend's duties. There was less excuse for their failure to anticipate hostile reactions than had been the case over the Stamp Act. Once again the colonists resorted to boycotts and non-importation agreements, though these had less impact on British opinion than previously. British anxieties about American unruliness were intensified by the Boston Massacre in March 1770 when five Bostonians were killed in a scuffle with British troops. Townshend had died unexpectedly in the summer of 1767. His successor as chancellor of the exchequer, Lord North, who became prime minister when Grafton resigned in 1770, had no desire to become embroiled in a bitter dispute in America, though he believed in the principle of parliamentary sovereignty and in Britain's rights to control imperial trade. North repealed all of Townshend's duties except that on tea. By doing so he hoped to show that the British had no intention of tyrannizing over the Americans. The retention of the tea duty upheld the principle of parliamentary sovereignty. It was also thought to be the only one of Townshend's duties which had brought in a reasonable return of about £12,000 a year. Perhaps if all went well there might still be a prospect, however distant, of raising revenue which would eventually provide for the costs of civil administration in North America. This hope proved illusory, but the tea duty meant that the fortunes of the American colonies and the British East India Company were inextricably linked and this was to have baleful consequences in 1773 when another crisis in the finances of the company compelled North to try to assist the company by stimulating sales of tea in America.

North had many of the attributes necessary for a competent first minister. He had the confidence of the king; he was a popular member of the House of Commons; he was a shrewd financier; he was a skilful and congenial debater. His good humour appealed to backbench country gentlemen. By temperament he was a conciliator. He had no wish to inflame passion or provoke violence in America. But like most British politicians of the time he firmly believed in the supremacy of parliament. He argued that supreme authority throughout the empire could reside only in Britain, that such an authority had to rest with parliament, and that it could neither be devolved nor abridged. He was aware that he could not afford to be insensitive to the wishes of the House of Commons or appear to be too submissive to intransigence and violence in the colonies. In normal times North would have been a successful and highly respected prime minister. But he was temperamentally unsuited to handling a crisis, especially if the conflict came to necessitate an appeal to arms. Intelligent and resourceful though he was, North lacked imagination: he had no conception of the true impact of British policies in America. Like Townshend and Grafton he thought that if some way could be found of raising revenue in the colonies to pay colonial administrators this would be no bad thing since it would make government in the colonies less deferential to popular pressures exercised through the colonial assemblies.[5]

In some degree the years 1770 to 1773 were a period of apparent calm in North America. North and his colleagues believed that their policy of upholding constitutional principle, while making appropriate gestures of conciliation, had worked. But the calm was deceptive. Many Americans resented what had happened and were now profoundly suspicious of British policy in America. Smuggling continued on a scale which irritated the British, and attempts to control it more effectively were viewed by many colonists as brutal

5. For Lord North see Thomas, *Townshend Duties Crisis*, chs 9–14; *idem*, *Tea Party to Independence*; *idem*, *Lord North* (1976); and Peter Whiteley, *Lord North: The Prime Minister who lost America* (1997), chs 8–11. For an American perspective on him, see Alan Valentine, *Lord North* 2 vols (Norman, OK, 1967).

and repressive. The *Gaspée* incident in 1772, when a revenue ship was ransacked and burned by a mob at Rhode Island, revealed how easily passions could erupt in violence. Those responsible for the outrage were never brought to justice. The Americans were now as resentful about British justice as they were about fiscal and commercial policy. They were more than ever inclined to believe that the British government would never hesitate to sacrifice American goodwill and prosperity to the demands of political opportunism and the pressures exerted by powerful groups in London. This meant that British motives were misunderstood and misrepresented.

In 1773 the East India Company was in a major crisis. The company owed massive debts and public confidence was low. North felt compelled to act. By his Regulating Bill he lent the company £1,400,000 to enable it to survive. The governor and council of Bengal were to be the supreme governing authority for those parts of India controlled by the company. Provision was made for the better administration of justice. Within its limits the Regulating Act was an intelligent and constructive measure. But, in the hope of stimulating the legitimate tea trade in America as a means of reviving the company's fortunes, North permitted the transportation of tea direct to America and its exemption from the payment of the English tea duty. This would bring down the price of tea in America and North was convinced that what he had done was in the interests of the company, while being beneficial to the Americans. Whether there was a reasonable prospect of undercutting the American smugglers is doubtful, for the margin of profit on each pound of tea remained small. But North refused to repeal Townshend's duty, when this was proposed as the best means of assisting the company and conciliating the Americans. He was reluctant to abandon any prospect of raising revenue, and in the back of his mind lurked a desire to keep the possibility of a colonial civil list open. On the basic principle of the supremacy of the British parliament North was adamant.

On 16 December 1773 some fifty Americans disguised as Mohawk Indians boarded the East India Company's ships, which were moored in Boston harbour, and poured the contents of about 200 chests of tea into the sea. When the news of the Boston Tea Party reached London the British government was shocked and angry and there was almost universal agreement among British politicians, in or out of office, that the perpetrators of a wanton and monstrous affront should be punished. The difficulty was that it was impossible to apprehend the individuals responsible for dumping the East India

Company's cargoes of tea into Boston harbour. This was itself a tribute to the remarkable level of support which the rioters had in Boston. The British were nevertheless reluctant to believe that majority opinion in America was anything other than loyal. Throughout the crisis the British exaggerated the strength of American loyalism. Even more they exaggerated the likelihood that loyalist feelings could be mobilized, whether politically or militarily. When it became clear that there was no prospect of arresting those who had organized and perpetrated the Boston Tea Party, the government stumbled down the perilous path of collective punishment. They were uneasy about doing so, but the alternative seemed to be to allow violence and disorder to go unpunished, and this was intolerable so far as the ministers and the majority of MPs were concerned.[6]

North's government therefore passed the notorious Coercive or Intolerable Acts, hoping that by doing so they would isolate and then destroy extremist opinion in America. They assumed that loyalists would rally to the cause when it was evident that the government was absolutely committed to the punishment of crime. Failure to act would ensure that the example of Boston would become widespread in America. It seemed sensible to try to detach Massachusetts from the other colonies and the town of Boston from the rest of Massachusetts. The Boston Port Act closed the port of Boston for all normal commerce, with the exception of ships carrying essential supplies, and transferred the customs houses to Salem. Until compensation had been paid to the East India Company and to other victims of disorder Boston would remain closed. The Massachusetts Bay Regulating Act provided for the upper house of the colonial legislature to be nominated by the crown, instead of being elected, and the powers of the governor were extended, particularly with respect to the dismissal of law officers. A third act allowed trials to be moved either to other colonies or to England in the hope that this would make it easier to convict those who had been accused of smuggling or riot by ensuring that they would not be tried before local juries who sympathized with their politics. A fourth act permitted the construction of barracks and the compulsory billeting of troops within Boston, should the authorities feel that this was necessary for the preservation of law and order.

6. The British reaction to the Boston Tea Party and its aftermath is meticulously analysed in Thomas, *Tea Party to Independence*, but see also Bernard Donoughue, *British Politics and the American Revolution: The Path to War* (1964).

The British wholly misjudged the mood of the Americans. Far from dividing the colonists from each other the Intolerable Acts drove them more closely together, united by a common sense of outrage at what the British had done. The colonists were horrified by the invasion of charter rights. If the British could intervene in the government of Massachusetts with impunity then they would soon be invading the rights of other colonies, reshaping colonial government as they saw fit. In fact, the British government had no such intention, but nothing the British did could persuade American radicals that there was no ambitious scheme for the subjection of the colonies. The Americans contrasted British policy in the Thirteen Colonies with concessions which North's government made to the French in Quebec by the Quebec Act of 1774. The good sense which North showed in dealing with the French Canadians added to American suspicions that the British were more liberal towards the Catholics of Quebec than to the Protestants of New England.

The call to arms

When it became evident that the Intolerable Acts had stimulated rather than curbed American resistance, and when colonial governors warned the British that some Americans were beginning to stock arms and talk of armed defiance, North and his colleagues were convinced that they had to assert the need to maintain law and order and to respond to the call for reinforcements. The British government was also perturbed by the conduct of the Philadelphia Congress. In September 1774 fifty-five colonial delegates had met in Philadelphia in order to coordinate American resistance. The king's ministers did not wish to do anything which would give a semblance of legality to what they regarded as an unconstitutional assembly. But they could not ignore what congress said or did. Opinion on the British side ebbed and flowed with every changing piece of news which crossed the Atlantic. General Gage, uneasily seeking to police Boston, wondered whether the Intolerable Acts might be suspended; Thurlow, the British attorney-general, considered the possibility of relinquishing all claims to tax the Americans, and then concluded that this would mean giving up any realistic chance of sustaining British rights in the colonies; Dartmouth, secretary of state for the colonies, believed that if it was incontrovertibly proved that coercion had failed then some attempt at conciliation should be made. George III objected to any suspension of the Intolerable Acts: if the Americans resorted to violence the king believed that force would have to be met with force. The king hoped that it would not come to such extremes, but he was convinced that any appearance of weakness would only make things worse. General Gage reminded the ministers in London that he had only 3000 troops; in his professional judgement it would need 20,000 men decisively to sustain British authority should an armed conflict break out.

At the beginning of 1775, in a desperate gesture of conciliation, North offered to pass on to the colonial assemblies the duty of raising taxes, with the general approval of the British government, with the Americans accepting responsibility for paying the costs of defence and colonial administration. Although North cited these proposals as proof of his desire for a peaceful settlement, they were wholly inadequate from the American point of view. The ministers began to prepare plans to blockade the New England colonies, and though bringing Gage's army up to the strength which the general demanded was impossible, they ruefully accepted the need to reinforce both the fleet and the army in North America. The tragedy was that the ministers failed to understand why the Americans were so recalcitrant, and offers which were sincerely meant to be conciliatory had already been overtaken by changes in American thinking. The original controversy over taxation had now been overshadowed by a wider concern for political liberty and securities for representative government.

General Gage had been told to be more active in searching out and seizing arms, and when this led to the first exchange of shots at Lexington and Concord (April 1775) the British government believed that it had no alternative but to resort to arms. When in June 1775 the British stormed Breed's Hill and Bunker's Hill at Boston, Gage was so shocked by the heavy casualties sustained that he thought his army would be ruined by many more such victories. The ministers in London were distressed by the loss of life, but still clung to the hope that order might be restored.

In July 1775 the American Congress defended the need to take up arms in the defence of liberty, but it also sent the Olive Branch Petition to King George III. The Americans denied that they wished to secede from the British empire, but reiterated their devotion to the defence of their constitutional liberties and reminded the British that they believed their cause to be just, while insisting on the strength of their resources and the real possibility of obtaining foreign help. George III rejected the petition. He could not accept it because it emanated from an assembly which had no legal status and from men who had taken up arms against the crown.[7] Yet the Olive Branch Petition had represented a victory for the moderates in the Philadelphia Congress over the radicals, and the rejection of the petition could only mean that many Americans came to believe that a reasonable offer of compromise had been contemptuously spurned. As late as December 1775 the American Congress held back from pressing for independence, but the publication of Tom Paine's *Common Sense* in January 1776 highlighted the case for separation, and after another six months of armed conflict congress issued the Declaration of Independence on 4 July 1776.

The British government was slow to realise the full significance of the declaration, and even those who believed themselves to be friends of America continued to call for conciliation after the Americans had affirmed their determination to seek independence. This was wholly in keeping with the consistent failure of British politicians to appreciate the evolution of American attitudes from the beginning of the controversy over taxation. Whenever American opinion moved forward – from apparently accepting the distinction between internal and external taxation to rejecting it, from disputes about taxation and the regulation of trade to a more searching concern with the nature of representation and self-government within the colonies, and finally from redress of grievances and a restoration of imperial harmony to a demand for secession from the British empire – the British failed to grasp what was happening. This ensured that even when gestures of conciliation were sincere and well meant they failed for the simple reason that they offered too little too late and were addressing a situation which had already been overtaken by events. The logic of a fundamental belief in the sovereignty of the British parliament, linked with the conviction that negotiations could be meaningful only after law and order had been restored and legal authority upheld in the colonies, dragged politicians who disliked the prospect of war down the road to conflict.

There was no premeditated conspiracy against American liberties, but there were decisive failures of understanding and catastrophic deficiencies in imagination which meant that what to the British seemed the straightforward assertion of rightful authority appeared to the Americans as tyranny. It has sometimes been said

---

7. George III's attitudes to the American crisis are best summarized in John Brooke, *King George III* (1972), ch. 5, but for his character and outlook, see also Stanley Ayling, *George III* (1972).

that this reflected the ignorance of the British governments of the time and their lack of first-hand experience of the colonies. Yet it is a further sign of the confusions of the conflict that some of the most obtuse comments about the Americans were made by naval and military officers who had served in the colonies, and whose prejudices were often elevated to the level of sober professional judgements by politicians looking for justifications for their actions. The orthodox interpretation of the British constitution prevented a succession of ministers from realizing that the Americans interpreted the traditional liberties of freeborn Englishmen in idiosyncratic and challenging ways. Because of their devotion to the sovereignty of the British parliament as the bastion of British liberties Grenville, Townshend, North and their colleagues failed to understand why the Americans regarded their policies in a sinister light, and their obstinate defence of parliamentary supremacy therefore brought about the dismemberment of the first British empire.

CHAPTER THREE

Britain's Imperial Sovereignty: The Ideological Case against the American Colonists

H.T. DICKINSON

The British imperialists deserve to have their motives and the justifications for their actions explored in as much depth as their colonial opponents, but this has rarely been attempted. This is partly because their cause ended in military defeat, whereas the Americans were remarkably successful. It is partly because the United States later became the greatest economic power and the foremost liberal democracy in the world, while imperial authority is widely condemned in the modern world. It is also due however to the fact that the historiographical debate on the American crisis has very much favoured the interpretation of that dispute advanced at the time by the American colonists. The colonists consistently argued that the crisis occurred solely because Britain abandoned a satisfactory relationship between mother country and colonies, and embarked on an attempt to increase its imperial authority at the expense of the existing rights and liberties of the colonists. Britain was portrayed as an aggressive imperial power, whereas the colonies were depicted as defending their hard-won freedom. The colonists argued that there would have been no conflict if Britain had not changed its policies from the early 1760s. It is possible to reverse this argument, however, though it has rarely been done.[1] It can be argued that the recent dynamic growth of the American colonies and the decline of British authority in America disrupted the status quo, forced Britain onto the defensive, and compelled the mother

---

1. It does however underpin the thesis in Robert W. Tucker and David C. Hendrickson, *The Fall of the First British Empire: Origins of the War of American Independence* (Baltimore, MD, 1982).

country to endeavour to restore its imperial authority over the colonies in order to protect its own vital interests and the security of the empire. American historians have rarely put the case in these terms and nor have British historians. Moreover, even the latter have generally examined Britain's unsuccessful imperial policy as if it were primarily a problem of practical politics, a failure to devise and support effective and acceptable measures towards the American colonies[2] – rather than as an ideological issue about motivation, argument and justification.

This chapter is not trying to argue that the American colonies did not have good cause to rebel against Britain. Nor is it seeking to claim that the British imperialist case was sensible, wise or morally superior, or to excuse, defend or justify British actions. Rather it attempts to understand and explain why the British imperialists thought they had good grounds for meeting the challenge to Britain's authority and why they were so convinced of the justice of their cause that they were prepared to resort to arms to defend it.

In advancing this case, this chapter hopes to demonstrate that there were elements of nobility and tragedy on both sides of the American Revolution. Both the British and the Americans shared the same reverence for the common law, constitutional liberties, the rule of law, government by consent, and the benefits of the Glorious Revolution of 1688. Both sides believed that they were compelled to use force to defend *their* interpretation of the British constitution and to secure their lives, liberty and property. To that extent, the American Revolution was a civil war *within* the British empire caused by an honest failure to advance policies which would promote in an equitable manner the interests of both Britain and the colonies in the new situation they found themselves in after 1763 and by an understandable inability to devise a constitution which could defend the liberties of Britons *and* Americans within the same framework and to the same extent.

In seeking to explain the British imperial case this chapter first explores the rationale behind British actions in the 1760s and 1770s. It then explains how the British attempted to refute the constitutional claims put forward by the American colonies. This campaign revealed that at the heart of the British case was a profound attachment to the concept of parliamentary sovereignty – an attachment which remains to this day. The concluding section tries to explain

2. See in particular Peter D.G. Thomas, *British Politics and the Stamp Act Crisis* (Oxford, 1975); *idem, The Townshend Duties Crisis* (Oxford, 1987); *idem, Tea Party to Independence* (Oxford, 1991).

why British imperialists were so attached to parliamentary sovereignty, as the principal defender of their constitutional liberties, that they went to war to preserve it.

The rationale for imperial policy

There is clearly not the space here to explain and justify in great detail Britain's policy towards the American colonies between 1760 and 1775. It is enough briefly to indicate that, while it may have been ill-judged, it was not part of a determined conspiracy to destroy the existing rights and liberties of the American colonies. Throughout these years successive British ministries, with the backing of majority support in parliament, argued that Britain, faced with the heavy expense of protecting the American colonies from their internal and external enemies and bearing itself a much heavier burden of taxes and debt, was justified in expecting the prosperous colonists to bear a fair proportion of these expenses.[3]

British policy was not solely concerned with easing the financial burden imposed by the need to defend British possessions in North America, however. It was also widely recognized that Britain's commercial links with the American colonies had grown rapidly in recent years and that this trade contributed significantly to Britain's burgeoning economic prosperity. If Britain were to retain its control over this trade and maximize the benefits to be gained from it, then the long-standing commercial regulations governing this trade, which had so often been evaded by the colonists in the past, had to be tightened and made more effective.[4] As their frequent use of the parent–child metaphor clearly revealed, British imperialists thought of the colonies, by definition, as subordinate and dependent, quite unable to defend themselves, and hence bound by their position to yield obedience to the mother country.[5] To many Britons the colonies had been established, nursed and protected by the mother country and hence they remained subordinate to her and existed for her benefit.[6] Since at least the 1690s British officials had intermittently

3. Lawrence Henry Gipson, *The British Empire before the American Revolution* 11 vols (New York, 1949–65), x, p. 231.

4. Thomas C. Barrow, 'Background to the Grenville program, 1757–1763' *WMQ* 3rd series, 22 (1965), pp. 93–104.

5. Jack P. Greene, 'An uneasy connection: an analysis of the preconditions of the American Revolution' in Stephen G. Kurtz and James H. Hutson, eds, *Essays on the American Revolution* (Chapel Hill, NC, 1973), p. 49.

6. *London Packet* 4 Jan. 1775.

expressed the fear that the colonies might one day throw off their dependence upon Britain and even become economic rivals of the mother country. These fears were expressed more frequently as the colonies grew and prospered in the earlier eighteenth century.[7] Josiah Tucker had predicted as early as 1749 that the American colonies would revolt as soon as they believed themselves to be strategically secure from the French threat and economically self-sufficient.[8] As the American colonies became increasingly important to Britain, in both economic and strategic terms, British officials became ever more anxious about the possible loss of imperial control over these colonies and they began to consider ways of shoring up imperial authority there. When the Seven Years War clearly exposed the weakness of imperial control, British ministers at last decided to force the colonies to contribute towards the costs of imperial defence.[9] The various government measures imposed on the American colonies from the early 1760s onwards were therefore not a determined conspiracy to destroy the rights and liberties of the colonists so much as an indication of Britain's fear that it was in danger of losing control over its precious American possessions. These measures were part of a strategy designed to tighten metropolitan control over the American colonies not so that Britain could exercise unlimited and arbitrary political power over them, but so that it could reap the financial and commercial benefits that colonial possessions were widely expected to bestow upon the mother country.

While the American colonies and some British critics of George III undoubtedly believed that there was indeed a conspiracy against liberty on both sides of the Atlantic in the 1760s and 1770s, no modern British historian would now maintain that such fears were fully justified. Britain was not trying to exercise unlimited or arbitrary power over the colonies, nor was it deliberately seeking to reduce the colonies to a condition of servitude. Rather it was seeking to make a reality out of the imperial powers that it was convinced it had the constitutional right to exercise. In seeking to explain the government's imperial policies therefore most British historians have agreed that these were primarily pragmatic responses to the genuine administrative problems of a recently expanded British empire and not part of a deliberate strategy to undermine the constitutional

---

7. J.M. Bumsted, '"Things in the womb of time": ideas of American independence, 1633 to 1763' *WMQ* 3rd series, 31 (1974), pp. 533–64.
8. Josiah Tucker, *Essay on Trade* 3rd edn (1749), pp. 93–6.
9. Bernhard Knollenberg, *Origins of the American Revolution 1759–1766* (1960).

rights of the king's American subjects. Britain did not pass the legislation that so angered the colonists in order to demonstrate parliament's sovereignty over the empire so much as resort to a defence of parliament's sovereignty over the empire *after* the colonies had argued that this legislation was unconstitutional. It was colonial resistance rather than British intentions that brought the intractable constitutional issue to the forefront of the dispute between Britain and the American colonies.

Before the mid-eighteenth century Britain – unlike France and Spain – had not developed a coherent imperial strategy or an effective machinery of empire. British politicians and the public saw the empire primarily as a way of expanding the commercial, fiscal and naval foundations of British power. The American colonies, in particular, were seen as the sources of raw materials and valuable colonial produce, and as a growing market for British manufactured goods. It was claimed that 'the colonies were acquired with no other view than to be a convenience to us; and therefore it can never be imagined that we are to consult their interests preferably to our own'.[10] These colonies served to increase the wealth and power of the British state and their management was perceived to be in the interest of Britain.[11] When the victories of the Seven Years War (1756–63) greatly increased the British possessions in North America, and greatly enhanced the commercial and strategic significance of the colonies to the mother country, Britain faced a political problem that no other society had resolved – how to preserve liberty over such a vast and varied empire and how to inculcate a sense of the common good among millions of people far removed from the political centre.

The acquisition of vast new territories in North America required Britain to devise new policies and to tackle long-standing American problems which had been neglected for years and which highlighted the weakness of metropolitan authority in the older American colonies. The most pressing problems were the financial burden of imperial defence and the widespread evasion of the trade laws. In endeavouring to solve these problems the British came up against the fact that the American colonists had little regard for either the interests or the authority of the mother country. In seeking to reform the empire and to impose its authority on these colonies, Britain did not deliberately seek to destroy the representative institutions of

    10. *London Chronicle* 31 July 1764.
    11. Thomas, *Townshend Duties Crisis*, p. 155; George L. Beer, *British Colonial Policy, 1754–1765* (1907), pp. 132–59.

the colonies or the rights of the colonists, but its actions were bound to restrict the scope of the colonies for independent economic and political activity. Thus, however unwittingly, Britain's imperial measures provoked a storm of protest in the colonies.[12] Although there were a variety of other grievances – over access to the wilderness, restrictions on the use of paper credit, the quartering of troops in the colonies, and the denial of jury trials in the vice-admiralty courts – the real source of American resistance to British policies were the efforts made by successive ministries to tax the colonies in order to meet part of the costs of the civil administration and military defence of the colonies. It was the Stamp Act of 1765 and the Townshend duties of 1767, in particular, that elevated minor irritants to the level of a major constitutional crisis.

From the imperial perspective the decision to tax the colonies seemed eminently fair and just. The Seven Years War had started in North America and there had been considerable military and naval operations in the colonies throughout the conflict. To meet the costs of these a heavy tax burden had been placed on the British people and the national debt had increased dramatically. The British believed, with some justice, that, while the American colonies were prosperous and were likely to benefit commercially from victories achieved in this successful war, they did not bear an equitable share of the financial burden of stationing troops and ships in North America. In view of the fact that the money that Britain proposed to raise from new taxes imposed on the colonies would be spent in America and that the tax burden would still be far lighter in the American colonies than in Britain, there seemed good grounds for asking the colonists to pay a modest portion of the costs of imperial defence. Imperialists argued that, in return for victory and continued protection, the Americans owed a financial obligation towards Britain.[13]

Even before he had introduced his Stamp Act, imposing an internal tax on the American colonies, George Grenville had convinced himself and a clear majority in parliament that Britain was justified, in practical and constitutional terms, in levying such a revenue in the colonies.[14] When the American colonists surprised

12. Jack P. Greene, 'The Seven Years War and the American Revolution: the causal relationship reconsidered' *JICH* 8 (1980), pp. 85–105.

13. [Anon.,] *An Address to the People of Great Britain . . . on the present Crisis of American Politics* (Bristol, 1776), p. 26.

14. John L. Bullion, *A Great and Necessary Measure: George Grenville and the Genesis of the Stamp Act 1763–1765* (Columbia, MO, 1982), pp. 99–163.

Britain with the strength of their protests against the innovation of levying an internal revenue on them, parliament repealed the Stamp Act of 1765, but soon resorted to levying revenue through the more usual practice of external taxes on trade, by means of the Townshend duties. British imperialists wrongly believed that the Americans would have no objections to revenue raised in customs duties on imported goods, since there were many precedents for such duties, and they were genuinely shocked when the colonies did raise violent objections to these duties. It appeared to British imperialists that, in order to avoid paying any taxes to the mother country, the Americans were changing their ground:

> The Americans have gone upon a system to gain step by step, to clear themselves from the control of this country. . . . They have taken that strange distinction between internal and external [taxation] . . . The next step to be taken, that you have no right to impose taxes in any case whatever. The next step to be taken is that you have no right to make laws binding them in any case whatever.[15]

Even when most of the Townshend duties were repealed, the Americans continued to object to the remaining tea duty. Their protest escalated into the violence of the Boston Tea Party, in December 1773, which provoked a tough response from the British government.

British imperialists were now convinced that any concessions to the American colonies were interpreted as signs of weakness and that the violent resistance in America was the work of a small, unrepresentative minority based in Boston.[16] They concluded that no government, indeed no political system, could long survive if it gave way to violence and the open repudiation of its authority.[17] An imperial power could not simply concede independence to a rebellious province without making some effort to reassert its authority or it would risk a dangerous collapse of its whole power in the American colonies and elsewhere. Colonial defiance could not be ignored and the laws had to be obeyed or anarchy would reign: 'It is now but too plain that the lenity and forbearance of Parliament have had no other effect than to aggravate the evil and to encourage the still further opposition to the supreme legislative authority.'[18]

---

15. Thomas, *Townshend Duties Crisis*, p. 259. See also William Knox, *The Controversy between Great Britain and her Colonies reviewed* (Dublin, 1769), pp. 34–5.
16. Fred J. Hinkhouse, *The Preliminaries of the American Revolution as seen in the English Press 1763–1775* (New York, 1926), pp. 159–62; Clarence E. Carter, ed., *The Correspondence of General Thomas Gage* 2 vols (New Haven, CT, 1931–3), i, pp. 89–92, 95, 196.
17. Thomas, *Townshend Duties Crisis*, pp. 168, 173.   18. Ibid., p. 195.

General Gage informed the British government from America: 'People agree now that, there has been a scheme for a revolt from the mother country long concerted between those who have most influence in the American councils, who have been preparing the people's minds by degrees.'[19] As early as 1770 Lord Barrington, the secretary at war, warned that universal anarchy was prevailing in the colonies and there appeared a general resolution of shaking off the authority of the British government: 'was not this, therefore, a period that called for the interposition of the military power? was not this a time for coercive measures?'[20] The king himself informed Lord North: 'we must either master them totally or leave them to themselves and treat them as aliens'.[21] While the Coercive (or in American eyes the Intolerable) Acts of 1774 shocked the American colonies, it is difficult to see how any imperial government could have responded with less firm measures without capitulating to the protesters and acknowledging the virtual independence of the colonies. The British ministers did not act arbitrarily or order the arbitrary use of force. They merely sought to arrest a revolutionary challenge through legally constituted civil officers empowered by constitutional acts of parliament. These measures were harsh when judged by earlier British responses to American resistance, but they were the minimum necessary if Britain were to restore its authority in Massachusetts. North's ministry had a choice only between imposing British authority on the colonies or acknowledging their *de facto* independence.[22] The coercive legislation of 1774 was therefore designed for the 'better execution of the laws and the just dependence of the colonies upon the crown and parliament of Great Britain'.[23]

By 1775 Lord Mansfield had concluded: 'We are reduced to the alternative of adopting coercive measures, or of forever relinquishing our claim of sovereignty or dominion over the colonies ... [either] the supremacy of the British legislature must be complete, entire, and unconditional; or on the other hand, the colonies must be free and independent.'[24] When actually faced with armed resistance in 1775, however, Lord North tried to avoid escalating the military conflict. He expressed a readiness to repeal the Coercive

19. Carter, ed., *Correspondence of General Gage*, i, p. 421.

20. *London Magazine* 39 (1770), p. 545.   21. *Corr. of George III*, iii, p. 154.

22. Jack M. Sosin, 'The Massachusetts acts of 1774: coercive or preventive?' *HLQ* 26 (1963), pp. 235–52.

23. *Journals of the House of Commons* (1803–13), xxxiv, p. 541.

24. *Parliamentary History*, xviii, pp. 269–71.

Acts and to abandon any attempt to impose parliamentary taxes on
the American colonies, but only if the colonies acknowledged the
constitutional authority of Britain and returned to their former
obedience. By 1775, however, the issue between the colonies and
the mother country had quite clearly gone well beyond the question
of Britain's right to tax the colonies. The real issue had become
Britain's claim, expressed as early as the Declaratory Act of 1766
and regularly repeated thereafter, that the Westminster parliament
could legislate for the colonies 'in all cases whatsoever'. Faced with
what they undoubtedly regarded as an unconstitutional threat to
their lives, liberty and property, the American colonies resorted to
armed resistance. Once fighting had broken out, British imperialists
faced a threat from which they could see no honourable retreat.
General Gage warned that 'the stroke is levelled at the British nation,
on whose ruin they hope to build their so much vaunted American
Empire, and to rise like a phoenix out of the ashes of the mother
country'.[25] The king himself concluded: 'The object is too important,
the spirit of the British nation too high, the resources with which
God has blessed her too numerous, to give up so many colonies
which she has planted with great industry, nursed with great ten-
derness, encouraged with many commercial advantages, and protected and defended at much expense of blood and treasure.'[26]
Long convinced that the loss of the American colonies would deal
a very serious blow to her economic power and render her vulnerable
to her European enemies,[27] British imperialists were not prepared
to stand idly by and lose a valuable empire that might eventually
fall prey to their traditional rivals. They were, though reluctantly,
eventually ready to fight a war in order to preserve Britain's control
over its American colonies.[28]

Refuting American claims

When they protested so forcibly against the Stamp Act in 1765 the
American colonies raised the fundamental constitutional issue of
'no taxation without representation'. British imperialists quickly

25. Quoted in Thomas, *Tea Party to Independence*, pp. 331–2.

26. *Parliamentary History*, xviii, p. 696.

27. 'Anti-Sejanus', *London Chronicle* 23 Jan. 1766; 'John Ploughshare', *London Chronicle*
20 Feb. 1766.

28. Richard W. Van Alstyne, 'Parliamentary supremacy versus independence: notes
and documents' *HLQ* 26 (1963), pp. 201–33.

recognized that American objections were not to the burden of taxation, or even to the mode of taxation, so much as to the fact that the British parliament was claiming the authority to tax the Americans even though the latter were not represented in the Westminster parliament and they possessed their own legislative assemblies. British imperialists promptly responded to this challenge to the constitutional authority of parliament by passing the Declaratory Act of 1766, which explicitly proclaimed that the parliament of Great Britain 'had, hath, and of right ought to have full power and authority to make laws and statutes of sufficient force and validity to bind the colonies and people of *America*, subjects of the crown of *Great Britain*, in all cases whatsoever'.[29] Over the next decade the American colonies sought, with a variety of arguments, to reject both the notion that parliamentary sovereignty was a legitimate feature of the British constitution and the British claim that parliament had ultimate authority over their lives, liberty and property. In response to this challenge, British imperialists sought to counter each one of these arguments. Whereas the colonists attempted to protect their constitutional liberties by appealing to their rights as emigrants, or to the terms of their charters, or to their historic liberties as Englishmen under the free British constitution, British imperialists challenged these claims and rejected the force of each argument deployed by the Americans.

The American colonists claimed that they had the right to enjoy the same liberties and privileges as Englishmen because the first colonists had emigrated as free men, they had carried the liberties of Englishmen with them when they migrated to America, and their descendants continued to possess them just as much as any inhabitant of Britain. British imperialists challenged the American interpretation of their rights as emigrants. Some imperialists claimed that the colonists had abandoned their rights as Englishmen on leaving England,[30] while others maintained that they had voluntarily given up their rights in return for the benefits to be gained in the new world. Others insisted that the emigrants had explicitly sought and secured legal permission to emigrate and so they remained subject to the authority which had allowed them to leave England.[31] There was no evidence that the migrants believed that they had given up their obligations as English subjects when they

29. *Gentleman's Magazine* 35 (1765), p. 561. The act is 6 *George III*, c.12.
30. *Lloyd's Evening Post* 11 May 1770.
31. [Anon.,] *The Rights of Parliament Vindicated, on Occasion of the Late Stamp Act* (1766), p. 15.

left for the new world or that the authorities in England had released them from their duties as subjects.[32] Lord Mansfield insisted that, prior to their departure, the first colonists had been subject to the sovereign authority in England and this he interpreted not as the king alone, but as the king-in-parliament.[33] The colonists emigrated in a position of constitutional subordination to parliament and they remained subordinate to parliament in their new circumstances across the Atlantic. In the same vein, Lord Lyttleton declared of the colonists in the House of Lords: 'They went out subjects of Great Britain and unless they can show a new compact made between them and the parliament of Great Britain (for the king alone could not make a new compact with them) they still are subjects to all intents and purposes whatsoever. If they are subjects, they are liable to the laws of the country.'[34]

The fact that the colonists were not represented in parliament, the imperialists argued, was not a reason for concluding that they were not subject to its enactments. If some had not possessed the vote before they emigrated, they could not complain about the lack of this right in the new world. If they had possessed the vote when they lived in Britain, they had voluntarily surrendered it on emigrating in return for the benefits to be gained in America.[35] If the colonies were still within the realm, the colonists had to face the same obligations as any British subject at home. If the colonies were without the realm, the colonists had no claims to the rights and liberties of British subjects. The colonists were not justified in claiming all of the benefits, while refusing all of the obligations, of those subjects living in Britain. George Grenville insisted on the dependent status of the colonies and concluded: 'If they are not subject to this burden of [the stamp] tax, they are not entitled to the privilege of Englishmen.'[36]

When the American colonists insisted that their colonial charters gave legal protection to their constitutional rights and liberties, British imperialists insisted that the charters were not embryo constitutions or documents conferring extensive constitutional rights on the

32. [Anon.,] *A Letter to a Member of Parliament on the Present Unhappy Dispute between Great Britain and her Colonies* (1774), pp. 13–14.

33. R.C. Simmons and P.D.G. Thomas, eds, *Proceedings and Debates of the British Parliaments Respecting North America 1754–1783* 6 vols (White Plains, NY, 1982–7), ii, p. 130.

34. Ibid., ii, p. 126.

35. John Wesley, *A Calm Address to our American Colonies* (1775), p. 11; [Anon.,] *Licentiousness Unmask'd; or Liberty explained* (n.d.), p. 42.

36. P.D.G. Thomas, ed., 'Parliamentary diaries of Nathaniel Ryder, 1764–7' *Camden Miscellany XXIII* Camden Society, 4th series (1969), vii, p. 256.

colonists, but were documents mainly concerned with trade and property rights. The charters had created corporations which could make by-laws, but they had not created independent governments exempt from parliamentary authority. Thomas Whately, an adviser to George Grenville, concluded:

> All [colonists] who took these grants [of charters] were British subjects, inhabiting British dominions, and who at the time of taking [them] were indisputably under the authority of parliament. . . . Those, therefore, to whom the charters were originally given, could have no exemption granted to them, and what the father never received, the children [could not] claim as an inheritance. . . . Nor was it ever an idea that they should; even the charters themselves, so far from allowing, guard against the supposition.[37]

According to British imperialists the colonial charters did not establish the political institutions and constitutional rights claimed by the colonists. Georgia, for instance, had no charter at all, and, while the third charter of Virginia (1611–12) did allow the colony's legislators to make laws for the good of the colony, they did not have authority to make laws 'contrary to the laws and statutes of our realm of *England*'.[38] The Connecticut charter of 1662 and that of Rhode Island too gave the same rights with the same restrictions. The charter of Pennsylvania allowed the colonists to tax themselves, but it also stated that subsequent acts of parliament could levy a tax on the colony. Only the 1633 charter of Maryland explicitly exempted the colony from taxation, but, it was pointed out, even this exemption referred to royal taxation not parliamentary taxation.[39] Moreover, since all charters had clearly been granted by a higher authority, the colonists were still subordinate to that authority and, as had occurred in the past, colonial charters could be amended or revoked by that superior authority.[40]

The American colonies claimed – and were allowed – many of the constitutional rights of Englishmen, including the right to a jury trial, the right to free assembly, the right to petition, the right

---

37. Thomas Whately, *The Regulations lately made concerning the Colonies, and the Taxes imposed upon them considered* (1765), pp. 109–11.

38. Francis Newton Thorpe, *The Federal and State Constitutions* 7 vols (Washington, DC, 1909), vii, p. 3806.

39. John Phillip Reid, *Constitutional History of the American Revolution* 4 vols (Madison, WI, 1986–93), i, pp. 163–5; ii, pp. 99–101; Thomas, ed., 'Parliamentary diaries of Nathaniel Ryder', pp. 254–5; Thomas Pownall, *The Administration of the Colonies* 2nd edn (1765), p. 89.

40. [Anon.,] *An Appeal to Reason and Justice in Behalf of the British Constitution, and the Subjects of the British Empire* (1778), p. 58; 'Royal charters subject to review' *Scots Magazine* 36 (1774), p. 120.

to freedom of conscience and to a free press, and the security of their life and property under the rule of law. What British imperialists would not concede was that the colonial assemblies possessed full legislative autonomy and were not subordinate to the authority of parliament. George Grenville, Lord Mansfield and other law lords maintained that there was a wealth of precedents to prove that parliament had repeatedly and consistently legislated for the colonies.[41] It was claimed that parliament in the reign of William III had explicitly declared that all by-laws or customs in the colonies contrary to any law passed at Westminster were illegal and hence void.[42] Dozens of other acts of parliament were cited as evidence of parliament legislating for the colonies so that 'no doubt can remain that the Legislature considered them as subordinate and dependent parts of the English empire, subject to commercial regulation, and liable to be modelled and governed, in all respects as the wisdom of parliament should, from time to time, think proper to direct'.[43] The colonial assemblies were not the equal of parliament, but were more like town corporations in England, with the right to make by-laws and levy local taxes, but with no right to challenge the superior constitutional and legislative authority of parliament. That authority included the right to levy taxes on the colonies and to legislate on any matter whatsoever: 'For without a right to tax, there can be no sovereignty – Sovereignty comprehends legislation, and government; without which, it cannot exist. And wherever the right of legislation and government is, there alone, exists the supreme right to tax. Wherefore, to have a right to the sovereignty, and yet no right to tax, is a political absurdity.'[44]

British imperialists accepted the principle of government by consent, but they rejected the colonial connection between taxation and representation. Detailed evidence from the government's law officers concluded (in direct opposition to the case made by the colonists and their British friends) that Wales, Durham and Chester

---

41. *Parliamentary History*, xvi, p. 173 (Lord Mansfield, 10 Feb. 1766); Thomas, ed., 'Parliamentary diaries of Nathaniel Ryder', pp. 254–5 (Grenville, 6 Feb. 1765); John Roebuck, *An Enquiry whether the Guilt of the Present Civil War in America ought to be imputed to Great Britain or America* (1776), p. 15; [Anon.,] *The Supremacy of the British Legislature over the Colonies, candidly discussed* (1775), p. 27.

42. The declaration was in cap. *7th–8th William III*, section 9. Thomas, ed., 'Parliamentary diaries of Nathaniel Ryder', p. 255 (Grenville, 6 Feb. 1765).

43. [Anon.,] *A Letter to a Member of Parliament on the Present Unhappy Dispute between Great Britain and her Colonies* (1774), pp. 18–19.

44. [Anon.,] *The Constitutional Right of the Legislature of Great Britain, to Tax the British Colonies in America, impartially stated* (1768), p. 5.

had all been taxed before they were allowed to send representatives to parliament.[45] This evidence provided a precedent for taxing the colonies even though they elected no MPs to the Westminster parliament. When drafting the Stamp Act, George Grenville had recognized that the issue of colonial representation had to be faced and answered. He insisted that parliament *virtually* represented the whole nation and not just those who possessed the right to vote, who were a clear minority of the nation.[46] This did not mean however that the majority who did not possess the vote were exempt from taxes or even that they were considered as not having given their consent to the decisions of parliament. The constitutional theory of representation in Britain was that the House of Commons spoke for all subjects and that all subjects were virtually represented by those chosen to sit in the House of Commons. Parliament gained strength by representing not individuals, but all the interests of the nation.[47] Soame Jenyns agreed with Grenville that not one in twenty men in Britain was directly represented, but he insisted no one would conclude that the others were exempt from paying taxes. The doctrine of virtual representation meant that Manchester and Birmingham, although they did not directly return MPs to parliament, were represented at Westminster and, by the same token, so were Albany and Boston.[48]

Parliament acquired power, weight and stability by representing the landed, financial, commercial and manufacturing interests of the nation, and also the official and professional men who served the country. All that mattered was that a sufficiently numerous, varied and responsible body of independent voters, representing a wide range of interests and constituencies, and qualified according to immemorial custom, should elect the nation's representatives. The system of representation ensured that MPs were elected by men of

45. Reid, *Constitutional History*, ii, pp. 19–20, 152–3, 374–5.

46. Thomas, *Stamp Act Crisis*, p. 89.

47. On the British theory of representation see H.T. Dickinson, *Liberty and Property: Political Ideology in Eighteenth-Century Britain* (1977), pp. 217–18, 281–3; Lucy S. Sutherland, 'Edmund Burke and the relations between Members of Parliament and their constituents', *Studies in Burke and His Times* 10 (1968), pp. 1005–21; Whately, *Regulations lately made*, pp. 108–9; [John Lind,] *Three Letters to Dr. Price Containing Remarks on his Observations on the Nature of Civil Liberty* (1776), pp. 120–1; Soame Jenyns, *The Objections to the Taxation of our American Colonies by the Legislature of Great Britain, briefly considered* (1765), pp. 6–8; [Anon.,] *Rights of Parliament Vindicated*, pp. 38–9; Samuel Johnson, *Taxation No Tyranny* (1775) in J.P. Hardy, ed., *The Political Writings of Dr. Johnson* (1968), p. 118; *Parliamentary History*, xvi, p. 99.

48. Jenyns, *Objections to the Taxation of our American Colonies* in *The Works of Soame Jenyns* 4 vols (1790), pp. 190–3.

property, who were free and independent, least likely to be influenced by wealthy and artful men and most likely to possess civic virtue and to understand the nation's true interests. It was just and appropriate that property not individuals should be represented because property was the real wealth and true interest of the nation. The non-electors were not entirely unrepresented because even their small property interests were represented and MPs were generally local men who understood the local circumstances of ordinary subjects. The non-electors were also protected from arbitrary laws and taxes being passed by their representatives because all MPs were required to own substantial property and all laws and taxes would affect them even more than poor men. MPs were therefore very unlikely to burden themselves (or their fellow subjects) with oppressive laws or unnecessary taxes.

While it was possible to criticize the British system of representation as irregular and even irrational, experience proved, it was claimed, that it worked because it consistently produced a House of Commons of the highest calibre. The defenders of the existing system of representation insisted that what was of greater importance was not who voted, but who was elected. An impartial examination of the composition of the House of Commons proved that men of the greatest wealth, highest status and most eminent talents were chosen to represent the people. These men were the best qualified to understand and the most likely to promote the public interest. They were far superior to the type of representative likely to be chosen by indigent and ignorant men, who were easily corrupted by rich men or readily manipulated by artful men. Since the best men were chosen as MPs, therefore, it mattered little how they were elected. A close scrutiny of the careers of MPs would reveal that many of those representing the largest counties and most populous boroughs rarely distinguished themselves in parliament. The chief men of business and the men of greatest talent were often chosen by a handful of voters in the smallest boroughs.

The theory of virtual representation emphasized that MPs represented all subjects (at home and abroad) and not just those who elected them to parliament. Each MP represented not only those electors who voted for him, but also those who had voted against him and even those who had not or could not cast a vote at all. Once an MP was elected, he ceased to be a representative of a particular county or borough, but became a representative of the whole nation.[49] By the same token, every individual was represented,

49. Whately, *Regulations lately made*, p. 109.

not by a particular MP, but by the whole House of Commons. It was therefore of little account whether certain towns or individuals (or, for that matter, distant colonies) were directly represented or not: MPs were not delegates, chosen only to speak for different constituencies or specific groups of people, but were the representatives of the whole nation given the task of pursuing wise policies that would benefit all subjects. As the voice of the whole nation, MPs were expected to act to the best of their abilities and in accordance with their independent judgement. They spoke for the whole community and that community was greater than the sum of its individual parts. MPs were not delegates, to be instructed or bound by their constituents to pursue certain courses of action in parliament, but the representatives of the nation given the task of pursuing the common good. Any attempt to constrain their independent judgement would destroy their role as representatives of the whole nation and would prevent them serving the whole community. The House of Commons was a deliberative chamber in which all members were concerned with the interests of all subjects (including those of the American colonists), not just of those who possessed the right to vote. Edmund Burke put this particularly well: 'parliament is a deliberative assembly of one nation, with one interest, that of the whole; where, not local purposes, not local prejudices ought to guide, but the general good, resulting from the general reason of the whole.'[50]

It was far too dangerous for the British parliament to deny the doctrine of virtual representation because it would mean that acts of parliament were not binding on non-electors in Britain or on British subjects in the colonies. British imperialists were keen to argue that the American colonists had repeatedly demonstrated that they believed they were indeed virtually represented in parliament by their acquiescence in a wide range of acts passed by that parliament. Most significant of all, in constitutional terms, was the fact that the Americans had accepted the decisions of parliament over the Glorious Revolution and the Hanoverian succession, when they had voluntarily transferred their allegiance to new monarchs according to the lead provided by parliament.[51] The American colonists themselves soon abandoned any serious challenge to the doctrine of virtual representation. They recognized that, while the franchise

---

50. Burke, 'Speech to the electors of Bristol' in Peter N. Miller, *Defining the Common Good: Empire, Religion and Philosophy in Eighteenth-Century Britain* (Cambridge, 1994), p. 252.

51. [Anon.,] *An Appeal to Reason and Justice*, p. 5.

was more widely spread in the colonies, not all colonists could vote and any claim for the direct representation of all men would raise the problem of all the poor men, native Indians and black slaves who were denied the vote in the colonies.[52] There was no particular colonial desire to campaign for a fully democratic system of representation at this stage. Moreover, the American colonists themselves could not see any effective way they could be represented in parliament. There was some discussion of how the colonists might be given representation in parliament,[53] but most commentators, on both sides of the Atlantic, quickly recognized that the practical problems involved were insurmountable.[54] It proved impossible to determine to the satisfaction of all how many representatives the colonies should be allotted or how the numbers could be changed as the wealth and population of the colonies expanded. Isaac Barré, though an MP well disposed to the American colonies, still admitted: 'The idea of representatives from that country is dangerous, absurd and impractical. . . . They will grow more numerous than we are, then how inconvenient and dangerous would it be to have representatives of 7 millions there meet the representatives of 7 million here.'[55] There were also other intractable difficulties: arranging travel to and from Britain in time for the meetings of parliament and the elections in the colonies; the cost of maintaining colonial MPs in an expensive capital city for months at a time without paying them and so making them dependent on their paymasters; and the task of keeping their American constituents informed of the issues under discussion at Westminster or colonial MPs informed of what was happening back in the colonies.[56] The American colonies quickly recognized the impracticality of securing effective representation in parliament, preferring to regard their own legislative assemblies as their best representatives. To ensure that was indeed the case, however, they had to insist that these colonial assemblies were equal in authority to the Westminster parliament and not subordinate to it. This meant challenging the central British claim: that parliament was the sovereign authority over the whole empire.

52. Josiah Tucker, *Tract V: The Respective Pleas and Arguments of the Mother Country, and of the Colonies, distinctly set forth* (Gloucester, 1775), p. v.

53. See, for example, Francis Maseres, *Considerations on the Expediency of Admitting Representatives from the American Colonies into the British House of Commons* (1770), pp. 9–12.

54. Thomas Pownall, *The Administration of the Colonies* 4th edn (1768), pp. xv, 130; W.J. Smith, ed., *The Grenville Papers* 4 vols (1852–3), iv, p. 317.

55. Simmons and Thomas, eds, *Proceedings and Debates*, ii, p. 144.

56. Reid, *Constitutional History*, iv, pp. 99–107.

The importance of parliamentary sovereignty

In the last resort the constitutional dispute between Britain and the American colonies was not about taxation nor about representation, but about sovereignty. What the colonists could not accept was the notion of parliamentary sovereignty: that the Westminster parliament was so supreme in the constitution of the empire – that its authority was so absolute, unlimited, uncontrolled, irresistible and arbitrary – that it could pass legislation for the whole empire 'in all cases whatsoever'. To the American colonists this meant that neither their colonial assemblies nor the common law and their customary rights could offer them any protection at all against the power of parliament. In the last resort, their lives, liberty and property would always be at the mercy of men living 3000 miles away and preoccupied with British interests. In contrast, the claim to parliamentary sovereignty over the empire was what Britain could never voluntarily surrender. The British valued parliamentary sovereignty because it preserved all of those interests considered indispensable to Britain's position as a great power: internal stability, economic prosperity, national security and imperial authority.

Largely unobserved and unappreciated in the American colonies, where a seventeenth-century interpretation of the English constitution still prevailed,[57] the British had developed since the Glorious Revolution the constitutional doctrine of the sovereign legislature of king-in-parliament as the ultimate, absolute and irresistible authority in the state.[58] Although a minority of British politicians shared the American attachment to an older view of the constitution, where overriding authority lay with the common law and fundamental law, and they believed with the colonists that parliament was constrained by the customary and immemorial rights of the people, a clear majority of the governing elite in Britain became committed supporters of the more recent constitutional doctrine that parliament's authority was absolute, omnipotent and irresistible. Fears of the kind of political instability experienced in the seventeenth century had generated the widely held belief that, in every state and in every empire, there had to be a final authority against whose decision

---

57. R.A. Humphreys, 'The rule of law and the American revolution' *Law Quarterly Review* 53 (1937), pp. 80–98; John Phillip Reid, *In Defiance of the Law: The Standing Army Controversy, the Two Constitutions, and the Coming of the American Revolution* (Chapel Hill, NC, 1981), esp. pp. 159–60, 169, 228.

58. H.T. Dickinson, 'The eighteenth-century debate on the sovereignty of parliament' *TRHS* 5th series, 26 (1976), pp. 189–210.

there could be no appeal and that this authority ought to rest in the legislature which made laws and raised taxes – in the case of Britain this was the combined legislature of King, House of Lords and House of Commons.[59] This being the case, stability could be secured throughout Britain's Atlantic empire only so long as the colonial assemblies were regarded as inferior legislatures, subordinate to parliament.[60] If parliament was not sovereign over the American colonies, then Britain had no constitutional authority to regulate Atlantic commerce in her own interests and might suffer a severe blow to her prosperity, power and status. Any colonial challenge to the superior constitutional authority of parliament must therefore be rejected. When the Americans protested against the Stamp Act of 1765, parliament was prepared to repeal the measure on purely practical grounds – because of its adverse effects on British trade with the colonies – but it explicitly refused to concede that it was persuaded to repeal the act because it did not have the constitutional authority to tax or legislate for the colonies. No MP or peer was prepared to introduce American petitions against the Stamp Act precisely because these petitions questioned the constitutional authority of parliament.[61] When repeal of the Stamp Act was being considered, William Blackstone even suggested in the House of Commons that the repeal should apply only to those colonies whose assemblies expunged from their records any resolutions challenging the sovereign authority of parliament. Alexander Wedderburn went further and wanted to make it a criminal offence to dispute parliament's right in books and pamphlets.[62]

Parliament was not in fact prepared to repeal the Stamp Act without also explicitly asserting its sovereign authority by passing the Declaratory Act of 1766, which insisted that parliament could legislate for the colonies 'in all cases whatsoever'. It was to assert and prove this claim that Charles Townshend levied his various duties on the colonies in 1767. Townshend informed the House of Commons that he was determined to take some steps which would

59. Dora May Clark, *British Opinion and the American Revolution* (New Haven, CT, 1930), p. 259; William Blackstone, *An Analysis of the Laws of England* 6th edn (Oxford, 1771), p. 3; *Parliamentary History of England*, xvi, pp. 170, 612; [Allan Ramsay,] *Thoughts on the Origin and Nature of Government* (1769), pp. 53, 55; Johnson, *Taxation No Tyranny*, pp. 108–9; R.L. Meek et al., eds, *Adam Smith, Lectures on Jurisprudence* (Oxford, 1978), pp. 311, 315, 319, 326, 433.

60. [Anon.,] *An Inquiry into the Nature and Causes of the Present Disputes between the British Colonies in America and their Mother-Country* (1769), p. 20.

61. *The Bowdoin and Temple Papers*. Collections of the Massachusetts Historical Society, 6th series, 9 (Boston, MA, 1897), p. 61.

62. Thomas, *Stamp Act Crisis*, pp. 238–9.

show 'the Americans that this country would not tamely suffer her sovereignty to be wrested out of her hands'.[63] His duties were not designed (like the Stamp Act) to raise substantial sums of money to meet some of the costs of defending the American colonies, but were levied to assert the principle of parliamentary sovereignty (by means of an external tax this time). Moreover, the money raised was to be used to pay the salaries of colonial governors, judges and other royal officials in order to render them financially independent of the colonial assemblies.[64] When American protests also led parliament to consider repealing these duties as uneconomic and injudicious, the tea duty was deliberately retained, not merely because it raised the most revenue, but because parliament wished to demonstrate that it had not completely surrendered its right to legislate for the colonies. Lord Hillsborough, the secretary of state for American affairs, warned: 'it was not the amount of the duties . . . that was complained of, but the principle upon which the laws were founded, the supremacy and legislative authority of Parliament – a principle essential to the existence of empire'.[65] George III himself insisted 'there must always be one tax to keep up the right'.[66] It was the obstinate decision to maintain the tea duty, even though the actual duty was later reduced to help the East India Company dispose of its surplus tea in the colonies in 1773, that provoked the Boston Tea Party at the end of that year and, in turn, led parliament in 1774 to pass the Coercive Acts, the strongest exertion of its authority over the colonies and the decision which soon provoked armed resistance. It was not the tea duty as such, or even the terms of the Coercive Acts, however, but the constitutional claims that allowed parliament to justify passing such measures, that the Americans regarded as intolerable. As Earl Gower later advised the House of Lords: 'A paltry tax upon tea, a particular insult, a single act of violence or sedition, was not the true ground of the present dispute. It was not this tax or that Act, nor a redress of a particular grievance; the great question in issue is, the supremacy of this country, and the subordinate dependence of America.'[67]

British imperialists had quickly recognized that the American crisis involved a colonial challenge to the sovereignty of parliament

63. Thomas, ed., 'Parliamentary diaries of Nathaniel Ryder', p. 344 (13 May 1767).

64. P.D.G. Thomas, 'Charles Townshend and American taxation in 1767' *EHR* 83 (1968), pp. 33–51. On Townshend's American policy see Cornelius P. Forster, *The Uncontrolled Chancellor: Charles Townshend and his American Policy* and L.B. Namier and John Brooke, *Charles Townshend* (1964).

65. Reid, *Constitutional History*, iv, pp. 130–1.   66. Ibid., ii, p. 226.

67. *Parliamentary History*, xix, pp. 320–1.

and their determination not to surrender parliament's supreme constitutional authority shaped their views from 1765 onwards. While they often retreated from the actual exercise of this authority – repealing or amending various measures and ultimately offering to repeal all offending legislation passed by parliament since 1763 – they would not abandon the *principle* of parliamentary sovereignty and never offered to repeal and annul the Declaratory Act. Proof of this absolute commitment to the principle of parliamentary sovereignty can be found in Lord North's belated, but sincere, efforts to achieve a reconciliation with the American colonies in 1775 and 1778. Lord North was genuinely horrified at the outbreak of war in 1775 and by 1778 he recognized that Britain faced a war with France and the real possibility of defeat. And yet his efforts at reconciliation were seriously hindered by his unwillingness – an unwillingness widely shared – to surrender the principle of parliamentary sovereignty. In preparing his peace offerings Lord North made it clear that Britain had finally abandoned for ever all efforts to levy taxes on the colonies by means of parliamentary legislation. By 1778 he was prepared to repeal all the offending legislation passed by parliament since 1763 and was ready to discuss in a spirit of goodwill any grievance the American colonies might have. What Lord North was not prepared to surrender, even when his back was to the wall, was the sovereignty of parliament: 'To be explicit . . . if the dispute in which the Americans have engaged goes to the whole of our authority, we can enter into no negotiation, we can meet no compromise.'[68]

Lord North was prepared to abandon parliamentary taxation, but he still required that the colonial assemblies should vote money to meet part of the administrative and defence costs of the empire. Parliament, however, not the colonial assemblies, would decide when to request money, how much should be paid in total, and what amount each colony should contribute. Moreover, parliament might still pass legislation to regulate imperial trade and the Declaratory Act would not be repealed. From a purely constitutional point of view, Lord North was seeking to elicit from the American colonies a tacit recognition that ultimate sovereignty lay with parliament, though he was ready to promise that this authority would not in practice be used.[69] As the Americans clearly recognized, however, even Lord North's offer to pass an act abandoning the practice of

68. Ibid., xvii, p. 320.
69. On North's attempts at reconciliation, see Weldon A. Brown, *Empire or Independence: A Study in the Failure of Reconciliation, 1774–1783* (Louisiana, 1941).

parliamentary taxation was an exercise in parliamentary sovereignty. More serious still, the very nature of parliamentary sovereignty meant that the Americans could never be given an absolute, watertight guarantee that a future parliament would hold to any bargain the colonies might strike with Lord North. Whatever solemn promises Lord North might make, even if they were fully endorsed by parliament at the time, were not necessarily permanent because, according to the doctrine of parliamentary sovereignty, no parliament could bind the decisions of a future parliament or even the acts of a subsequent session of the same parliament. Once they conceded the theoretical point of parliamentary sovereignty, the Americans could have no future security at all for their lives, liberty and property.[70] William Knox, one of the most committed imperialists,[71] admitted that the Americans were being asked to place their trust in the honour and goodwill of every future parliament because they could be offered no absolute legal securities for their rights and liberties once they acknowledged the sovereignty of parliament:

> Whatever the terms we may give them, they can have no security for our adherence, but our own good faith. . . . They cannot, indeed, compel us to the performance of *any* terms when they have once submitted, but they may justly think, that to whatever terms the public faith shall be solemnly pledged in an act of Parliament . . . the honour and probity of the English nation will compel an adherence on the part of government.[72]

Given their experiences over the previous decade or so, it is not surprising that the Americans rejected any attempt to make the security of their lives, liberty and property dependent upon the goodwill and probity of a British parliament. They were determined to seek other more effective ways of providing constitutional security for their rights and liberties. This was an understandable decision. What still needs explaining, however, is why British imperialists were so attached to the *principle* of parliamentary sovereignty, much more than they were committed to the practical exercise of it, that they were prepared to continue with a bloody, expensive and ultimately disastrous war, and to lose the American colonies, rather than surrender this cherished principle.

70. Reid, *Constitutional History*, iv, pp. 129–50.
71. On Knox and the American colonies, see Leland J. Bellot, *William Knox: The Life and Thought of an Eighteenth-century Imperialist* (Austin, TX, 1977).
72. Reid, *Constitutional History*, ii, p. 239. See also *Parliamentary History*, xix, p. 850; John Erskine, *Shall I go to War with my American Brethren* (1769), p. 12.

The attachment to parliamentary sovereignty

By 1774–5 the dispute over parliamentary sovereignty had proved intractable and it produced a gulf between Britain and the American colonies that neither side believed could be bridged with constitutional safety. There was no peaceful solution to the crisis because there was no supreme judicial tribunal which could produce a binding final judgement on whether parliament had the right to pass laws for, or levy taxes on, the colonies. The issue had to be resolved by force of arms. As a London newspaper commented:

> The dispute with America is now become more serious than ever. It is reduced to the decisive question, whether the right of taxation be *here* or *there*. There is no medium which can be adopted with honour or safety on either side. No problem of expediency can now be started, for the opposition in America is not to the sum levied but to the right of levying it.[73]

Lord North clearly appreciated what the crisis was about:

> We are now disputing . . . with those who have maintained that we have as a Parliament no legislative right over them. That we are two independent states . . . we are not entering into a dispute between internal and external taxes, not between taxes laid for the purpose of revenue and taxes laid for the regulation of trade, not between representation and taxation, or legislation and taxation. But we are now to dispute the question whether we have or have not any authority in that country.[74]

Given the enormous cost of disputing that question, particularly on a point of principle only, why did Lord North think it was worth the effort?

The majority of Britons (not just the committed imperialists) were enormously proud of the eighteenth-century British constitution and this admiration was widely shared in Europe by such distinguished commentators as Voltaire, Montesquieu and De Lolme. Even most parliamentary and extra-parliamentary critics of eighteenth-century administrations almost always praised the principles of the constitution and concentrated their fire on ministers who were corrupting, betraying or undermining this constitution. In seeking to explain the practical virtues of the constitution its admirers pointed to all the positive benefits which the nation had reaped since the Glorious

---

73. *London Evening Post* 27 Jan. 1774.
74. Thomas, *Tea Party to Independence*, p. 51.

Revolution of 1688. The constitution was credited with saving the country from the evils of absolutism and Catholicism, with establishing the rule of law, government by consent and the many liberties of the subject, with creating a stable system of public finance, and with promoting an unparalleled period of economic advance, material prosperity and imperial expansion. Under its much-lauded constitution Britain had become a major world power and had triumphed over its domestic enemies and its external rivals. Most significant of all, it had achieved the ultimate objectives of all good government: the preservation of liberty, the security of property and the maintenance of law and order, all under laws based on the consent of the people. The British constitution was compared favourably to any other that had ever existed in the history of the world.

It was widely argued that the British constitution possessed these inestimable virtues and achieved these enormous benefits because it was both a mixed government and a balanced constitution. It was generally agreed that there were three pure forms of government: monarchy, aristocracy and democracy.[75] While each had its merits, each was also weakened by a serious threat to liberty or stability. Monarchy avoided disputes over who could exercise authority and it allowed the sovereign to act promptly in an emergency; but it placed liberty and property at the mercy of one individual who might act as an arbitrary tyrant. Aristocracy provided an able elite capable of leading and of offering an inspiring example to the nation, but it too often degenerated into a narrow oligarchy of warring, self-interested factions. Democracy offered the greatest liberty to the ordinary subject, but it was slow to reach decisions and was so inherently unstable that it invariably soon collapsed into anarchy and mob rule. Britain, however, had devised a mixed form of government which secured the benefits while avoiding the disadvantages of those three governments in their pure form. A government which mixed elements of monarchy, aristocracy and democracy, maximized the constraints on power and prevented its abuse, provided good leadership to society while securing the rights of the subject, and preserved liberty while maintaining stability.

The benefits of mixed government were achieved in practice by the balanced constitution of King, Lords and Commons. Each of these institutions had its own peculiar privileges and distinct functions. As chief magistrate the king was above the law, was the fount

75. On mixed government and the balanced constitution, see Dickinson, *Liberty and Property*, pp. 143–59, 272–80.

of honour, was the unchallenged head of the executive, and retained various prerogative rights, including the power to summon, prorogue and dissolve parliament. The Lords enjoyed the highest honours in the state, sat in the upper chamber of parliament as of right, and formed the highest court of justice in the land. The Commons were the representatives of the people, and, as such, defended the liberties of the subject and put forward their grievances for redress and their proposals for legislation. They also enjoyed the privilege of initiating all money bills which gave them control of the public purse. Besides these distinct and individual functions, all three institutions of King, Lords and Commons combined together to form the sovereign legislature. No bill could become law unless it was approved by all three in the same session of parliament. There was no strict separation of powers even though the king was the head of the executive, the Lords were the supreme court of law and the Commons voted the public revenues. The executive and the judiciary interacted with the legislature, since the king's ministers and senior public servants sat in both houses of parliament, the judges sat in the Lords to offer their advice on legal matters, and all three institutions formed the sovereign legislature. The concept of the balanced constitution involved each part having its independent role, while all three were dependent on each other when passing legislation. The British constitution therefore was a complicated system of checks and balances. It preserved the privileges of crown, nobility and people, while seeking to secure a harmonious relationship between all three. It was this delicate balance and equilibrium that ensured those twin goals of any well-regulated state: liberty and stability.[76]

Britain's mixed government and balanced constitution was widely praised as the best political system that human wisdom had ever contrived. It was credited with bringing unity to the British Isles as Wales was absorbed into the English political system in 1536, Scotland agreed an incorporating union in 1707 and sent representatives to the Westminster parliament, while Ireland was denied legislative independence or equality, and later joined an incorporating union in 1800. Parliament sought to extend its sovereignty to the American colonies in the 1760s and 1770s and was alarmed to see its efforts rejected. The American constitutional challenge aroused the deepest fears of its British opponents. The deep and

76. William Blackstone, *Commentaries on the Laws of England* 4 vols, 7th edn (Oxford, 1771), i, pp. 154–5.

prolonged constitutional conflicts of the seventeenth century had taught educated Britons that the delicate balance of the constitution could be destroyed by three challenges: an over-powerful monarch, popular radicalism and religious dissent. The American crisis convinced them that all three challenges were recurring at the same time. The ministerial instability of the 1760s and the career of John Wilkes had already convinced some British politicians that the ambitions and extensive patronage of George III were threatening to disturb the balance of the constitution. Edmund Burke protested that 'the power of the crown, almost dead and rotten as prerogative, has grown up anew, with much more strength, and far less odium under the name of influence'.[77] When he was later seeking to curb crown patronage by economical reforms, Burke claimed: 'formerly the operation of the influence of the crown only touched the higher orders of the state. It has now insinuated itself into every creek and cranny in the kingdom.'[78] To such critics of crown influence the American colonies posed an alarming threat to the constitution. In seeking to reject parliamentary sovereignty, the Americans insisted that their colonial assemblies alone could tax, and legislate for, the people of the colonies and that the colonists were subordinate and owed allegiance solely to the king.[79] To many in Britain this meant a return to the pre-1763 situation, when Britain had been able to exercise little authority over the colonies[80] or, more alarmingly if the colonies did accept only the king's authority, it threatened to increase the power of the crown to a dangerous degree and to undermine the liberties of the king's British subjects.[81]

Parliament was particularly alarmed when the colonies addressed their petitions against the Townshend duties to the king alone and when they appealed to the king to veto parliamentary bills.[82] George Grenville opposed schemes to raise money in the colonies by requisitions sanctioned by the crown, rather than by parliamentary taxation, because such a proposal would strengthen the independence of the crown while weakening parliament's financial control of the king.[83]

77. Edmund Burke, 'Thoughts on the cause of the present discontents' (1770) in *Works of Edmund Burke* 6 vols, Bohn edn (1854–6), i, p. 313.

78. *Parliamentary History*, xx, p. 1297.

79. Jack P. Greene, 'Competing authorities: the debate over parliamentary imperial jurisdiction, 1763–1776' *PH* 14 (1995), pp. 47–63.

80. Tucker and Hendrickson, *Fall of the First British Empire*, p. 410.

81. *London Packet* 10 and 11 Mar. 1774; Thomas, ed., 'Parliamentary diaries of Nathaniel Ryder', p. 267.

82. Reid, *Constitutional History*, iv, pp. 153–6.

83. Thomas, *Townshend Duties Crisis*, pp. 101, 158, 174–5.

Another imperialist MP, John Moreton, warned the House of Commons 'of the danger of raising money in America by requisitions from the crown; by which revenue, so raised, the king might be able to govern this country without parliament'.[84] The American colonies floated the idea of a federal solution to the imperial crisis by suggesting that they might be self-governing states sharing the same monarch as Britain. This would endanger the existing British constitution where the monarch was not a figurehead, but a very active player in politics. If George III was monarch of America, while being independent of the British parliament so far as America was concerned, he would gain additional power that might be used to subvert the independence of parliament and the liberties of the subject within Britain. It was not surprising therefore that in 1775 a loyal address to the king, protested 'against the principles of those men, who by asserting the dependence of America on the crown, exclusively of the parliament of Great Britain, endeavour to point out a distinction, that in future times, may be productive of the most fatal consequences to both'.[85] Fortunately for the preservation of parliamentary sovereignty, George III had no intention of accepting the American claims that their only constitutional connection with Britain was through the crown. The response of the loyal address from Oxford was 'heart-felt pleasure, that your Majesty has not been tempted to endanger the constitution of Great Britain, by accepting the alluring offers of an unconstitutional increase of your prerogative'.[86]

The second threat which was posed to parliamentary sovereignty was the radical claim that ultimate sovereignty lay with the people. Parliament was dominated by propertied men who had a low opinion of the common people, whom they often regarded as 'rash and precipitate, giddy and inconstant, and ever the dupes of designing men who lead them to commit the most atrocious crimes'.[87] Charles James Fox spoke for many MPs when he declared that the House of Commons was the true voice of the people, not the 'irregular and riotous crowd', who 'are but ill-qualified to judge truly of their own interest, or to pursue it, even if they form a right judgment'.[88] British imperialists were convinced that the American colonists were

84. *Parliamentary History*, xix, p. 803.   85. *London Gazette* 25 Nov. 1775.
86. Ibid., 14 Nov. 1775. See also Lord North's response to Charles James Fox, when he accused the Americans of supporting Tory principles. *Parliamentary History*, xviii, p. 771.
87. Josiah Tucker, *Four Letters on Important National Subjects* (1783), p. 98.
88. John Derry, *English Politics and the American Revolution*, pp. 17–18.

British subjects and that therefore parliament could pass laws and levy taxes which the colonists had to accept. They maintained that no laws and taxes would ever be enacted if a legislature had to have such measures ratified by every single subject. Josiah Tucker protested: 'no man in his senses will pretend to say, that the laws and edicts of parliament are not binding, 'till they have received the sanction of some patriotic club, or popular assembly convened for that purpose:- or that taxes ought not to be levied, *'till the people shall appear to be willing to pay them.'*[89] James Scott, writing as 'Anti-Sejanus', concluded: 'The *right of Taxation* over the colonies is a point which none but a *republican leveller*, or the wildest visionary in politics would dare to dispute; and the necessity of *enforcing the tax*, after it has been violently and rebelliously withstood, is evident to every man, who has the credit and dignity of the British legislature at heart.'[90]

When the Americans first challenged parliamentary sovereignty they had done so on the basis of their historic rights as Englishmen. Increasingly, however, the more radical among them began to appeal to natural rights. Conservative writers in Britain had often opposed the radical theories of John Locke and contemporary reformers, and they poured scorn on the notion of the original contract and the claim that all men possessed equal and inalienable natural rights, including the right to participate in the decision-making processes of the state.[91] Claims to natural equality were highly dangerous because they encouraged men to seek an equality of property as well as an equality of rights, and this would 'occasion such tumult, disorder, and anarchy, as would necessarily dissolve the constitution; and give rise to some new kind of government, fatal in all probability to Britain'.[92] The colonists' claim to equal natural rights was seen by British imperialists as a direct threat to the British constitution and the first step towards anarchy: 'To say then that the colonists have a right of judging for themselves what laws they shall obey, and which they may protest against, is, in effect, to invest them with a right incompatible with the officers of subjects, and utterly subversive to the end of all human institutions.'[93]

89. Josiah Tucker, *The Respective Pleas and Arguments of the Mother Country, and the Colonies, distinctly set forth* 2nd edn (1776), p. 23.

90. *London Magazine* 35 (1766), p. 73.

91. [Ramsay,] *Thoughts on the Origin and Nature of Government*, pp. 8–9; H.V.S. Ogden, 'The state of nature and the decline of Lockean political theory in England 1760–1800' *AHR* 46 (1940), pp. 21–44.

92. [Anon.,] *Constitutional Right*, pp. 48–9.

93. [Ramsay], *Thoughts on the Origin and Nature of Government*, p. 16.

From the later 1760s British imperialists had begun to accuse the leaders of the colonial opposition of being factious, turbulent spirits, who were misleading their supporters and disguising their true aim of seeking independence from the mother country.[94] By 1775 there was a widespread belief in Britain that there had long been a conspiracy by a few wicked men to throw off the authority of the mother country.[95] In that year many loyal addresses denounced the American colonists as 'Sons of Anarchy', 'Mob and Rabble led by mad Enthusiasts and desperate Republicans', and rebels producing 'the miseries of a democratical tyranny'.[96] Colonial violence, particularly in New England, convinced British imperialists that American anarchy had to be met by a firmer exertion of parliamentary sovereignty:

> Democracy is too prevalent in America, and claims the greatest attention to prevent its increase, and fatal effects. It is necessary too that Great Britain should not only assert, but also support that supremacy which she claims over the members of the Empire, or she will soon be supreme only in words, and we shall become a vast empire, composed of many parts, disjointed and independent of each other, without any head.[97]

British imperialists therefore rejected the American claim that they were justified in taking up arms. William Blackstone argued that there was no case for resisting Britain's present admirable constitution and granting people the right to replace it with another: 'For this devolution of power, to the people at large, includes in it a dissolution of the whole form of government established by that people; reduces all the members to their original state of equality; and, by annihilating the sovereign power, repeals all positive laws whatsoever before enacted.'[98]

The third threat posed to the British constitution was an attack on its religious foundations. Since the sixteenth century the English had stressed not only the unity of king and parliament, but the maintenance of a national state church under royal and parliamentary authority. The Church of England was a state church, not a 'gathered church', and the whole nation was regarded as being members of it. The church received certain benefits from the state

---

94. Thomas, ed., 'Parliamentary diaries of Nathaniel Ryder', p. 344.
95. Ira D. Gruber, 'The American revolution as a conspiracy: the British view' *WMQ* 3rd series, 26 (1969), pp. 360–72.
96. Paul Langford, 'Old Whigs, old Tories, and the American revolution' *JICH* 8 (1980), p. 125.
97. Thomas, *Townshend Duties Crisis*, p. 217.
98. Blackstone, *Commentaries*, i, p. 162.

(including financial support, the right to hold ecclesiastical courts, and the political privileges secured by the Test and Corporation Acts), while the church did nothing without the civil magistrate's leave or approbation.[99] The church possessed considerable political power: the king was its supreme governor, its bishops sat in the House of Lords, and its clergy played a major role in education, and in preaching loyalty and obedience to the powers that be. The clergy usually regarded themselves as the custodians of an ordered, hierarchical society. During the American crisis there was a marked resurgence of conservative propaganda emanating from the Church of England. The Anglican clergy were the most consistently pro-government body in the nation during the American Revolution. They regularly emphasized order, obedience and submission to those in authority, and praised the virtues of the existing constitution and the rule of law. They feared licentiousness, stressed the sinfulness of revolt, and gave almost unanimous support to the policy of coercion.[100]

The church's authority had been extended to Wales and Ireland since the sixteenth century and its adherents monopolized all political offices under the crown. In the seventeenth century its hegemony had been seriously challenged by Protestant Dissenters of various persuasions, but the Glorious Revolution and the Act of Settlement of 1701 respectively helped to secure its privileges by ensuring that the monarch would first support and then be in communion with the Church of England. Many commentators stressed the political benefits flowing from this alliance of church and state. Edmund Burke, for example, regarded the established church as a great national benefit and a public blessing. He insisted that the English did not see the church as a mere political convenience: 'They consider it as the foundation of their whole constitution, with which, and with every part of which, it holds an indissoluble union. Church and state are ideas inseparable in their minds, and scarcely is the one ever mentioned without mentioning the other.'[101]

By the eighteenth century Dissent was supported by less than 10 per cent of the English population, though Rational Dissenters still offered the most vocal criticisms of the existing order in church

99. Norman Sykes, *Church and State in England in the XVIIIth Century* (Cambridge, 1934), pp. 315–21.

100. James E. Bradley, 'The Anglican pulpit, the social order, and the resurgence of Toryism during the American revolution' *Albion* 21 (1989), pp. 361–88; and Paul Langford, 'The English clergy and the American revolution' in Eckhart Hellmuth, ed., *The Transformation of Political Culture in Britain and Germany in the Later Eighteenth Century* (Oxford, 1980), pp. 275–307.

101. *Burke's Writings and Speeches*, viii, p. 149.

and state. When the Dissenters sought an extension of religious toleration in the early 1770s, their campaign alarmed the defenders of the established church. True churchmen were urged to unite: 'It being evident that the Dissenters in general want to subvert the constitution.'[102] In the American colonies, by contrast, Protestant Dissenters were a majority of the population and they were often among the most vocal critics of Britain's policy. In the early 1760s they were particularly worried about the archbishop of Canterbury's desire to appoint a Church of England bishop in the colonies.[103] Without going so far as those who claim that the American Revolution was a war of religion,[104] it is true that colonial opposition ensured that no bishop and no ecclesiastical courts of the Church of England were established in the American colonies and American Dissenters were in the forefront of critics of parliamentary sovereignty. They saw parliamentary sovereignty as an affront to God's sovereignty as expressed by fundamental law and they preferred to advocate the sovereignty of the people under God. Edmund Burke, more well disposed to the American colonists than most Britons, certainly saw their particular religious principles as predisposing the colonists to oppose British authority:

> Religion, always a principle of energy in this new people, is no way worn out or impaired; and their mode of professing it is also one main cause of this free spirit. The people are protestants; and of that kind, which is the most adverse to all implicit submission of mind and opinion. . . . the dissenting interests have sprung up in direct opposition to all the ordinary powers of the world; and could justify that opposition only on a strong claim to natural liberty. Their very existence depended on the powerful and unremitted assertion of that claim. All protestantism, even the most cold and passive, is a sort of dissent. But the religion most prevalent in our Northern Colonies is a refinement on the principle of resistance, it is the dissidence of dissent; and the protestantism of the protestant religion.[105]

Conclusion

By 1775 the British government had shifted its policy towards the American colonies from the legislative imposition of parliamentary sovereignty to what proved to be a fatal attempt to impose

102. *London Chronicle* 30 Sept. 1775.
103. Knollenberg, *Origins of the American Revolution*, pp. 81–4.
104. J.C.D. Clark, *The Language of Liberty 1660–1832* (Cambridge, 1994).
105. Edmund Burke, 'Speech on conciliation, 22 March, 1775' in *Burke's Writings and Speeches*, iii, pp. 121–2.

parliament's authority by military support. Despite various suggestions for compromise put forward in the colonies and in Britain, it proved impossible to find any middle ground between colonial submission to parliament on the one hand and the American colonies' complete submission on the other. This failure was not entirely inevitable, though it is difficult to see how the British could have avoided the resort to arms to resolve the crisis. It is true that successive British ministries were guilty of ignorance, misjudgements and miscalculations and they were often preoccupied with other issues (including George III, John Wilkes and the East India Company) and so did not devote enough attention to the situation in the American colonies. British ministers and parliament in general consistently and seriously underestimated the depth and extent of colonial opposition to their imperial policies and the capacity of the colonies to resist these measures by political and military means. On the other hand, their policies were endorsed by most minor government officials, who were much better informed about the colonies and who devoted most of their time to thinking about the American situation.[106] Britain's imperial policy failed not because of the personal frailties of particular ministers, but because of the strength of the ideological beliefs that underpinned their policies. The political nation in general believed it needed to exert its authority over the American colonies and it believed it was constitutionally justified in doing so. Since the colonists were fiercely opposed to both of these propositions, a serious crisis was extremely difficult to avoid.[107]

In the last resort, therefore, the dispute between Britain and her American colonies was fundamentally a constitutional crisis in which both sides were so deeply attached to their respective positions that they could not retreat from them even if it meant war. Both thought they were defending rights, liberties and privileges preserved and protected by the British constitution. Both had learned a great deal from the constitutional conflicts of the seventeenth century and both praised the political settlement reached by the Glorious Revolution. The American colonists, although their political *practices* had undergone rapid development in the eighteenth century, remained attached to the seventeenth-century version of the English constitution. They were afraid of absolute, arbitrary authority and sought protection from it in the common law, customary rights and the

106. F.B. Wickwire, *British Subministers and Colonial America 1763–1783* (Princeton, NJ, 1966).

107. Jack P. Greene, 'The plunge of the lemmings: a consideration of recent writings on British politics and the American revolution' *South Atlantic Quarterly* 67 (1968), pp. 141–75.

fundamental laws of the constitution. Their British opponents, on the other hand, had also changed their political practices in the eighteenth century, but their interpretation of the British constitution had also changed in tune with their practices. They did not fear and indeed positively welcomed the development of a sovereign parliament because they had learned to manipulate and control that parliament. Annual sessions of parliament and parliamentary involvement in all major affairs of the state and, increasingly, in the social and economic life of the people, gave its members great power and prestige. The system of public credit and parliamentary control of revenue-raising gave the House of Commons greater control over the executive and effectively limited the *power* of the crown. At the same time, the expansion of crown *patronage* provided members of both houses of parliament with a wide range of honours, offices and rewards. The electoral system, the development of parliamentary lobbying through a wide range of pressure groups, the growth of a free press and the existence of a public conscious of its rights, made parliament far more accountable to the British people than it ever was or could be to the American colonists and this also ensured that parliamentary sovereignty was never seriously abused. In contrast, the American colonists, although not subject to any parliamentary measure that could fairly be described as tyrannical, were fully justified in believing that their lives, liberty and property were not safe when controlled by a sovereign parliament meeting at Westminster and elected only by men living in Britain. The Americans could legitimately argue that they had no security so long as supreme constitutional authority over their political and economic interests was located in the Westminster parliament and not in their own legislative assemblies. British imperialists, on the other hand, could reasonably claim that British lives, liberty and property were better protected under a sovereign parliament than they had ever been in the past and this was a benefit worth fighting for. General John Burgoyne asked the House of Commons, before he left for the war in America: 'Is there a man in England (I am confident there is not an officer or soldier in the King's service) who does not think the parliamentary rights of Great Britain a cause to fight for, to bleed for, to die for?'[108] Until military reverses taught them to think otherwise, a majority in parliament was indeed ready to take up arms in an effort to impose British authority over the American colonies and to resist the colonial demand for independence.

---

108. Simmons and Thomas, eds, *Proceedings and Debates,* v, p. 477.

CHAPTER FOUR

The Parliamentary Opposition to the Government's American Policy 1760–1782

FRANK O'GORMAN

The conflict with America gave rise to intense, if intermittent, discussion in the parliamentary opposition of the Rockingham Whigs and the followers of the Elder Pitt. Until the later stages of the conflict their opposition was neither coherent nor effective nor popular. It was not coherent because their opposition to government policy rested their disagreement on two somewhat contradictory propositions; on some occasions they demanded a more conciliatory policy, on others a more vigorous assertion of parliamentary sovereignty. It was not effective because they failed to alter or amend the drift of ministerial policy. Their opposition to the policy of Lord North may have been ultimately vindicated by the failure of British arms in America but for many years they had little to offer that was politically constructive. The fact that North's policy failed does not prove that the opposition's political judgement was right nor that its philosophical generalizations were sound. It was not popular because these critics failed to weaken the powerful national consensus on imperial questions which existed down to the later 1770s.[1]

The principle of parliamentary sovereignty

From the outset there was little in principle to distinguish the policy of the parliamentary opposition from that of successive governments. George Grenville's Stamp Act of 1765 had aroused a storm

1. I.R. Christie, *Crisis of Empire: Great Britain and the American Colonies, 1754–83* (1966); Ian R. Christie and Benjamin W. Labaree, *Empire or Independence, 1760–76: A British–American Dialogue on the Coming of the American Revolution* (Oxford, 1976).

of opposition in the colonies and a degree of commercial protest which persuaded the weak Rockingham administration (1765–6) to repeal the act in 1766. It was less, however, any generosity of spirit on the part of the government which characterized its policy than its adherence to traditional imperial attitudes and the maintenance of the old imperial system. The Rockingham ministry did not doubt that legislative adjustment would restore the harmony of old imperial relationships since the colonists were essentially good and loyal imperial citizens. Indeed, it was their customary mentality which won the support of the provincial commercial lobby, whose exertions in the winter of 1765–6 after colonial protests against the Stamp Act persuaded the government of the necessity for its repeal. So controversial was the policy, however, that the repeal was accompanied by a Declaratory Act, a severe recitation of parliamentary sovereignty over the colonies 'in all cases whatsoever'. The repeal of the Stamp Act may have signified the reluctance of the ministry to stand by the principle of the right of parliament to tax the colonists directly, but its other measures confirmed its willingness to raise a colonial revenue in other ways. The administration's overhaul of the commercial structure of the empire – the reduction of the molasses duty from 3d. to 1d., the lowering of the duties on cotton and sugar and the establishment of free ports at Kingston and on Dominica – represented a continuing assumption in London that the interests of the empire remained subordinate to those of the mother country. Ministers, however, also continued to subordinate the interests of its constituent parts to those of the mother country. The Declaratory Act, together with these other assertions of parliamentary sovereignty, hung like a stone around the necks of the Rockingham party whenever in the future they ventured to criticize the policy of the governments of George III which were, after all, simply seeking to enforce such sovereignty.[2] In this manner, expediency rather than a principled commitment to the colonial cause typified the Rockinghamite position in 1765–6.

Such a traditional view of the empire was thoroughly acceptable to the Elder Pitt and his small but influential band of supporters. It has long been recognized that Pitt's political philosophy did not begin and end with a simple belief in parliamentary sovereignty over the empire. He displayed (as did many American colonists) a view more common in the seventeenth than the eighteenth century,

---

2. Whigs of an older generation, such as Hardwicke and Newcastle, were privately uneasy at the sweeping nature of the sovereignty claimed in the Declaratory Act.

a belief in a fundamental law lying behind the sovereignty of parliament, to which he appealed against parliament in a succession of issues ranging from the Middlesex election to the Declaratory Act. In the early 1760s little was known about Pitt's attitude to the colonial problem. He had not, for example, been present during the parliamentary debates on Grenville's policy in 1764 and 1765. Consequently, when he came to deliver his opinions on the Stamp Act it was natural that contemporaries would react strongly. On a famous parliamentary occasion on 14 January 1766 Pitt announced his opposition to the act on the grounds that the colonists were not represented in parliament. Arguing that the act was contrary to the fundamental constitutional principle of no taxation without representation, he proceeded to make a distinction between the imposition on the colonists of internal taxes, which he viewed as unconstitutional, and external taxes, such as customs levies, whose legitimacy he accepted because he supported the underlying right of parliament to regulate imperial trade.[3] This was why, at the same time, he demanded an unequivocal assertion of the rights of parliament over the colonies. As he declared on 24 April, within the empire Britain 'was the conducting head, the animating heart, the inspiring soul, which gave life to all the rest'.[4] No wonder that some of the colonists regarded Pitt as no friend of America.[5] As Derek Jarrett has tellingly remarked: 'Pitt had conquered an empire for the sake of the old colonial system, with colonies serving as sources of raw materials and as markets for manufactured goods, and he intended that it should remain that way.'[6] In general, then, the position of the Rockingham ministry and that of Pitt were not too different. Pitt's removal of internal taxation from the scope of parliamentary sovereignty, however, was to have momentous consequences.

After the fall of their ministry in 1766 the Rockingham Whigs continued to vindicate the principle of parliamentary supremacy over the colonies. They continued to defend the Declaratory Act and consistently demanded its enforcement in the colonies. Indeed, little more than parliamentary tactics divided them from the policy of successive ministries. They did not oppose the principle of the

3. G.H. Guttridge, *English Whiggism and the American Revolution* (Berkeley, CA, 1966), pp. 63–4.

4. Jeremy Black, *Pitt the Elder* (Cambridge, 1992), p. 259, quoting the Harris memo, 24 April 1766.

5. Peter D.G. Thomas, *British Politics and the Stamp Act Crisis* (Oxford, 1975), p. 367.

6. Derek Jarrett, *The Begetters of Revolution: England's Involvement with France, 1759–89* (1973), p. 83.

Townshend duties in 1767 because the duties did not contravene the Declaratory Act. The danger they saw in the Townshend duties was that they might provoke the Americans to question – and even demand the repeal of – other revenue measures. To repeal the Townshend duties might encourage the colonists to question the Declaratory Act. If they came to challenge, and thus to weaken, parliamentary sovereignty then opinion in Britain might be outraged. Such a polarization of opinion might lead to further conflict. Privately, Rockingham had his doubts about what Townshend was doing. Although he deplored the violent reaction against the duties in the colonies, he believed that British sovereignty over the colonies could be achieved by 'merely commercial regulations'. It was, he maintained, madness to try to make 'a Revenue Mine' out of America.[7] Sadly, these reservations were never thought through, partly through lethargy but partly also because of a distinct stiffening of British public opinion against the colonies in these years. Rockingham's own instincts were those of moderation and conciliation. Even at this early stage, he seems to have been gripped with the fear that unwise and extreme actions on either side of the Atlantic might endanger the unity of the empire.[8] After all, the Rockingham Whigs viewed themselves as the heirs of the Whigs of the Glorious Revolution, with a unique destiny to maintain the liberties of Britain, her people and her constitution. And now, her empire. Since the beginning of the present reign, when George III and Lord Bute appeared to be establishing a new and sinister form of secret government, in which power and influence were not vested in the official and responsible ministers but reposed in 'ministers behind the curtain', relations between the mother country and her colonies had been soured. It would need Whig statesmanship of the highest order to restore traditional colonial relationships.

Nevertheless, the Rockingham Whigs were no less emphatic than their ministerial opponents in demanding that law and order should be enforced in the colonies. Indeed, on 13 May 1767 they attacked the government for its feebleness in disciplining the recalcitrant colony of New York and joined the Grenville Whigs in demanding that the colony pay for its own defence in the future. They had little sympathy for arguments based on the theoretical rights of the

---

7. Sheffield Public Library, Wentworth Woodhouse MSS, Rockingham to Joseph Harrison, 2 Oct. 1768. See also ibid., Rockingham to Harrison, 19 May 1769.

8. And possibly because Rockingham himself had begun to adopt a conspiratorial view of American affairs, blaming 'vain men [who] are now the fomentors of all the disturbances'. Ibid., Rockingham to Joseph Harrison, 2 Oct. 1768.

colonists. They wished to maintain the harmony of the empire because of the mutual benefits of commerce and because of the larger interests of Britain in the world. There is, therefore, no reason to depict the Rockingham Whigs at this time as 'Friends of America'. They were a small party struggling to keep their heads above water after their departure from office in 1766, anxious to maintain their independence against the pretensions of a conniving court cabal. Towards this objective, they were pursuing the goal of a united opposition, anxious to conciliate other factions and individuals. In the years after 1766 they were anxious to protect their negotiating position and endeavoured to keep open their lines of communication with Charles Townshend, whom they believed they could detach from the ministry, with the Earl of Chatham, as Pitt had now become, and even with the Grenville and Bedford Whigs, the authors of the Stamp Act. In truth, the Rockinghams lacked a comprehensive plan for America distinct in any way from that of their opponents.

This was made embarrassingly clear in 1770 when Lord North repealed the Townshend duties with the exception of the duty on tea, a conciliatory measure which reserved British sovereignty. The Rockinghams supported an amendment demanding the abolition of the tea duty but put forward no programme of their own. Well might Lord North ridicule the Rockinghams for falling back upon the Declaratory Act, while refusing to support measures which might enforce it. At this time, they had little that was constructive to offer, preferring to attack successive examples of administrative failure. In May 1770 Burke moved for an enquiry into the causes of the American disorders, denouncing both the incompetence of members of the government and the rising influence of the crown, while condemning the pettiness and inconsistency of colonial policy over the previous three years. Yet what was North doing in 1770 that the Rockinghams had not done in 1765–6? Surely North was striving to preserve British sovereignty, while choosing to exercise it in a prudent and pragmatic manner by responding sensibly to American grievances. What was the tea duty if it was not a practical symbol of British sovereignty? It is difficult to avoid the conclusion that in this way, the Rockinghams chose to exaggerate the (in reality, slight) differences which separated them from the North government. Symptomatic of the general convergence of opinions between government and opposition on America in these years was the appointment of Lord Dartmouth as secretary of state to the Colonial Department in August 1772. As a former Rockingham Whig, it was difficult for the Rockinghams to attack their erstwhile colleague. In the early 1770s, as the American issue slipped from view, and as British public opinion drifted into a less tolerant disposition towards the colonists, the Rockingham Whigs were less than prepared for the great colonial crisis of 1773–4.

Rockingham Whigs in opposition

Ever since the Townshend duties of 1767 the Rockingham Whigs had adopted a circumspect attitude towards the colonists. Their reaction to North's tea duty of 1773 was entirely typical. They did not oppose the tea duty because it seemed to them to be a practical expression of the Declaratory Act. Rockingham himself was more concerned for the independence of the East India Company from government control than he was for the political and economic welfare of the colonists. The only member of the party to oppose the Tea Act was William Dowdeswell. Yet even his concern did not arise out of any solicitousness for the colonies, but out of his fear that the colonists would refuse to purchase the tea, with damaging consequences for the East India Company.[9] The party entirely failed to anticipate the consequences of the act and they were just as shocked as the rest of British opinion at the Boston Tea Party.[10]

The tea party horrified British public opinion, with its defiant and intentional destruction of property and its apparent disregard for the consequences of the incident for imperial relations. The colonists received little sympathy and understanding in Britain. An outraged propertied elite, and much public opinion, rallied around Lord North's coercive legislation in the parliamentary session of 1774. The Rockingham Whigs had always been susceptible to public opinion. Consequently, although they opposed the coercive legislation, they did so without enthusiasm and with little effect. Indeed, so horrified had they been at the receipt of the news of the Boston Tea Party that they were at first unwilling to take up the colonists' cause. Even when they did steel themselves to oppose the coercive policy they did so while deploring the violence and damage to property which had characterized the actions of the colonists. While the House of Commons was debating the first of the coercive bills, the Boston Port Bill, Edmund Burke confided to a friend:

9. William Clements Library, Dowdeswell MSS, Dowdeswell to Rockingham, 14 Aug. 1768.
10. W.M. Elofson, *The Rockingham Connection and the Second Founding of the Whig Party, 1768–73* (Montreal, 1996), p. 170.

Those who spoke in opposition, did it, more for the acquittal of their own honour, and discharge of their own consciences . . . than from any sort of hope . . . of bringing any considerable Number to their opinion; or even of keeping in that opinion several of those who had formerly concurred in the same general Line of Policy with regard to the colonies.[11]

The bill met with no opposition in principle from the Rockinghams. Reservations were expressed by Dowdeswell and Lord John Cavendish, both of whom thought the bill inexpedient and that it might agitate the situation in the colonies. The only Rockingham Whig to oppose it outright was the Duke of Richmond in the Lords who applauded the Bostonians: 'They would be in the right to resist, as punished unheard, and, if they did resist, he should wish them success.'[12] As so often, however, Richmond spoke for nobody but himself.

It was only on the Massachusetts Regulating Bill that the Rockingham Whigs organized themselves effectively, arguing that the bill was both an illegitimate attack upon chartered rights and an unjustified reinforcement of the powers of the officers and ministers of state. They were, however, helpless to delay its passage and on 2 May it passed the Commons by 239 votes to 64. Similarly, the Rockinghams made a poor showing on the third coercive bill, the Impartial Administration of Justice Bill, when their major division issued in a ministerial victory by 127 votes to 24 on its third reading on 6 May. The fourth coercive measure, the Quartering Bill, met with no opposition at all.[13] By now the opposition was exhausted and in no fit state to deal comprehensively with the Quebec Act, which was introduced by the government very late in the session. They opposed the measure on a number of grounds; it made provision for a nominated rather than an elective council; it contained an excessive measure of toleration for Roman Catholics and for the Roman law of France. Nevertheless, opposition met with the same sort of response as it had on the Coercive Acts, going down to defeat on the third reading by 105 votes to 29 on 26 May.[14]

In view of the reputation later acquired by the Rockingham Whigs on colonial rights and American independence it is important to place in some perspective their lukewarm reaction to Lord North's

---

11. *Burke's Corr.*, ii, p. 528. Burke to the Committee of Correspondence of the General Assembly of New York, 6 April 1774.

12. A. Francis Steuart, ed., *The Last Journals of Horace Walpole during the Reign of George III, 1771–1783* 2 vols (1859), i, p. 364.

13. For details of the opposition to the last three coercive bills, see Frank O'Gorman, *The Rise of Party in Britain: The Rockingham Whigs, 1760–82* (1975), pp. 329–30.

14. Ibid., pp. 312–13.

coercive legislation. Their opposition to the ministry was particularly weak and ineffective, no doubt because they were no less affronted by the Boston Tea Party and no less impressed by the strength of British public opinion than the government. Where they parted company with the ministry they were on rather stronger ground. Thus they performed better on the Massachusetts Bay Bill than on the Boston Port Bill because their fear for the future of chartered rights rested on genuine grounds and received the endorsement of public opinion. Nevertheless, it remains the case, as Guttridge remarked over half a century ago, that 'throughout the session of 1774 the conduct of the Rockingham Whigs was tactical rather than constructive on the American question'.[15] Although a noticeable moderation informed their activities, together with an anxiety that the Americans might be driven to greater extremes, the policy that they advocated – of clinging to the Declaratory Act while repealing the tea duty – was simply no longer realistic after the Boston Tea Party. The Americans were no longer willing to tolerate either the spirit or the letter of the Declaratory Act.

The reaction of Lord Chatham and his friends to the coercive legislation was little different to that of the Rockingham Whigs and was vulnerable to the same criticisms. Even Chatham's usually liberal friend, Isaac Barré, voted in support of the Boston Port Bill. The friends of Chatham roused themselves on the Massachusetts Regulating Bill, opposing the policy of coercion and leading the opposition to the bill. Dunning distinguished himself in a magnificent speech, ridiculing the language of ministers: 'The language was, Resist and we will cut your throats – Acquiesce and we will tax you.'[16] Chatham himself came down to the Lords on 28 May 1774 to oppose the Quartering Bill and to put himself forward as the only man in England who 'could assert the authority of England and compose the differences in America'.[17] He could not, however, command their lordships and Richmond's motion was lost by 57 votes to 16. As on other occasions, both wings of the opposition performed unevenly, failing to react with vigour and incapable of understanding the new mood of exultant freedom which was sweeping the colonies. The coercive legislation of 1774 completely failed to restore peace and order in North America. Rockingham and Chatham were appalled as the situation there drifted out of control. All sections of the opposition agreed that what was urgently and

15. Guttridge, *English Whiggism*, p. 73.
16. Steuart, ed., *Last Journals of Horace Walpole*, i, p. 359.   17. Ibid., i, p. 369.

immediately needed was the restoration of trust between mother country and her colonies. But this could not be achieved by coercive legislation from one side and subsequent defiance and disorder from the other. The prospect of a military solution horrified both Rockingham and Chatham. Both sections of the opposition agreed that such an outcome would drive the colonies to further extremes while leaving Britain vulnerable to foreign intervention by the European powers.[18] But how was trust to be re-established and harmony in the empire restored?

Conciliation plans: Burke and Chatham

Between April 1774 and November 1775 Edmund Burke delivered three famous speeches which together may be regarded as his project for peace and conciliation in the colonies: a speech on Rose Fuller's motion for the repeal of the tea duty in April 1774 and his two speeches for conciliation of 22 March and 16 November 1775.[19] Burke delivered the first of his speeches on 19 April 1774 on a motion for the repeal of the duty on tea (although the speech did not appear in a published form until the following year). In it, he continued to adhere to the Declaratory Act, while seeking to conciliate the Americans by advocating the repeal of the tea duty. He argued that Britain had in recent years departed from her traditional policy of legislating purely for mercantile reasons. In true Rockinghamite fashion, Burke advocated the retention of British sovereignty, but forebore to exercise it in the interests of imperial harmony. He retained the right to tax, but the purpose of such taxation would not be to raise a revenue but to regulate commerce. Furthermore, Burke was prepared to allow the colonial legislatures such powers as 'are equal to the common ends of their institution' but it was by no means clear what that entailed.

Burke's first speech for conciliation was delivered almost a year later, on 22 March 1775 when he moved his 'Proposals for Conciliation'. By this time, the situation had become more serious, with the use of force to quell the colonial protest a real possibility. Burke passionately denounced the use of force. 'It may subdue for a moment,' he announced 'but it does not remove the necessity of subduing again.' The old imperial connection must be restored on

18. For these dilemmas of leadership, see O'Gorman, *Rise of Party*, pp. 327–30.
19. For Burke's speeches, see ibid., pp. 313–14, 332–5, 344–5. For the texts of the speeches, see *Burke's Writings and Speeches*, ii, pp. 406–63, iii, pp. 102–69, 183–220.

the basis of trust, consent and mutual self-interest. Even now Burke did not question Britain's right to govern North America, even at this time of rapid change and overwhelmingly serious contention. Even now, Burke did not doubt Britain's unique imperial role. By assuming the mantle of Providence to civilize the American wilderness Britain had brought positive benefits to North America. Yet Burke brought to this essentially British view of empire some fresh and invigorating perceptions. For Burke, the empire was an association of different states under a common monarchy, an empire in which the constituent parts enjoyed and should enjoy considerable local autonomy. Exactly how much autonomy they should enjoy would be a matter of compromise. Adopting an argument which might have surprised many of his contemporaries, who assumed as a matter of course that the colonies were an economic drag on the home country, Burke argued that both Britain and her colonies derived much common benefit from their commercial intercourse. It was madness to threaten that benefit through sterile argument about questions of right. To this end he was prepared to repeal those measures which had done so much damage: the tea duty, the coercive legislation of 1774 and the hated Admiralty courts. What Burke advocated was a new spirit which, 'by restoring the former unsuspecting confidence of the colonies in the mother country', would restore the old harmony within the empire. The details of conciliation were less important than the dramatic and overriding need for conciliation. 'The proposition is peace, not peace to depend on the juridical determination of perplexing questions; or the precise marking the shadowy boundaries of a complex government. It is simple peace.' Burke's concept of empire, moreover, did not rest on statutes and laws but on common cultural and linguistic sentiments, 'the close affection which grows from common names, from kindred blood, from similar privileges and equal protection . . . ties which though light as air, are as strong as links of iron'. Nevertheless, Burke's speech failed to persuade a majority of MPs and his motion was lost by 270 votes to 78.

In his second speech, on 16 November 1775, Burke went a little further, proposing not merely the repeal of the Coercive Acts but also the repudiation of parliament's right to tax the colonies. He had by now reached the conclusion that parliamentary sovereignty should only be exercised with the agreement of the colonial legislatures. He was prepared to recognize the Congress and even to pronounce a general amnesty as a preliminary to comprehensive peace negotiations. Yet the old imperial structure would continue.

The trade and Navigation Acts would stand and sovereignty would remain with King, Lords and Commons. Within this imperial structure, however, Burke was prepared to allow a considerable amount of devolved government. Congress would enjoy legislative authority while local colonial assemblies would raise and spend customs duties. Yet again, however, parliament refused to listen. Although Burke won the votes of 105 MPs, exactly twice as many voted against him.

There was much that was enlightened and statesmanlike about Burke's conception of empire and his proposals for conciliation. They were certainly far-reaching, conceding practically everything that the first Continental Congress had demanded. They were years ahead of their time in catching something of the dynamic spirit of empire and in abandoning legalistic disputes about sovereignty. The problem with Burke's conciliation plans is that, with the benefit of hindsight, they would not have conciliated the Americans. (It goes without saying that if they failed to pass the Commons, it is unthinkable that they would have passed the Lords; and they would have been greeted with apoplexy by George III.) Burke's eloquent distinctions between theory and practice, and between the exercise and the non-exercise of sovereignty, were too sophisticated for the average country gentleman, who wanted plain speaking, positive solutions and some ready response to American defiance of British law and order. It was surely too late by 1775 to imagine that the colonial legislatures would have accepted Burke's plan. It was all very well to demand a new spirit of conciliation, much more difficult to translate that demand into reality. It may be harsh to recognize the fact, but Burke failed to provide realistic and practical solutions to either the political, administrative or financial problems facing the empire in North America which might have prevented the outbreak of hostilities at Concord and Lexington in April 1775. By November 1775 and Burke's second conciliation speech it was too late. It was all very well for Burke to preach peace but, as Dean Tucker demanded, 'what is this heaven born pacific scheme?' He went on: 'Why, truly: if we grant the colonies all that they shall require, and stipulate for nothing in return; then they will be at peace with us. I believe it; and on these simple principles of simple peacemaking I will engage to terminate every difference throughout the world.'[20] By now, Burke's optimistic yet continuing assumption that the American colonists were interested in reforming and renewing the imperial relationship had been left behind by events. In

20. Josiah Tucker, *A Letter to Edmund Burke Esq.* (1775), pp. 44–5.

general, then, we may conclude that Burke's rhetoric and oratorical power could not entirely conceal the actual impracticability of his ideas. At this critical juncture, the American Revolution found the Rockinghamite opposition incapable of producing an innovative and effective practical response.

Yet, as we have noticed, the Rockinghams were not the only influential group in the parliamentary opposition and they were not alone in bringing forward proposals for conciliation. Indeed, Burke's imperial ideas had in part been formed by the need to negotiate tactical differences within that opposition. Consequently, Burke's speeches on conciliation may be viewed to some extent as an attempt to rally support in the House of Commons from the independent country gentlemen and thus as a means of securing ascendancy within the opposition. This was particularly urgent because down to 1774, at least, Chatham could undoubtedly claim to be a more sincere 'Friend of America' than any Rockingham Whig because he had espoused the notion, dear to the colonists, that there should be 'no taxation without representation'.

Chatham's first major pronouncement on the colonial issue after the passage of the coercive legislation came in January 1775. On 20 January he moved a resolution in the Lords for the withdrawal of British troops from Boston. He asserted that the colonists be free to tax themselves while the imperial parliament should confine itself to the regulation of colonial commerce and the enforcement of the navigation laws. In his speech Chatham warned the government that the colonists could not be held down by force of arms. A few regiments against 3 million colonists could not hope to prevail. Yet a majority in the House of Lords, in no mood for conciliation, agreed with the ministers that the hotheads in Boston represented nobody but themselves. Chatham's motion went down by 68 votes to 18. However, on 1 February Chatham introduced his conciliation plan into the Lords.[21] The plan affirmed British sovereignty while offering a number of important concessions to colonial opinion. Chatham was now prepared not only to negotiate with the Congress, but to recognize it as a permanent institution within the imperial structure of government, with its own revenues and powers of taxation. He abandoned any British claim to taxation in the colonies. The power of the purse was to be exercised only with the consent of the colonial legislatures. He renounced the use of force against the colonies and promised first the suspension and ultimately the

21. *Parliamentary History*, xviii, pp. 150–60.

repeal of all the legislation passed since 1764 once Congress had recognized the supremacy of parliament. Chatham was also anxious to recognize the inviolability of colonial charters and the independence of the colonial judiciary. These were weighty concessions, indeed, but were balanced by Chatham's insistence that the colonists grant a permanent revenue to finance British forces in the colonies.

Chatham's plan went much further than Burke's. Yet it, too, was totally unacceptable to the colonists. It did not specifically abandon the Declaratory Act, the colonists would not have tolerated the military provisions of the plan and they would not have agreed to finance their own submission to the mother country. Chatham's empire would still have been much too centralized for a people who had now progressed so far that within little more than a year they were to declare for independence. On the other hand, it went much too far for British opinion. Its recognition of the Congress seemed rash and likely to succeed only in encouraging the colonists to take the road leading to independence. Even though the Rockinghams felt uncomfortably obliged to vote for Chatham and his plan it was thrown out by the respectable, but decisive, division of 61 votes to 32.

Could Chatham have rescued the empire? Could the statesman of conciliation have averted American independence? It is extremely doubtful. For one thing, it is unlikely that many in the colonies still shared Chatham's high opinion of his own reputation there. He might have been the object of admiration in the colonies in the mid-1760s but that was no longer the case a decade later. To some extent this was his own fault. As Marie Peters devastatingly concludes: 'Advice from his American contacts was ignored or overridden.'[22] His distinction between internal and external taxation had largely been overtaken since 1766 and the Americans no longer respected it. Furthermore, by now hardly anyone in Britain believed that the colonists would agree to impose taxes on themselves. However conciliatory Chatham wished to be towards the colonies he could never have brought himself to concede the case for independence. He could not see that to the colonists the real issue was not taxation but *sovereignty*. So far as he was concerned, American independence would destroy the unity of the empire which he had in his own career done so much to fashion. Independence would damage that commercial intercourse and prosperity upon which British strength

22. Marie Peters, *The Elder Pitt* (1998), p. 220.

rested. The only possible consequence of American independence was a divided empire and a weakened Britain, both now vulnerable to Bourbon intervention. At the political level, too, Chatham made serious tactical errors. He did not take the trouble to seek to influence domestic opinion out-of-doors, especially in the City of London and among the provincial mercantile communities. Less significant, perhaps, was Chatham's inability to consult with other sections of the parliamentary opposition. Both on 20 January and 1 February 1775 the Rockinghams came down to the House without prior knowledge of the substance of Chatham's proposals. Although they agreed with many of Chatham's ideas, they did not agree with all of them. For example, his readiness to give statutory expression to the distinction between internal and external taxation was unacceptable to them because such a distinction violated the central principles of the Declaratory Act.

Indeed, Chatham was an imperialist politician of an earlier generation. His thinking falls into relief when it is compared with that of a number of leading British intellectuals, such as Adam Smith and Josiah Tucker, dean of Gloucester. Rejecting the common assumption that British markets in the Americas depended upon the continued dependence of the colonies upon the mother country, they argued that the laws of supply and demand, not the dictates of political sovereignty, should regulate trade. The fact that the navigation laws were widely evaded showed that they were both inoperative and unjust. Tucker's solution to the American problem – to dissolve the political connection between Britain and the colonies – was self-evidently unthinkable before the later 1770s.[23] Smith's solution was to incorporate the colonies within the British political system through processes of representation.[24] Not only would the colonists have resisted this measure but it was also politically unrealistic since it would have required the extensive relief of Protestant Dissenters in England, a measure that was half a century ahead of its time. Smith himself concluded his great work *The Wealth of Nations* (1776) with the statement:

> If any of the provinces of the British empire cannot be made to contribute towards the support of the whole empire, it is surely time that Great Britain should free herself from the expense of defending

23. George Shelton, *Dean Tucker and Eighteenth-Century Economic and Political Thought* (1981), pp. 182–213; Robert E. Toohey, *Liberty and Empire: British Radical Solutions to the American Problem, 1774–76* (Lexington, KY, 1978), pp. 156–60; and John Derry, *English Politics and the American Revolution* (1976), pp. 162–7.

24. R.H. Campbell and A.S. Skinner, eds, *Adam Smith, An Enquiry into the Nature and Causes of the Wealth of Nations* 2 vols (Oxford, 1976), ii, pp. 624–6.

those provinces in time of war, and of supporting any part of their civil or military establishments in time of peace, and endeavour to accommodate her future views and designs to the real mediocrity of her circumstances.[25]

Such free-trade ideas may have been anathema to Chatham but they profoundly influenced Lord Shelburne,[26] his political disciple in the early 1760s and his secretary of state during the administration of 1766–8. Shelburne shared his master's belief that conciliation was possible provided that Britain respect the constitutional and political rights of the colonists. He continued in the 1770s to hope that the colonists could be persuaded to accept some measure of political subordination to the mother country. Once that hope had been dashed, he nevertheless dreamed that even though American independence might be inevitable it might be accompanied by the establishment of a great Anglo-American free-trade area which would outflank the hostility of Bourbon absolutism. Ironically, Shelburne was the British prime minister when American independence had ultimately to be conceded in 1783, and the terms on which independence was ultimately negotiated were to owe much to his thinking.

The war effort: government and opposition

The conciliation plans of Burke and Chatham were overtaken by events, not least the outbreak of fighting on 19 April in Lexington. The news reached England on 26 May 1775. The Rockinghams were devastated at the news and Rockingham himself worried about its consequences: 'If an arbitrary Military Force is to govern one part of this large Empire, I think & fear if it succeeds, it will not be long before the whole of this Empire will be brought under a similar Thraldom.'[27] Characteristically, Rockingham viewed the colonial conflict as an extension of his party's domestic preoccupations about the king and the alleged system of secret influence which had afflicted the country since the beginning of the reign of George III.[28] For a time, the outbreak of the war brought the two wings of the

25. Ibid., ii, p. 947.
26. On Shelburne, see John Norris, *Shelburne and Reform* (1963) and Peter Brown, *The Chathamites* (1967), pp. 34–108.
27. Lord Edmond Fitzmaurice, *The Life of William, Earl of Shelburne* 2 vols (1912), ii, pp. 9–10.
28. On which see O'Gorman, *Rise of Party, passim*; and *idem*, 'The myth of Lord Bute's secret influence' in Karl W. Schweizer, ed., *Lord Bute: Essays in Reinterpretation* (Leicester, 1988), pp. 57–81.

opposition closer together. Burke's conciliation speech on 16 November, demanding the repeal of the legislation passed since 1766 and his abandonment of the right to tax, saving the navigation laws and the right to regulate commerce, brought the Rockinghams' policy very close to that of Chatham. Both sections of the opposition were alarmed at the replacement in the same month of the conciliatory Lord Dartmouth as secretary of state by one who was thought to be an advocate of coercion, Lord George Germain.[29] At the beginning of the new session of parliament, therefore, both wings of the opposition declared against the use of force in the colonies. Thereafter they continued to protest about the injustice and maladministration which accompanied the prosecution of the war. They moved motion after motion demanding papers relating to the war, denying the government the right to send more troops to the colonies and demanding details of war objectives and of the conditions under which peace might be restored. Even now, however, the Rockinghams continued to express their view that with a change of men and measures conciliation might still be achieved and trust might yet be forged. By clinging to the Declaratory Act, however, they failed to realize that conciliation on such terms was impossible.

Such illusions were finally dispelled by the Declaration of Independence of 4 July 1776, news of which reached London on 10 August. This came as little surprise to the government, which had for some time been expecting it. For a time, the real significance of the declaration did not sink in. Until now, British opinion had never seriously envisaged the possibility that the colonists would commit themselves to republican independence. They could not entertain the possibility that the new world would ever cross the psychological boundary of declaring itself independent of the old. Consequently, it was inevitable that the North administration would opt for a military response to the declaration. It was not just that Britain believed in her right to rule in America. What also concerned ministers was the likely reaction of the Bourbon powers in this new situation. France, in particular, was carefully watched for signs of military intervention on the side of the colonies.

The opposition reacted to the Declaration of Independence by opposing the war in America, but even at this late hour they could not bring themselves to support American independence. In view

29. On these ministers, see B.D. Bargar, *Lord Dartmouth and the American Revolution* (Columbia, SC, 1965); Gerald S. Brown, *The American Secretary: The Colonial Policy of Lord George Germain, 1775–1778* (Ann Arbor, MI, 1963); and Alan Valentine, *Lord George Germain* (Oxford, 1962).

of the state of opinion among the propertied and parliamentary classes in 1776 it would have been politically suicidal to have done so. Even now, however, they continued to advocate the hopeless cause of conciliation. They took genuine pleasure in the heroic defiance which they assumed the colonists to be displaying in the cause of liberty in their uneven struggle against the forces of authoritarian and unconstitutional government. In this way, the Rockingham Whigs depicted even the Declaration of Independence as a projection of their domestic struggles, not ceasing to reflect on the status of their accusations that ministers were waging war in another continent in order to keep their system of secret influence intact. Their best course of action lay in hoping that a change of ministers in London would lead to a healing of wounds and the restoration of the unity of the empire. Meanwhile, they would oppose the war with vigour and with energy.

There was, indeed, room for informed comment upon and criticism of the government's policy towards the Americans, in particular of the delays and the administrative complexities which hindered the war effort. In large measure, their criticisms were justified: three separate departments supplied the armed forces and four transported them.[30] The army in America was poorly trained. It was a collection of regiments subjected to no regular system or drilling. Delay and duplication together with inter-departmental rivalry weakened the cohesion of the war effort. Yet North made the best of a bad job. Dartmouth gave way to Germain in November 1775 and a more resolute note was struck. Furthermore, the somewhat rash accusations of political corruption that the opposition continually directed at North were both unfair and unfounded. For example, their major accusation concerned the assignment of war contracts to his own political supporters. In a system in which contracts, supplies and loans were negotiated on a private basis, such charges were perhaps inevitable. Yet we now know that North kept his own hands clean and that despite the natural tendency of such business to gravitate towards individuals and companies which were sympathetic to the government 'the maintenance of supply to the British army in America was a successful operation, in the face of immense physical and organizational problems'.[31] Furthermore, North was able to finance the war successfully while still finding time to bring forward improvements to the conduct of Treasury business, improvements, however, which were implemented by his successors.

30. Piers Mackesy, *The War for America 1775–1783* (1964; rev. edn 1993), p. 12.
31. Peter D.G. Thomas, *Lord North* (1976), p. 98.

If their accusations against the government's conduct of the war were at times exaggerated, then the opposition's depiction of the North administration as tyrannical and unconstitutional was unrealistic and unconvincing. It is extremely dangerous to take too seriously the constitutional assumptions of the opposition and to accept their view that they were unquestionably and consistently in the right during the years of the American war. Their portrayal of an authoritarian government, goading the helpless colonies into rebellion, was very wide of the mark. The idea that George III and Lord North might have turned a victorious army upon domestic freedoms was simply madness, yet the opposition tried to convince themselves that it was true. Even the normally sensible Duke of Richmond 'dreaded the return of that army to these kingdoms' because it might subvert the remains of freedom.[32] No less nonsensical was the continuing determination of the Rockingham Whigs to cultivate their belief in a system of secret influence. They believed that the highly suspect personal influence of Lord Bute in the earliest years of the reign developed into a system of secret influence after that nobleman retired from politics. Thereafter, it was asserted that Bute's mantle had been assumed by certain individuals: the lawyer Lord Mansfield or, more usually, Charles Jenkinson. The function of such individuals in Rockinghamite ideology was to provide explanations for what was otherwise inexplicable, their own exclusion from office, the outbreak of the war in America and the continuing existence of Lord North's ministry despite its internal weakness and its military disasters. Burke suspected 'that Jenkinson governs everything' and that, further, 'To follow Jenkinson, will be to discover My Lord Bute, and My Lord Mansfield, and another person as considerable as either of them.'[33]

Such illusions and exaggerations perhaps performed an intrinsically valuable role in explaining and justifying the proceedings of an opposition which had few political prospects in 1776–7 and certainly no hope of office. Once these are placed into their correct perspective, we can recognize the fact that in many respects the opposition was not as diametrically opposed to the position of Lord North's government as they liked to think. They were little less fervent than Lord North in their desire to maintain the integrity of the empire and in their attachment to British sovereignty over it. It is by no means clear that an administration led by either

32. *Parliamentary History*, xix, p. 404.
33. *Burke's Corr.*, iii, pp. 89–90. Burke to Rockingham, 5 Jan. 1775.

Chatham or Rockingham would have been more successful either in preventing the outbreak of hostilities in 1775 or in preventing the Declaration of Independence, or even in prosecuting the ensuing war with any more success than the hapless Lord North. After all, what were George III and Lord North fighting for if it were not the sovereignty of parliament over the colonies, a good Whig position and one which the attachment of the Rockingham Whigs to the Declaratory Act vindicated?

As British forces began to seize the upper hand in the military conflict with the colonists in the second half of 1776 and as the colonists began to negotiate the entry of France into the war,[34] the position of the Rockinghams was seen to be increasingly untenable. They still refused to recognize that it was illogical to continue to embrace a policy of conciliation when both the British government and the Congress could now only envisage a military solution to their differences, when American independence had become a reality and when France appeared to be on the point of entering the war. They could not support American independence and they could not support the war to end it. Yet by opposing the war constitutionally they were surely implicating themselves in what they condemned as the system of secret influence and tyrannical government which had instigated and which continued to sustain that war. After months of hesitation, the party decided in January 1777 upon a policy of seceding from parliament, a public repudiation of the war and an ultimate disavowal of the system of secret influence. By keeping their hands clean of the conflict they could leave the ministers to destroy themselves. Then the king would surely come to his senses, call in the opposition to restore peace and harmony in the empire and save the country from Bourbon intervention.

For a few unconvincing months, the party remained in secession. In fact, the secession was never total. The Chathamites took no notice of it and some influential members of the Rockingham party, not least Sir George Savile and the rising star Charles James Fox, continued to attend parliament. The ministry took advantage of the secession of the principal elements in opposition to rush through parliament a bill to suspend the operation of habeas corpus. When they tried in April to pay off debts of £600,000 on the civil list the Rockinghams rushed back to town, convinced that the forces of secret influence and corruption were gaining ground in their absence.

34. The dramatic appearance of Benjamin Franklin in Paris in December 1776 marked the beginnings of a process that culminated in the Franco-American entente which ultimately brought France into the war in 1778.

That put an end to the secession. It did not, however, put any fresh life into the opposition which remained tentative and weak.

It was at this point – in May 1777 – that Burke published his *Letter to the Sheriffs of Bristol*. This was nothing less than an apologia for the conduct of the Rockingham Whigs. Noting that the temper of the public was hostile both to the Americans and to the opposition, Burke repeated his demand for conciliation. The significance of the *Letter*, however, is his recognition that America could not now be coerced. If the repeal of all the legislation passed since 1763 – including, presumably, the Declaratory Act – would not persuade the colonists to return to their former loyalty then there was nothing for it but independence. The only alternative was a long and damaging war in which British liberties would be the first casualty. Burke's *Letter* elicited a notable reply, that from the Earl of Abingdon.[35] In his *Thoughts* on Burke's *Letter*, Abingdon attacked the doctrine of parliamentary supremacy, preferring to acknowledge that power rested with the people. 'What is the difference between the despotism of the King of France, and the despotism of the parliament of England'? Well might Burke deplore the impression given by such controversies of weakness and division within the opposition.[36]

Accepting American independence

What ultimately resolved many of these uncertainties was the British surrender at Saratoga on 13 October 1777. The news came through on 3 December 1777. At once the pulse of politics quickened as the opposition sensed that great events were at hand. Saratoga at least seemed to confirm the wisdom of Burke and others who had already expressed doubts that the war could be won and that the Declaratory Act might no longer be enforceable. As yet, however, neither the Rockinghams nor the Chathamites would budge on the vexed question of American independence. Chatham would not even discuss it. To Rockingham he wrote in December 1777: 'I will as soon subscribe to Transubstantiation as to sovereignty in the colonies.'[37] Rockingham and his followers took refuge in endless attacks on the ministry, demanding the papers on the Saratoga campaign and denouncing the new system of raising troops

35. Willoughby Bertie, 4th Earl of Abingdon, *Thoughts on the Letter of Edmund Burke, Esq., to the Sheriffs of Bristol, on the Affairs of America* (Oxford, 1778).

36. *Burke's Corr.*, iii, pp. 368–70. Burke to Abingdon, 26 Aug. 1777.

37. Fitzmaurice, *Life of Shelburne*, ii, pp. 9–190.

by private subscription. Although he shivered at the prospect of recognizing the reality of American independence, Rockingham was coming round to the view that the prospect of reconquering America was by now remote and unlikely. Chatham was furious at this and refused to have anything to do with other elements in opposition. This was unfortunate because on 2 February 1778 the opposition enjoyed one of their best parliamentary performances for years. In the Lords Richmond moved that no more troops be sent to America, losing by the respectable, if predictable, figures of 94 votes to 31. In the Commons, however, Fox's similar motion attracted no fewer than 165 votes, against the ministry's 259. It was a clear defeat for the opposition but it was something of a pyrrhic victory for the government since many independents came out in support of Fox. The opposition kept up the attack in the subsequent days. For example, on 6 February Burke attacked the government for using Indian troops, whose uncivilized and barbarous conduct he proceeded to exemplify in a famous yet exaggerated onslaught which ministers were able to repel with some ease. If the opposition thus failed to achieve a significant breakthrough in the aftermath of Saratoga, it appeared that by now events were beginning to run in their favour. Most damaging of all for North's government was the confirmation in the middle of March that the Americans had signed a military and commercial treaty with France. North had failed to localize the conflict. The War of American Independence now became a war in several continents and threatened to be a prolonged danger to Britain.

The entry of France into the war gradually brought the Rockingham Whigs to recognize American independence. At first, they took the reports of this crucial event as the occasion to demand the resignation of the ministers. Although North was able to take refuge in his majorities, by 263 votes to 113 in the Commons and by 100 votes to 36 in the Lords on 17 March 1778, the issue of the war was beginning to be embroiled in the constitutional issue of the appointment and dismissal of ministers. By now the Rockingham Whigs had already begun to steel themselves to take decisions of lasting consequence. At a party meeting of members of both houses on 15 March they, in effect, crossed this important psychological Rubicon by deciding that Richmond should move a motion for the withdrawal of British troops from America. This he did on 23 March 1778. The failure of his motion by 56 votes to 28 is less important than the fact of the motion itself and the readiness of the Rockinghams at last to make a public declaration in support of the policy of American independence. There was by now, indeed, much to be said in favour of such a policy. To end the war in America would free British energies to take on the Bourbons and, perhaps in the not too distant future, wrench control of American policy from the hands of the sinister cabal which, they believed, continued to govern the country.

The decision of the Rockingham Whigs to accept the reality of American independence had at last come, but it had been a protracted and difficult resolution. Arguably, the legitimacy of a parliamentary opposition was much more clearly established than it had been, say, in Walpole's time, but the Rockinghams had been patently chastened at the prospect of an opposition publicly advocating such a divisive and contentious policy, especially when they clearly lacked the solid support of public opinion. It was much less obvious to contemporaries than it was to become to the Whig historians of the nineteenth century that the policy of the government was unjust and tyrannical. In spite of what the opposition might claim, the king and the government were not seeking to erect a despotism in America. For the Rockinghams to desert the Declaratory Act and to recognize American independence went against the grain of a substantial public opinion and, to a very large extent, their own political instincts. The unpopularity of the idea of dismembering the empire was a serious factor inhibiting the development of their thinking. For many years there was little or no public support for the idea. It was particularly important that in 1776–8 the mercantile community had little inclination to support the policy of independence. There was little or no mercantile support for independence, as there had been in 1765–6 for the repeal of the Stamp Act. Burke, at least, thought that if a conciliatory policy which enjoyed the support of mercantile circles both in Britain and America had been adopted in the winter of 1774 then there might have been some prospect of a peaceful solution to the American problem. And he deplored endeavours by those sympathetic to the government 'in all the manufacturing parts of the Kingdom to perswade the people concerned, that the reduction by force of the disobedient Spirit in the Colonies is their sole security for trading in future with America'.[38] Significantly, merchants looked to the government to restore their trade just as they had in 1765–6. In the war of petitions for and against the government's policy in 1775

38. *Burke's Corr.*, iii, pp. 94–7, Burke to Richard Champion, 10 Jan. 1775; ibid., iii, pp. 133–6, Burke to the Committee of Correspondence of the New York General Assembly, 14 Mar. 1775.

the Rockinghams found it hard going, even in Rockingham's native county of Yorkshire. Although we now know that the number of petitions against the coercive policy was not too far behind those supporting it, the fact remains that there was no clear and undisputed wave of public opinion supporting the opposition and resisting the coercive legislation.[39] The most that can be said is that some communities, especially in the North of England, were seriously divided on the American issue. Only in East Anglia and possibly Wales was there anything resembling widespread hostility to the war.[40] Thereafter the wave of patriotic reaction which followed the outbreak of hostilities further inhibited the opposition's readiness to consider a policy of supporting American independence.

No doubt, too, the reluctance of Chatham to embrace the cause of American independence was a factor in the evolution of Rockinghamite strategy. Angered by the willingness of the Rockingham Whigs to ignore his opinions on this issue, he decided to make one last effort to impose his ideas and his personality upon the political scene and to save the empire he had done so much to establish. On 11 May he dragged himself down to the Lords to outline and to defend his views on the war and on the empire. Arguing that the colonists must be conciliated and the unity of the empire upheld, he predicted that national humiliation and economic ruin would follow upon American independence. Appealing against 'the dismemberment of this ancient and most noble monarchy', he argued that the hearts of the colonists could not be won on the battlefield. It was nonsense to argue, as Richmond had, that Britain was incapable of retaking the colonies and defeating France at the same time. As Richmond rose to contest this point, Chatham, draped in flannel and supported on crutches, collapsed.[41] He lingered for five weeks but died on 11 May 1778.

Without Chatham's towering presence in the House of Lords, the task of the parliamentary opposition became more formidable, especially since the outbreak of war with France had raised patriotic emotions to such an extent that any criticism of war-time sacrifices might seem unpatriotic and unprincipled. Nevertheless, the removal of Chatham from the scene opened the door to a more outright commitment to American independence than had previously been possible. The opposition therefore had to underline

---

39. James E. Bradley, *Popular Politics and the American Revolution in England: Petitions, the Crown, and Public Opinion* (Macon, GA, 1986), p. 127.

40. Linda Colley, *Britons: Forging the Nation, 1707–1837* (1992), pp. 138–40.

41. For this famous parliamentary occasion, see *Parliamentary History*, xix, pp. 1012–28.

their own patriotism while trying to persuade their fellow country-men that British forces could not accomplish the re-conquest of North America. Indeed, if Britain continued to waste her armies and her money in North America she might only succeed in bring-ing Spain into the war in support of her Bourbon neighbour, France (as soon occurred in any case). Surely, the time had now come to recognize American independence and then to attempt to establish a clear and mutually profitable commercial relationship with the new republic, leaving Britain free to settle her account with France. This was the line that Fox took when he opened the debate on the address on 26 November 1778, stressing that the war against France was a legitimate struggle against the national enemy, but that the war against America was a bottomless pit of expense and effort, as futile as it was expensive. Significantly, Fox did not contest the legitimacy of the American War, only its expediency, a familiar Rockinghamite tactic. As for the Declaratory Act, Fox wisely chose to ignore it. His motion failed by 226 votes to 107, a disappointing division, but by the end of the session there were signs that the opposition's tactics, as well as its patience, were beginning to pay off. On 29 March 1779 they succeeded in persuading the ministry to agree to the establishment of a Committee of Enquiry into the Conduct of the War. The committee sat from 22 April to 30 June 1779 and on several occasions the opposition ran the ministry very close indeed. On 29 April, for example, opposition motions to con-sider the conduct of General Cornwallis were beaten off by only 180 votes to 155 and 181 votes to 158.

By this time, however, domestic issues were to be determined almost entirely by military and diplomatic developments. After the humiliating surrender at Saratoga, Britain decided to prosecute an essentially naval campaign, but for some time the naval situation proved to be dark and threatening. For a time, indeed, in 1779 Brit-ain faced a serious invasion threat. Spain entered the war towards the end of June 1779. The combined French and Spanish fleets assembled 30,000 troops in 60 ships in the Channel which man-aged to slip inside the defences of the English Channel fleet. The invasion scare continued for several weeks until the Bourbon fleets, plagued by illness, decided to withdraw. Thereafter, the threat of invasion may have lifted, but the Bourbon fleets continued to enjoy the freedom to roam the Channel and even controlled the waters of the Caribbean. On the mainland, however, at the same time, the prospects for the British had been steadily improving. In May 1779 Cornwallis took Charleston. South Carolina and Georgia were then secured and he now moved into North Carolina. He failed to follow up his advantage, however, and the campaign dragged on indecisively for over a year. For several months the military situation hung in the balance until in May 1781 Cornwallis ventured, against instructions, into Virginia where he established a base at Yorktown. In the confusion which followed, the navy was unable to provide him with supplies and reinforcements. When a French fleet isolated his army by cutting his lines of supply to New York, Cornwallis was doomed. The surrender of the last British army in North America heralded final defeat in the British attempt to cling on to the North American colonies. When the news reached London on 25 November 1781 it was greeted with disbelief.

The immediate effect of the surrender at Yorktown was a recognition among both government and opposition that the war in America must be scaled down. In effect, it was at an end. Yet even now the opposition was enfeebled by its own divisions and thus incapable of profiting fully from the difficulties of the government. The Chathamites, now under the leadership of Shelburne, still shrank from conceding independence. The Rockingham Whigs, on the other hand, argued that only a British recognition of American independence would free the country to wage full-scale war against the Bourbon powers. Choosing to single out Lord Sandwich, the First Lord of the Admiralty, as the chief architect of Britain's disasters, Fox moved a motion of mismanagement against him on 7 February 1782, which was repulsed by the excitingly narrow margin of 205 votes to 183. On 20 February Fox repeated his attack, moving a motion of censure against Sandwich, which was, again, repulsed only narrowly, by 236 votes to 217. Two days later Conway's motion against the principle of prosecuting the war was lost by only one vote, 194 votes to 193. The days of the administration of Lord North were clearly numbered. On 27 February Conway repeated the attack, this time to win by 234 votes to 215. Analysis of these division lists reveals the stark fact that a large number of independents, as well as some friends of the government, were deserting North. The end could not be delayed indefinitely. On 20 March 1782, as the opposition moved up to a final assault demanding that the king remove the government, North came down to the House to announce his resignation.

The government of Lord North was succeeded by a joint administration led by the leaders of the opposition. The establishment of the Rockingham–Shelburne ministry, however, did not end the divisions between the Rockinghams and the old Chathamites. The disposal of offices was perfectly structured to exacerbate existing differences. Fox, as foreign secretary, was charged with responsibility for the peace negotiations with the European powers. Shelburne, however, as colonial secretary, enjoyed the responsibility for negotiating peace with the colonies. Much to the satisfaction of George III, the new government refused to authorize unconditional independence for the American colonies, thus leaving Shelburne with some room for manoeuvre in his schemes to maintain some sort of political connection, however symbolic. These divisions blighted the government's peace strategies and had not been composed when Rockingham died on 1 July 1782. He was succeeded by Shelburne, who ultimately negotiated the peace terms, agreed in the Treaty of Versailles, which formally ended the American War of Independence. Consistent with his earlier principles, Shelburne was anxious to develop harmonious relations with the new republic and the peace terms were notably generous. The Americans were given the freedom not only to colonize the western lands of the continent beyond the Ohio river but also to enjoy the commercial privileges of Englishmen in matters of trade. Many MPs could not understand this bewildering liberality towards an ungrateful and rebellious republic with whom we had recently been at war and who had dragged in the Bourbon powers in order to defeat Britain. Consequently, the peace preliminaries were thrown out by the House of Commons on 24 February by divisions of 224 votes to 208 and 207 votes to 190. Shelburne was forced to resign, the victim of that American independence against which he had fought for so long. Nevertheless, the signature of the Treaty of Versailles in September 1783 formally recognized American independence and fixed the boundaries of the new nation.

Conclusion

American independence came about, then, as the direct consequence of military failure and political exhaustion. The 'Friends of America' in Britain's parliament played a relatively small part in this momentous development. Indeed, the scope for a parliamentary opposition during war-time was very limited. Even in normal times in the eighteenth century, the power and influence of an opposition was limited. It was limited by the abiding popular suspicion of the theory and practice of opposition. It was limited by the knowledge, the information and the understanding that the leaders and followers of opposition were able to accumulate: in spite of the care which Burke and Rockingham took to remain abreast of American developments they were singularly unsuccessful in understanding the minds of the Americans, particularly after 1774. It was limited by the disharmony and division which frequently afflicted eighteenth-century oppositions. In this respect the constant differences between Chatham and the Rockinghams were no less serious and debilitating than those between the Tories and the opposition Whigs of the age of Walpole. On all of these counts, the opposition to the American War of Independence was found wanting. Furthermore, the parliamentary opposition tended to measure its political wisdom by the consistency with which they clung to their earlier principles and pronouncements, particularly their denunciations of the alleged system of secret influence. Further, they found refuge in clinging tenaciously to political achievements of the past – notably the Declaratory Act – as a guide to political conduct in the present. At a time when political, military and diplomatic situations were rapidly changing, often with bewildering rapidity, such a nostalgic mindset was perhaps unhelpful. Admittedly, the parliamentary opposition was at times faced with political choices which were agonizingly difficult to make. When they had managed to align themselves with a substantial body of British public opinion – for example, over the need to react to the Boston Tea Party with punitive legislative action – they forfeited whatever credibility they might have enjoyed with the Americans. Yet when they came closer to American opinion, as they did over independence in 1778, they parted company with a large body of their fellow countrymen, who were deeply suspicious of the close links which politicians such as Burke and Chatham cultivated with the colonists. If this was not the most united and the most successful opposition of the eighteenth century, it must be conceded that at times their situation was particularly unenviable.

Yet something can be said for the parliamentary 'Friends of America', both Rockinghamite and Chathamite. Their belief in moderation, peace and conciliation had in it something noble. Their opposition to the war, while understandably expressed within a familiar context of domestic politics, sought to embrace higher principles than those of expediency and pragmatism. In ruminating upon their problems and in searching their souls they elevated the language of politics above and beyond the immediate situation and sought solutions at a level of political wisdom which was to impact upon politics after 1783 and to influence and inspire the government of the British empire in India and ultimately throughout the world.

CHAPTER FIVE

The British Public and the American Revolution: Ideology, Interest and Opinion

JAMES E. BRADLEY

The question of British public opinion during the American Revolution is a difficult, vexing and highly contested issue that has evoked a considerable body of literature.[1] The subject entails the analysis of categories that are not only hard to measure, but difficult to define: the meaning of the term 'public' elicits a variety of definitions, and the notion of 'opinion' obliges an equally wide and yet subtle gradation of meaning. Edmund Burke understood the 'British public' to be that body of men who were sufficiently aware of political issues to make an informed decision, and sufficiently interested to seek to influence public policy.[2] The 'public', however, was anything but a static entity. When, during the course of the American conflict, the doors of parliament were opened to newspaper reporting, the controversy engaged the public more directly, and

1. Dora Mae Clark, *British Opinion and the American Revolution* (New Haven, CT, 1930); J.H. Plumb, 'British attitudes to the American revolution', in *In the Light of History* (New York, 1972), pp. 70–87; Mary Kinnear, 'British friends of America "without doors" during the American revolution', *The Humanities Association Review* 27 (1976), pp. 104–19; John Sainsbury, 'The pro-Americans in London, 1769–1782' *WMQ* 3rd series, 35 (1978), pp. 423–54; *idem, Disaffected Patriots: London Supporters of Revolutionary America 1769–1782* (Kingston and Montreal, 1987); James E. Bradley, *Popular Politics and the American Revolution in England: Petitions, the Crown and Public Opinion* (Macon, GA, 1986); Kathleen Wilson, *The Sense of the People: Politics, Culture and Imperialism in England, 1715–1785* (Cambridge, 1995); Alfred Grant, *Our American Brethren: A History of Letters in the British Press during the American Revolution, 1775–1781* (Jefferson, NC, 1995); Jerome R. Reich, *British Friends of the American Revolution* (Armonk, NY, 1998); H.T. Dickinson, *Politics of the People in Eighteenth-Century Britain* (1995), chs 7, 8.
2. Edmund Burke's *Works* 6 vols (Bohn edn, 1868–76), 'Letters on a regicide peace' (1796), v, p. 190. To qualify as the public, people required means of information, leisure for discussion and independence of will.

issues of taxation and representation were inevitably extended to a broader audience. The public was thus transformed by its newly acquired access to information and by rapidly changing perceptions of self-interest.

But the matter is further complicated by historians' appeal to a wide variety of historical sources and techniques. Both qualitative and quantitative evidence have been used to investigate public opinion, and the ideas expressed in published sources have, on occasion, been pitted against the interests and behaviour of the political elite, thereby revealing not only different methods, but widely differing philosophies of history as well. The topic also necessitates a discussion of the larger historic meaning of the era. Recently it has been argued that political, legal and religious issues in England coalesced around imperial politics in such a way that opinion about America actually tells us as much about domestic social divisions as it does about the colonies.[3] Indeed, the topic is pivotal for the question of the origins of English radicalism, because the British response to the American crisis provides a crucial link between the Wilkite radicalism of the late 1760s and the later radicalism of the Association movement. The question of public opinion thereby entails a variety of complex matters, ranging from sources of data, to the emerging, and thus changing, meaning of public opinion, to the broader interpretation of the revolution. This chapter investigates some of the assumptions governing the scholarship on public opinion, explores the appropriateness of using different types of evidence, and suggests possible avenues for further inquiry.

Divided opinions

Opinion about the popularity of the war and sympathy for the colonists was divided. Early in the conflict, Lord North worried that the government did not have the public's support: writing to George III in August 1775 about ways of encouraging army recruitment in England, he observed, 'the cause of Great Britain is not yet sufficiently popular'.[4] Much later, when the conflict was over and North was seeking to justify his own role in the tragedy, he declared: 'It was the war of the people.' Speaking before the House of Commons,

---

3. James E. Bradley, *Religion, Revolution and English Radicalism: Nonconformity in Eighteenth-Century Politics and Society* (Cambridge, 1990); and Wilson, *Sense of the People*.
4. *Corr. of George III*, iii, p. 249, North to George III, 25 Aug. 1775.

North claimed that the crown alone could not have obtained the majorities in parliament, 'or', he added, 'if the influence could have produced these majorities within doors, could it have produced the almost unanimous approbation bestowed without doors, which rendered the war the most popular of any that had been carried on for many years'.[5] North's claim, however, was paradoxical at best, for in the end he wished to be vindicated by an instrument that he had eschewed for most of his career. His late appeal to public authority revealed the extent to which the conflict itself had created a new awareness of the importance of the 'people' and their will.

While the parliamentary opposition could not argue with the government's substantial majorities within doors, they strongly contested the claim that the war was popular, and they based their views on public opinion without doors. In the summer of 1775, Temple Luttrell, opposition MP and arch-opponent of North, toured England and canvassed, in his words, 'a multitude of persons widely different in station and description'. He reported in October that 'the sense of the mass of the people is in favour of the Americans'. Lord Camden, brilliant lawyer and former lord chancellor, agreed. Camden put the case in precisely the opposite terms to those of Lord North: 'three to one in our House, and two to one in the other, can be resisted by nothing but the voice, nay, indeed, the clamour of the public'.[6] In a speech of 15 November 1775 against the coercive policy of the government before the House of Lords, he declared, 'You have not half of the nation on your side', and Camden based his claim explicitly on the number of popular petitions for peace that he had seen.[7]

Americans have always wanted to believe that the English people favoured their cause, and they have been encouraged in this view by Whig historians on both sides of the Atlantic. W.E.H. Lecky and G.M. Trevelyan sympathized with the Americans and liked to imagine that there was genuine, popular support for the parliamentary opposition.[8] Leading national historians of nineteenth-century America, such as George Bancroft and Richard Frothingham, believed the same; the Rockingham Whigs had correctly interpreted the will of the English people, but even with the support of the English people, leaders in parliament could make no progress against a corrupt

5. *Parliamentary History*, xxxiii, p. 849, 7 May 1783.
6. Quoted in Kinnear, 'British friends', p. 117.
7. *Parliamentary History*, xviii, p. 759, 26 Oct. 1775; Camden's remarks are recorded in *London Evening Post*, 14–16 Nov. 1775.
8. G.M. Trevelyan, *History of England* (Garden City, NY, 1953), iii, p. 75.

administration and a villainous king.[9] The Americans and the Whig historians were thus united in their acceptance of the myth of the malicious intent of George III, a myth which included the malevolent influence of his counsellors, the resurrection of the Tory party, and a plot to ruin the constitution.

Sir Lewis Namier almost single-handedly destroyed the myth of a secret cabinet, the influence of the king and the rise of a new Toryism.[10] But in dismantling Whig historiography, he also cut the foundation from underneath the notion of a viable public opinion. Namier believed that the political movements of men and nations were as unconnected to human opinion as the movement of plates beneath the earth; at one point he likened the English people's response to the American crisis to the plunging of lemmings into the sea.[11] The deterministic philosophy of Namier and his school was confirmed by their preferred sources and methods: the directives of political managers tended to exhaust the meaning of politics, and local interests predetermined the outcome of most elections. Three volumes in Namier's projected series *England in the Age of the American Revolution* were completed and each book denied the importance of public opinion in favour of the Americans.[12] The series as a whole argued that England's most populous, open boroughs, including Bristol, Norwich, Newcastle-upon-Tyne, Liverpool, Coventry and Worcester, were controlled by local issues.[13] All of the impressive research invested in these monographs and powerfully summarized in *The History of Parliament* thus confirmed the conclusion of the earlier work of Dora Mae Clark: 'Coercion was a popular policy.'[14] In a study for the bicentennial of the revolution

9. George H. Bancroft, *History of the United States of America from the Discovery of the Continent* 6 vols (Boston, 1876), iv, pp. 131, 134–5, 197, 494, 498; Richard Frothingham, *The Rise of the Republic of the United States* (Boston, 1872), pp. 406–8.

10. Lewis Namier, *England in the Age of the American Revolution* 2nd edn (1961), pp. 154–5, 160, 182, 190–2; *idem, The Structure of Politics at the Accession of George III* 2nd edn (1957), pp. 212–14, 218; *idem*, 'King George III: a study of personality' in *Personalities and Powers* (1955), p. 55; Ian Christie, *Myth and Reality in Late-Eighteenth-Century Politics and Other Papers* (1970), pp. 7–108.

11. Namier, *England in the Age*, p. 41. Sir Herbert Butterfield noted the deleterious effect of Namier's approach on the study of public opinion in 'George III and the constitution' *History* 43 (1958), p. 33.

12. John Brooke, *The Chatham Administration, 1766–1768* (1956), p. 220; Ian Christie, *The End of Lord North's Ministry, 1780–1782* (1958), p. 285; Bernard Donoughue, *British Politics and the American Revolution: The Path to War, 1773–1775* (1964), pp. 155–6, 199, 230, esp. pp. 287–8.

13. Christie, *End of North's Ministry*, pp. 83, 128, 142–3, 153; Sir Lewis Namier and John Brooke, eds, *The House of Commons, 1754–1790* 3 vols (1964), i, p. 342.

14. Clark, *British Opinion and the American Revolution*, p. 92. In Lewis Namier and John Brooke, eds, *The House of Commons 1754–1790*, the opinion of 'the mass of the

co-authored by the British and American historians, Ian Christie and Benjamin Labaree, the view was put categorically: 'In the decision to crush rebellion the North ministry was carrying out Parliament's – indeed, the country's will.'[15]

In the late 1960s and early 1970s, these views began to be challenged by a new generation of historians. The earliest, detailed studies of the Commonwealthman tradition revealed a more widespread and more coherent body of radical thought than was previously believed to exist. The well-known studies of Caroline Robbins and Bernard Bailyn thereby helped modify the notion that the English people were united in favour of coercion.[16] This new, chastened version of the older Whig school argued that there was a viable, continuous tradition of True Whig or Commonwealthman ideas shared by Englishmen and colonists alike. While the True Whigs comprised a small minority, their ideas provided significant encouragement to both American colonists and English radicals by emphasizing such things as the consent of the governed, the importance of limiting the authority of the crown, and the need for greater accountability in parliament. In the mid-1970s, the broad surveys of John Brewer, H.T. Dickinson and Colin Bonwick strongly reinforced an appreciation for the importance of political ideas in England.[17] Brewer's work on John Wilkes and Dickinson's study of ideology extended considerably beyond metropolitan politics and showed that popular opposition to the government was widely dispersed in the nation. These studies effectively expanded our understanding of the political nation beyond the parliamentary classes in a way that began seriously to embrace Burke's 'British public'.

Specialized studies of those groups that sympathized with the American colonists began to appear at about the same time, and scholars have characteristically categorized such 'friends of America' under

nation' is used to explain the slowness of the government's retreat from coercion (i, p. 80).

15. Ian R. Christie and Benjamin W. Labaree, *Empire or Independence, 1760–76: A British–American Dialogue on the Coming of the American Revolution* (Oxford, 1976), p. 234.

16. Caroline Robbins, *The Eighteenth Century Commonwealthman* (Cambridge, MA, 1959); Bernard Bailyn, *The Ideological Origins of the American Revolution* (Cambridge, MA, 1967).

17. John Brewer, *Party Ideology and Popular Politics at the Accession of George III* (Cambridge, 1976); H.T. Dickinson, *Liberty and Property: Political Ideology in Eighteenth-Century Britain* (1977); Colin Bonwick, *English Radicals and the American Revolution* (Chapel Hill, NC, 1977); the earlier study by George Rudé, *Wilkes and Liberty* (Oxford, 1962) was very influential. See also, Robert E. Toohey, *Liberty and Empire: British Radical Solutions to the American Problem, 1774–1776* (Lexington, KY, 1978).

five headings.[18] We now know much more about the Rockinghams, the rise of party and the composition of parliamentary opposition during the American crisis.[19] Paul Langford and Frank O'Gorman fully credited English public opinion at the time of the Stamp Act and they even took the views of the Americans seriously.[20] Thus, early in the conflict, a species of public opinion was now accepted: the merchant petitions of 1765 against the Stamp Act played a role, however minor, in parliament's repeal of the act. A second, broad field of study was found outside parliament. The English radicals, and particularly the Dissenting ministers in London, were well served by the studies of Colin Bonwick and they continued to receive careful scrutiny.[21] An entire journal was devoted to the study of the leading Rational Dissenters, and since the published sermons of Dissenting ministers and liberal Anglicans were readily available, we now know a great deal about the pulpit rhetoric that favoured the colonists.[22] The Dissenters not only provided a ready audience for the Whig myth of the government of George III, their ministers were a chief source for the popular propagation of the myth, thus linking them ideologically with the colonists. A third, related group of pro-Americans was comprised of leading publicists, such as Granville Sharp, Josiah Tucker and Catharine Macaulay, and several of them

18. Plumb and Kinnear adopt the same broad categories: Plumb, 'British attitudes', pp. 74, 83; Kinnear, 'British friends', p. 105.

19. Paul Langford, *The First Rockingham Administration, 1765–1766* (Oxford, 1973), esp. pp. 109–98; Frank O'Gorman, *The Rise of Party in England: The Rockingham Whigs, 1760–82* (1975), esp. Part 4, pp. 297–467. Older studies like G.H. Guttridge, *English Whiggism and the American Revolution* (Berkeley, 1966) seem more valuable in the new climate. See also Elliott R. Barkan, ed., *Edmund Burke On the American Revolution: Selected Speeches and Letters* (New York, 1966).

20. Langford, *First Rockingham Administration*, p. 175, where repeal of the Stamp Act is attributed in part to public opinion.

21. In addition to Bonwick's *English Radicals and the American Revolution*, see also *idem*, 'An English audience for American revolutionary pamphlets' *HJ* 19 (1976), pp. 355–74, and 'English Dissenters and the American revolution' in H.C. Allen and Roger Thompson, eds, *Contrast and Connection* (1976), pp. 88–112. See also Verner W. Crane, 'The club of Honest Whigs: friends of science and liberty' *WMQ* 3rd series, 23 (1966), pp. 210–33, and Donald Davie, 'Disaffection of the Dissenters under George III' in Paul J. Korshin and Robert R. Allen, eds, *Greene Centennial Studies; Essays Presented to Donald Greene in the Centennial Year of the University of Southern California* (Charlottesville, VA, 1984), pp. 320–50; and Ernest R. Payne, 'Nonconformists and the American Revolution' *Journal of the United Reformed Church Historical Society* 1 (1976), pp. 210–27.

22. *The Price-Priestley Newsletter* became *Enlightenment and Dissent* in 1982 and numerous articles still deal with the thought of Price and Priestley. Durward T. Stokes, 'British sermons favorable to the American revolution' *Social Science* 48 (1973), pp. 131–41; Henry P. Ippel, 'Blow the trumpet, sanctify the fast' *HLQ* 44 (1980), pp. 43–60, and *idem*, 'British sermons and the American revolution' *Journal of Religious History* 12 (1982), pp. 191–205; Bradley, *Religion, Revolution and English Radicalism*, pp. 159–92.

have had individual monographs devoted to their thought.[23] The politically powerful Common Council of the City of London, first studied in detail by Lucy Sutherland and George Rudé, constitutes a fourth category of mostly consistent pro-Americans and friends of John Wilkes. John Sainsbury's detailed analysis of popular politics in London revealed fresh new evidence of the links between the followers of Wilkes and the supporters of America.[24] Finally, the American merchants trading in London and their agents were naturally strong patriots, and their activities on behalf of their business associates have been carefully studied.[25]

Arguably, however, at least two of these groups could not be appealed to as representing anything approaching English public opinion. The self-interest (if not the self-serving) of the parliamentary opposition when out of office, and the obvious interest of the American traders and agents, evidently disqualify them as representative of the public. Similarly, it could be argued that the views of the Dissenting intellectuals, the leading publicists and the city radicals were anything but typical of the public. Moreover, if one were to combine all those who spoke or wrote on behalf of the colonists from the beginning of the conflict to its end, the total would comprise only several hundred persons at best. In addition, all of the studies to date relied principally on qualitative, verbal evidence, and the links that were made with the colonists were based largely on the ideology of a thoroughly discredited Whig myth.

Grass-roots opinion

In a brilliant essay, first published in 1964, J.H. Plumb recognized that if one hoped to obtain a reading of genuine public opinion, a different approach to the evidence was needed. As a social historian, Plumb appreciated the insights of Trevelyan, and on the basis of scattered, anecdotal materials from diaries and correspondence, he challenged the then regnant Namieran view; widespread 'sympathy

23. The most recent study is Reich, *British Friends of the American Revolution*. See also the anthology by Paul H. Smith, ed., *English Defenders of American Freedoms, 1774–1778* (Washington, DC, 1972). Book-length studies have appeared on Thomas Pownall, Josiah Tucker, David Hartley, James Burgh and Catharine Macaulay.

24. L.S. Sutherland, *The City and the Opposition to Government, 1768–1774* (1959); Rudé, *Wilkes and Liberty*, pp. 149–71; Sainsbury, 'Pro-Americans in London'.

25. Jack Sosin, *Agents and Merchants: British Colonial Policy and the Origins of the American Revolution 1763–1775* (Lincoln, NE, 1965); Michael Kammen, *A Rope of Sand: The Colonial Agents, British Politics and the American Revolution* (Ithaca, NY, 1968).

for America and tenacious adherence to liberal and radical sentiments' did indeed reach down to the 'grass roots'.[26] But hard evidence actually to substantiate Plumb's claim was lacking, and his essay
remained largely unknown.

Two complementary approaches seemed to hold significant promise for investigating public opinion at the grass roots: local history
and quantitative studies. A different approach to the evidence was
first taken by John Money, one of Plumb's students, and Money's
work was soon followed by the studies of Peter Marshall, Thomas R.
Knox, H.T. Dickinson and John Sainsbury. Local evidence supplied
what was lacking in the qualitative evidence of published sources:
in a wide variety of counties, boroughs and unenfranchised cities,
solid evidence for genuinely popular pro-Americanism began to
emerge. Using an impressive array of rare, local sources, Money
investigated communications networks, debating societies and book
clubs, taverns and coffee houses, and he found that during the age
of the American Revolution, local identities were changing and the
meaning of politics was broadening to embrace a much wider
world.[27] Not only in Birmingham, but also in Coventry, Worcester,
Wolverhampton and Walsall, Money found that people were turning against the idea of virtual representation and he discovered
'serious divisions' caused by the American War.[28] Peter Marshall
studied the local history of Bristol and found that at almost every
level of society, including the artisans, Bristolians were divided
throughout the war. Marshall then turned to Manchester, formerly
thought to be a bastion of Toryism, and by supplementing local
history with a close, quantitative analysis of the signatures on the
Lancashire petition circulated in the city, he delineated a vibrant
tradition of support for the colonists.[29]

26. Plumb, 'British attitudes', p. 74. Plumb's sympathy for G.M. Trevelyan is sug-
gestive. See J.H. Plumb, *Men and Places* (1963), pp. 224–49.
27. John Money, 'Birmingham and the West Midlands, 1760–1793: politics and
regional identity in the English provinces in the later eighteenth century' *Midland
History* 1 (1971), pp. 1–19. The title of his Cambridge dissertation, upon which his
later monograph, *Experience and Identity: Birmingham and the West Midlands, 1760–
1800* (Manchester, 1977), is based, is noteworthy: 'Public opinion in the West Midlands, 1760–1793'. See *idem*, 'Taverns, coffee houses and clubs: local politics and
popular articulacy in the Birmingham area in the age of the American Revolution'
HJ 15 (1971), pp. 15–47, and ch. 8, 'The war for America', pp. 185–218 in his
Experience and Identity.
28. Money, 'Birmingham', p. 19.
29. Peter Marshall, *Bristol and the American War of Independence* (Bristol, 1977);
idem, 'Manchester and the American Revolution' *Bulletin of the John Rylands University
Library of Manchester* 62 (1979), pp. 168–86.

If the midlands and south-west showed signs of divisions, so did the north-east. H.T. Dickinson found significant popular opposition to the government, both local and national, in Northumberland and Durham. There was opposition over Wilkes and the Middlesex election affair at Morpeth and Berwick, as well as in the counties, and it was possible to trace clear lines of continuity in radicalism between the issues over Wilkes, America and the Association movement. Strong pro-American activity was clearly expressed in the debates over taxation in the Philosophical Society of Newcastle-upon-Tyne.[30] In the very borough where Namier and Christie found nothing but local interests, Brewer found only a few expressions of support for Wilkes, but Dickinson and Thomas R. Knox located a 'substantial, sustained support for Wilkes' and expressions of popular radicalism for the American cause as well.[31] All of these studies exploited new sources, little used by previous scholars, and they demonstrated that local history, 'deeply and systematically pursued', was the indispensable medium needed to investigate popular radicalism.[32] While the political elite of London had previously received careful study, John Sainsbury applied quantitative techniques to the metropolis and discovered significant elements of pro-American feeling among the populace.[33] With the appearance of these studies, scholars could no longer neatly separate national issues from local interests: national issues were the means by which local concerns became focused and then reinterpreted in the light of the broader imperial crises. The provincial introversion of previous generations was evidently transcended by the American conflict, at least in many urban settings, and the British public was in the process of being awakened to its own peculiar interests.

Local studies offered the possibility of putting the question of public opinion on a more empirical basis, but such studies were still limited by geographic provenance and size of sample. To advance the discussion, more quantitative approaches were needed, but the first general statistical survey remained hidden in a little-known dissertation of 1973. Mary Kinnear had taken an innovative approach to parliament by studying pro-American MPs in connection with

---

30. Harry T. Dickinson, *Popular Politics in the North-East of England in the Later Eighteenth Century* (Durham, 1979), pp. 5, 9–10.

31. Thomas R. Knox, 'Popular politics and provincial radicalism: Newcastle upon Tyne, 1769–1785' *Albion* 11 (1979), p. 225; see also his 'Wilkism and the Newcastle election of 1774' *Durham University Journal* 72 (1979–80), pp. 23–37.

32. For the newer method, distinguished even from Rudé's and Brewer's work, see Knox, 'Popular politics', p. 224 and Dickinson, *Popular Politics*, pp. 1–2.

33. Sainsbury, 'Pro-Americans in London', and his *Disaffected Patriots*.

the specific kind of constituencies that they represented. First, she defined 'pro-American' MPs on the basis of the minority in three parliamentary division lists of 1775 and 1778. By locating these members on eight other division lists, she argued for a high level of ideological consistency among some 207 pro-Americans: they were 'aware of the arguments justifying the course taken, and that that course was consistent'.[34] The counties, as against many of the boroughs, had a relatively broad franchise, and despite the possible influence of patrons, the large number of voters rendered them somewhat less susceptible to corruption.[35] Broadly speaking, county constituencies were thought to reflect public opinion more accurately than many boroughs, although the representative nature of parliament was the subject of much debate, both then and now. Kinnear found it remarkable that 'more than half of the eighty county members of Parliament were pro-American [in the parliament of 1774–80] and nearly a quarter of all pro-Americans represented English counties, as compared with only seven per cent of the other [pro-government] members of Parliament'.[36] She rightly concluded that this fact tended to corroborate the Whig opposition's contention that the government's majorities could be traced to the use of influence in the smaller boroughs.

Further evidence in support of the claim that pro-American members were more representative of public opinion than their opponents was found in the large freeman boroughs with constituencies of more than 1000 electors. When these boroughs were combined with the counties, Kinnear found that 44 per cent of the pro-American MPs sat for populous constituencies with more than 1000 voters, compared to only 20 per cent of the pro-government members. This was exactly reversed for the small boroughs with electorates of less than 100; 44 per cent of the pro-government MPs sat for small boroughs, compared to 22 per cent of the pro-Americans.[37] This innovative analysis suggested, though it did not prove, that sympathy for the colonies had a broader public base

---

34. Mary Kinnear, 'Pro-Americans in the British House of Commons in the 1770s', unpublished PhD dissertation (University of Oregon, 1973), p. 104.

35. Support for candidates who opposed the government's American policy is found in seventeen elections in 1774, and in 1780 the opposition actually gained a number of seats in the Commons. This evidence, however, had been used in the past to argue that America was not an important electoral issue. Donoughue, *British Politics*, pp. 195–7; Christie, *End of North's Ministry*, pp. 156–61. See also John Phillips, *Electoral Behavior in Un-reformed England: Plumpers, Splitters and Straits* (Princeton, NJ, 1982), pp. 143–4.

36. Kinnear, 'Pro-Americans', p. 71. 37. Ibid., pp. 72–3, 298.

than support for the government, and it was the first hard data that
could be used to challenge North's contention about the popularity of the war.[38]

Petitions and addresses

Evidence for a broader quantitative study of popular politics first
appeared in two independent but complementary studies in 1980.
Paul Langford was the first to show that a great number of signed
addresses favouring coercion had survived, and his analysis of leaders
and signatures connected government majorities in parliament with
an older, Tory tradition. Nevertheless, because Langford was only
aware of the addresses in favour of coercion, his study confirmed
the belief that there was 'widespread endorsement' for North's
policies, and little popular sympathy for America.[39] John Phillips
discovered three additional boroughs in which both signed, loyal
addresses and opposition petitions had survived – to Manchester
could be added Bristol, Colchester and Coventry – and his study
was the first to hint that there were many more boroughs in which
signed petitions favouring peace had survived.[40] A search of the
London and provincial press and the Home Office papers revealed
that altogether 205 documents had ascended to George III concerning the American crisis. Historians had overlooked these documents
because studies of the press had paid little attention to provincial
newspapers, particularly the press's handling of the crucial last
six months of 1775, and because the Public Record Office had
catalogued the documents under the misleading heading, 'Condemnation of the American Rebellion by . . .'.[41] These documents

38. Ibid., pp. 74–6. Prosopographical analysis of the 207 pro-Americans and their
484 pro-government counterparts was not greatly illuminating; only minor differences in age, religion, social background and education distinguished the two groups.
39. Paul Langford, 'Old Whigs, old Tories, and the American Revolution' *JICH* 8
(1980), p. 112. Relying only upon the government organ, the *London Gazette*, and
with no awareness of the local studies of the 1970s, Langford was able to conclude:
'The loyal addresses which in late 1775 finally made it clear that the verdict at least
of the countryside and small towns was irreversibly behind coercion rather than
conciliation in America owed much to such [old Tory] families, as the names of
those MPs entrusted with the presentation of the addresses to the King reveal',
p. 124. Historians continue to see only one side of the evidence: see Grant, *Our
American Brethren*, ch. 3.
40. John A. Phillips, 'Popular politics in unreformed England' *JMH* 52 (1980),
pp. 611, 620.
41. List of petitions and addresses, PRO, Home Office List B/20A x/Lo4508. The
government organ, the *London Gazette*, published all the coercive addresses.

proved that there was in fact widespread popular agitation over the American crisis that in numbers and geographic extent rivalled the agitation over the Middlesex election affair, and actually exceeded that of the Association movement. Between 1775 and 1778 some 60,000 people had signed their names to petitions and addresses either opposing or supporting the government's use of force in the colonies.[42]

In 1775 there were two flurries of petitioning activity, the first to parliament and the second to the crown. In January 1775 English merchants from thirteen centres of trade petitioned parliament on behalf of peaceful concessions to the colonists.[43] Six boroughs had sent loyal addresses favouring coercion, indicating that merchants were already divided over the use of force, and parliament voted to disregard all such documents, a decision grounded in the majority's determination to narrow the conflict to the single question of colonial submission. On 7 February, parliament declared the colonists in a state of rebellion.[44] This strategic decision to enforce the coercive legislation of the previous session led to a major shift in the people's approach to the government. From March 1775 onwards, petitions from both the colonies and Britain were addressed to the crown. But in April the king decided to receive no more petitions while seated upon the throne, that is, publicly, in his royal capacity; thereafter petitions were presented to the lord in waiting, or at the levee, and in either case, they were easily disposed of.[45] The evil of

42. Quite apart from the normal channel of parliamentary elections, at least 44,000 Englishmen were involved in popular agitation over America in the period 1775–8. If the petitions in the spring of 1775, and those from London and the counties of Cumberland and Kent are added, the total reaches about 60,000. Bradley, *Popular Politics and the American Revolution*, pp. 121–2. On the other periods of agitation, Rudé, *Wilkes and Liberty*, pp. 128, 211; Ian Christie, *Wilkes, Wyvill and Reform* (1962), pp. 97 n. 1, 122. On the history and practice of petitioning, see Sheila Lambert, *Bills and Acts: Legislative Procedure in Eighteenth-Century England* (Cambridge, 1971), pp. 52, 82, 87–105, and P.D.G. Thomas, *The House of Commons in the Eighteenth Century* (1971), pp. 17–19, 57–60.

43. London, Bristol, Norwich, Dudley, Liverpool, Manchester, Wolverhampton, Birmingham, Leeds, Bridgport, Nottingham, Whitehaven, Huddersfield. On the growth of pro-Americanism before 1775, see Mary Kinnear, 'Pro-Americans', ch. 1; Bradley, *Popular Politics and the American Revolution*, ch. 2; and Sainsbury, *Disaffected Patriots*, pp. 3–21. Six places sent documents in support of coercive measures: Birmingham, Leeds, Trowbridge, Huddersfield, Nottingham, Poole. See *Journals of the House of Commons* xxxv(1775), pp. 71–3, 77, 78, 80–1, 82, 89, 90, 108, 123, 124, 139, 141, 144, 151, 164, 186, 198.

44. Ibid., xviii, pp. 18, 221–33, 265–92.

45. *City Addresses, Remonstrances, and Petitions to the Throne, Presented from the Court of Aldermen . . . Commencing the 28th October, 1760, with the Answers Thereto* (1865), pp. 36–7: Hertford to the Lord Mayor, 11 April 1775; *Corr. of George III*, iii, p. 235: George III to Lord North, 26 July 1775; ibid., p. 273: George III to Lord North, 23 Oct. 1775.

unanswered petitions became one of the colonists' major objections in their long litany of complaints against the British government.

News of the military skirmishes at Lexington and Concord reached Britain in late May, but it was not until 23 August 1775 that the king publicly declared the colonists in a state of rebellion. The royal proclamation of colonial rebellion triggered dozens of addresses to the crown expressing support for the government and coercion, and the loyal addresses stimulated, in turn, an equally strong reaction in favour of peaceful concessions. Because the king damned 'aiding or abetting' the colonists in 'any manner or degree', it was widely believed and reported in the press that popular petitions in support of peace were tantamount to treason. Rumours of colonial advances into Canada reached Britain in November, the same month in which the majority of these documents ascended to the throne. The petitions in favour of peace thus arose when the conflict was well advanced and when both parliament and the king had declared the colonists in a state of rebellion. Considerable risk was involved in circulating and signing documents in favour of concessions, since in many people's eyes, such acts at home encouraged the rebellion abroad.

In 1769 the Middlesex election affair resulted in petitions from eighteen counties and twenty boroughs, but only two of these counties and four of the boroughs sent opposing petitions favouring the government.[46] The American crisis, in contrast, prompted popular documents from eleven counties and forty-seven boroughs, and of these, five counties and twenty-one boroughs were so seriously divided that they sent signed, conflicting documents over whether coercive or conciliatory measures should be pursued.[47] The number of addresses in favour of coercion outnumbered the petitions for peace, but the petitions actually collected more signatures, since many of the addresses came from corporate bodies and were unsigned.[48]

---

46. Rudé, *Wilkes and Liberty*, pp. 112, 118–31; Bradley, *Popular Politics and the American Revolution*, p. 123; *London Gazette* 4–7 Feb., 23–7 May 1769.

47. See tables 3.1–3.3 in Bradley, *Popular Politics and the American Revolution*. All but three of the Scottish counties sent addresses, as did the majority of Scottish parliamentary boroughs. In Ireland only four towns addressed the throne; in Wales there were three.

48. The twenty-one English towns and boroughs for which both addresses and petitions survive are London, Southwark, Bristol, Coventry, Newcastle-upon-Tyne, Nottingham, Worcester, Colchester, Taunton, Great Yarmouth, Southampton, Cambridge, Bridgwater, Poole, Lymington, Abingdon, Westbury, Wallingford, Leeds, Halifax and Bolton. The five counties for which opposing documents survive are Middlesex, Berkshire, Hampshire, Lancashire and Staffordshire. We know that there were conciliatory documents from Cumberland and Norfolk and coercive ones from

The twenty-one boroughs and five counties that sent opposing documents do not exhaust the evidence of division over America, however. Study of the provincial press shows that resistance to the government's policy of coercion was pervasive and nationwide. In eleven cities that sent addresses only, and in ten additional boroughs and towns that neither petitioned nor addressed, there is solid evidence for disaffection with the government's measures.[49] The newspapers show that different political views were deeply felt and vividly expressed: one finds the language of parties 'extremely inveterate against each other' at Liverpool, of 'great riot and tumult' at Manchester, and correspondents at Warwick and Exeter expressing the conviction that 'the sense of the people' or the 'majority' of the people were against coercive measures.[50] How representative is this sample? In seventeen, or more than half, of England's twenty-eight large freeman boroughs with electorates of more than 1000 we can now document political division over America, and to these must be added the large unrepresented cities of Manchester, Birmingham and Leeds. Altogether, at least fifty English boroughs and towns were divided over coercion (a number equal to one-fourth of all parliamentary boroughs), and in the majority of these boroughs the conflict extended to the point of a contest, either in the form of petitioning or parliamentary elections.[51]

The popular documents concerning America fall into two distinct categories; they either support the government and urge the use of coercive measures, or they express concern for the Americans and appeal for conciliatory measures. Typically, the loyal addresses voiced their abhorrence of the rebellion in America and of those factions in Britain that had encouraged the spirit of opposition. References to seditious, disloyal people at home were characteristic of the documents which supported coercion. Support for George III and North's administration was thus commonly wedded to an expression of belligerence towards the colonists, and the use of force was encouraged

---

Herefordshire, Devonshire, Worcestershire and Kent. See Bradley, *Popular Politics and the American Revolution*, pp. 65–9.

49. Bradley, *Popular Politics and the American Revolution*, ch. 3, tables 3.4 and 3.5, and pp. 81–4; and *idem, Religion, Revolution and English Radicalism*, pp. 321, 342. Manchester, Liverpool, Carlisle, Warwick, Lancaster, York, Bewdley, Gloucester, Leicester, Exeter, Winchester. The ten with neither petition nor address are Portsmouth, Kendal, Appleby, King's Lynn, Ludlow, Salisbury, Birmingham, Hexham, Morpeth, Carmarthen.

50. *General Evening Post* 16–18 Nov. 1775; *Cumberland Packet* 28 Sept. 1775; *London Evening Post* 14–16 and 28–30 Dec. 1775; *Morning Chronicle* 5 and 13 Oct. 1775.

51. Bradley, *Popular Politics and the American Revolution*, pp. 86–8. See pp. 24–35 for a discussion of the geographic provenance of the petitions.

with promises of local assistance forthcoming if necessary. Of all the loyal addresses, only four equivocated on the use of force as the best policy, and even these allowed that force might be desirable.[52] Conversely, the majority of petitions in favour of peace explicitly stated that they were advanced in response to the misrepresentations of the coercive addresses; the petitioners sought to rectify the impression that the people were united in support of coercive measures. A handful of petitions can be attributed to the inspiration of Rockingham Whigs, and others are similarly moderate in tone,[53] but a number of petitions neglected the doctrine of parliamentary supremacy, and still others championed the natural as well as the chartered rights of the colonists, thereby witnessing to a more radical element in numerous boroughs.[54]

While the practice of petitioning was not itself a radical act, in the mid-1770s, opposition to petitioning was outspoken and intense.[55] In the assemblies that met to petition parliament in the period before Lexington and Concord, fears were commonly expressed about taking a stand in favour of the colonists, since the colonists had resisted the authority of parliament.[56] But after Lexington and Concord, and following the royal proclamation of 23 August declaring the colonists in a state of rebellion, such perceptions became pervasive. In this context, petitioning the king on behalf of the Americans was associated by some with mob activity and was, accordingly, strongly resisted by loyalists. Advocates of strong coercive measures were very concerned about tumults at home, since, they said, 'The dispute, Sir, is no longer between America and Administration, it is a contention for power, with the people at large, and the meanest individual is deeply interested in the success of our troops.'[57] As John Sainsbury has observed, 'Instead of simply

52. Cambridge, Plymouth, Exeter and Hereford, PRO, Home Office 55/10/16; 10/10; 11/7; 10/7.

53. The petitions from Bristol, London, Abingdon, Westbury, Berkshire and possibly Leeds, Nottingham and Bridgwater are attributable in part to Burke and his associates. See Bradley, *Religion, Revolution and English Radicalism*, pp. 336–7.

54. Southwark, Taunton, Newcastle-upon-Tyne, Southampton, Lymington, Coventry, Leeds, Staffordshire, Middlesex, Worcester and Wallingford. *Public Advertiser* 4 Dec. 1775; PRO, HO 55/8/3; ibid., 28/29; ibid., 11/20; ibid., 11/56; *London Evening Post* 21–4 Oct. 1775; HO 55/21/39; *London Evening Post* 12–14 Dec. 1775; HO 55/13/2; *London Evening Post* 9–11 Nov. 1775; HO 55/28/21.

55. Linda Colley, 'Eighteenth-century English radicalism before Wilkes' *TRHS* 5th series, 31 (1981), pp. 11, 13.

56. *Cambridge Chronicle* 7 Jan. 1775. See Bradley, *Popular Politics and the American Revolution*, pp. 112–17, for a full discussion of the risk involved in petitioning.

57. *York Courant* 1 Aug. 1780.

supporting colonial dissent, the pro-Americans were now of course aligning themselves with armed opponents of the crown.'[58]

The language of the petitions themselves was highly stylized and conventional, but the speeches at the borough and county meetings where the petitions originated were often more spirited; here, viewpoints of opposing factions were articulated with precision and at length, and these speeches take us behind the petitions to the political commitments of the principal leaders. The tenor of some of these meetings was clearly threatening to observers on both sides of the debate.[59] The provincial press also made the political associations and proclivities of the petitioners manifest. Readers of local newspapers who also signed petitions were often well-informed concerning the political issues; week by week, reports of the debates in both houses of parliament were printed. Government documents, such as the royal proclamation and the activities of radical groups such as the London Association were also widely published.

The loyal addressers consistently viewed the conflict as an 'unnatural rebellion', while the petitioners thought of it as an 'unnatural civil war'. But were the differences grounded in political principles? Despite the relative clarity of the issues, and despite the simplicity of the choice put before the public, a number of contemporary observers were either sceptical about the motivation of the petitioners or doubtful whether the petitions reflected genuine political awareness.[60] Can signed petitions be used as valid indicators of eighteenth-century public opinion?

Contemporary observers sometimes viewed the petitions and addresses as valid indicators of informed public opinion; some even construed them as arbiters of which side was more popular. At Colchester it was observed, 'There were upwards of 500 respectable signatures to the above address [i.e. petition]. – The [loyal] address which was lately presented from the same place, was signed by 125 only. – A proof that there, as well as many other places in the kingdom, a great majority of the people are quite averse to the American war.'[61]

58. Sainsbury, *Disaffected Patriots*, pp. 90, 95.

59. For example, see the speech of the Clerk of the Peace of the County in Hampshire, *Morning Chronicle* 21 Nov. 1775; Thomas Wooldridge's speech in Staffordshire, *Worcester Journal* 2 Nov. 1775; and Sir Joseph Mawbey's speech at Southwark, *Public Advertiser* 11 Nov. 1775. Wooldridge was associated with Wilkes, and Mawbey was a member of the Society of the Supporters of the Bill of Rights.

60. *Parliamentary History*, xviii, pp. 847, 1105–6, 719–20.

61. *Cambridge Chronicle* 3 Feb. 1776. Clearly the popular will was becoming increasingly meaningful to some. For identical observations relating numbers to popularity, see *London Evening Post* 30 Nov.–2 Dec. 1775.

Higher standards, however, are required of contemporary tests of validity. In select cases, it is possible to determine if individual people behaved consistently over time, and this test may be implemented by comparing petitioners to voters in parliamentary elections. Four independent studies involving eleven different boroughs demonstrated that there was a strong, statistically significant relationship between voting and petitioning or addressing.[62] Even though a year or more separated the events of voting and petitioning, in large and small boroughs alike, individuals behaved consistently in both political acts, and thus it seems reasonable to assume that they acted freely upon the basis of their own convictions. A second test of the political consistency of addressers and petitioners is found by comparing the petitions to lists of subscribers to funds which supported wounded British soldiers and their families.[63] In five boroughs, between 22 and 70 per cent of all subscribers to government funds also signed loyal addresses to the crown (an average of 46 per cent) and of all those who addressed, an average of 24 per cent subscribed to the government fund. Conversely, only 0.8 per cent to 7.8 per cent of the petitioners subscribed (an average of 3.3 per cent). Contrary to the views of government critics, petitioners appear to have both understood and remembered the political content of the documents they signed, and one in four possessed the means and inclination to support the government with a voluntary contribution.[64]

A final test of validity is found in the continuity between the petitions over the Middlesex election affair and the American petitions. Thanks to John Sainsbury's study of London, we now know that there was both ideological congruence and historical continuity in leaders and radical techniques between the London

62. Thomas R. Knox studied the Wilkes' petition of Newcastle in 'Wilkism and the Newcastle election of 1774', p. 31; Phillips, 'Popular politics in unreformed England', pp. 618–20, studied Colchester, Coventry, Bristol, Liverpool, Newcastle and Nottingham; John Sainsbury studied London, *Disaffected Patriots*, p. 119. On Great Yarmouth, Southampton, Cambridge, Bridgwater, see Bradley, *Popular Politics and the American Revolution*, pp. 172–3, and the discussion in *idem*, 'Religion and reform at the polls: nonconformity in Cambridge politics, 1774–1784' *JBS* 23 (1984), p. 38.

63. A subscription was begun in London on 18 October 1775 and approved by the king. The names of subscribers were printed every week in the London papers along with the amount they subscribed; lists exist for London, Bristol, Leeds, Nottingham and Poole. These lists were compared to the addresses and petitions from each borough. For further details, see Bradley, *Popular Politics and the American Revolution*, pp. 152–6. This subscription remained open until 15 Jan. 1777.

64. For petitioning from the government's perspective, see *The False Alarm* (1770) in Donald J. Greene, ed., *Samuel Johnson's Political Writings* (New Haven, CT, 1977).

pro-Wilkites in the 1760s and the pro-Americans in the 1770s.[65] The same continuity can also be traced in the provinces. Local studies demonstrated continuity in leadership at Bristol, Newcastle-upon-Tyne, Coventry, Southwark and Southampton.[66] Here, as elsewhere, the petition and address stirred up considerable debate in the press, and as elsewhere, the issue was of more than passing importance: a viable radical tradition in opposition to the government can be shown to have continued throughout the war in each of these boroughs.

Religious and social divisions

Based in part on this evidence, several recent studies have referred to the nation as 'seriously fractured', or to 'the fissures within the nation at large', with the people 'deeply divided'.[67] If there is an emerging consensus on the divisive nature of the conflict, there is no agreement on the meaning of these divisions. J.C.D. Clark has argued that the differences over America were at bottom religious differences: with an emphasis on the heterodoxy of Dissent, the war was truly a war of religion.[68] Conversely, John Sainsbury's study of London showed little evidence of religious differences among the rank-and-file in the metropolis, and he believed the divisions could be accounted for principally on the grounds of wealth and social class.[69] Summarizing the quantitative data from these earlier studies, Kathleen Wilson argued that statistical analyses obscured the

65. Sainsbury, *Disaffected Patriots*, pp. 5–18, 24–5, 31–42, 52–4, 82–8; he convincingly ties the London Wilkites to the London Association (pp. 24–5, 31–42, 112, 119, 146–7).

66. Bradley, *Religion, Revolution and English Radicalism*, pp. 330–1; Marshall, *Bristol and the American War of Independence*, p. 24; Knox, 'Wilkism and the Newcastle election', pp. 30–1; *London Evening Post* 11–14 Nov. 1775; *Public Advertiser* 1 Dec 1775; *Newcastle Chronicle* 30 Dec. 1775. Accounts of Coventry in *Morning Chronicle* 19 Oct. 1775; *London Evening Post* 19–21 Oct. 1775; *General Evening Post* 17–19 Oct. 1775; Bradley, *Popular Politics and the American Revolution*, p. 133.

67. Linda Colley, *Britons: Forging the Nation, 1707–1837* (1992), p. 137; Wilson, *Sense of the People*, p. 244. Paul Langford, however, depicts North's ministry enjoying 'widespread support', *A Polite and Commercial People: England 1727–1783* (Oxford, 1989), p. 538, and Peter D.G. Thomas, *John Wilkes: A Friend to Liberty* (Oxford, 1996) writes as if there were no petitions in support of conciliation (pp. 159, 168–70).

68. J.C.D. Clark, *The Language of Liberty 1660–1832: Political Discourse and Social Dynamics in the Anglo-American World* (Cambridge, 1994); and the brief overview in *idem*, 'The American Revolution: a war of religion?' *History Today* 39 (1989), pp. 10–16.

69. Sainsbury, *Disaffected Patriots*, pp. 80–2, 117–19. Rudé also ignored metropolitan Dissenters, *Wilkes and Liberty*, pp. 145–6. My study, *Religion, Revolution and English Radicalism*, attempted to integrate social motivation with secular and religious ideology.

divisions at all levels of society, and she located the causes of pro-American sentiment in people's reaction to the structures of state power, both local and national, thereby throwing the explanation for the divisions back on ideas and competing interpretations of the state.[70] In different ways, each of these studies tended to view material, local interests at odds with ideas, and they each implied that a choice must be made between the material and ideological sources of opinion. Political opinion, however, has always arisen from a combination of ideas and interests that reflect, however indirectly, a person's social, religious and economic status.

Paradoxically, the very evidence that most strongly supports the documents' value for measuring public opinion reveals with some precision significant differences in the petitioners' social, professional and religious location in British society. In other words, as in every age, political opinion in the age of the American Revolution arose in a specific socio-economic, political and religious matrix. British society was divided, and those divisions were clearly expressed during the revolutionary crisis. An analysis of individual addressers and petitioners shows conclusively that there was a coherent, reasonable and in some cases predictable connection between the stance a person took on the American War and his social, professional and religious status. Coherent patterns of public opinion can thus be positively correlated to political principle, but the principles of a person were not formed in a vacuum. Opinion was rationally connected to interest. By comparing the signatures of the petitions and addresses to religious records, such as the Dissenters' non-parochial registers of births and baptisms, and by examining parliamentary poll-books and city directories with the use of modern sampling techniques, it was possible to develop a profile of more than 2000 individuals in six large freeman boroughs and several smaller boroughs.

The dominant features that emerge from a social analysis of petitioners and addressers are, in a way, not surprising. The clearest predictor of opinion over America was religion. The Presbyterians, Congregationalists, Baptists and Quakers, who stood outside the Anglican communion and still felt the legal and political disabilities imposed by the Test and Corporation Acts were, statistically speaking, the most devoted friends of the Americans. The Dissenters' prominence in petitioning was particularly evident in Bristol,

70. Wilson, *Sense of the People*, pp. 271–2. Though Wilson eschews the idea of a resurgence of party, she credits the power of the Whig myth (pp. 246–7, 273–4).

Coventry, Nottingham and Taunton. At Newcastle-upon-Tyne, where Dissenters were inactive as voters in parliamentary elections, and at Colchester, where a variety of circumstances conspired against their outstanding partisanship in elections during the American crisis, they were exceptionally dedicated friends of America.[71] In seven boroughs, it was possible to identify thirty-two Dissenting ministers who signed the petitions for peace, and only one Dissenting minister who signed a coercive address. The Dissenting laity, as well, were overwhelmingly in favour of peace, comprising one-fourth of all petitioners.[72]

Many of the Dissenting ministers who had signed the petitions preached constitutionally informed sermons that strongly favoured the Americans.[73] In the preponderance of the Dissenting signatures we see coherent behaviour, for the laity were thereby acting in accordance with the sermons that they had heard from the Dissenting pulpits. 'Nonconformity' was the key category for these expressions of opposition to the government, not specific denominations; an analysis of individual denominations across the boroughs shows that the Presbyterians, Congregationalists, Baptists and Quakers behaved similarly. Neither did the theological distinction between Rational Dissenter and Heterodox Dissenter make any statistical difference in the religious response to the American War. J.C.D. Clark is the most recent in a long line of historians to argue that heterodox theology was the key component in the Dissenters' disaffection with the government, and clearly, the dozen or so most well-known Dissenting publicists, such as Richard Price, Joseph Priestley, Joseph Towers and James Burgh, were heterodox.[74] But numerous Orthodox Dissenters, such as Robert Robinson, James

71. Of the seven boroughs studied, in Liverpool alone were the Dissenters ambivalent about the American Revolution. Bradley, *Religion, Revolution and English Radicalism*, pp. 392–3, and Jan Marie Albers, 'Seeds of contention: society, politics and the Church of England in Lancashire, 1689–1790', unpub. PhD diss., 2 vols (Yale University, 1988), pp. 437–9, for a full discussion of the uniqueness of Liverpool.

72. Though in each borough the Dissenters comprised only a small proportion of the total population, on average 26.4 per cent came from the Dissenting communions, while Dissenting addressers averaged only 9.6 per cent of all addressers who favoured coercion. Bradley, *Religion, Revolution and English Radicalism*, pp. 389–91. In the earlier study of five smaller boroughs, the proportion of Dissenting signers of petitions was 16.7 per cent and of signers of addresses 8.4 per cent, thus broadly corroborating the pattern. Bradley, *Popular Politics and the American Revolution*, p. 192.

73. A few Dissenting ministers, L.L. Peters, John Martin and Henry Hunter, preached sermons in favour of the government, but the loyalist Dissenters were a tiny minority.

74. J.C.D. Clark, *English Society, 1688–1832* (Cambridge, 1985), pp. 252, 293, 304; *idem, Language of Liberty*, pp. 13, 32, 217, 276.

Murray, Caleb Evans and Rees David, also published works expressing sympathy for the colonists. *The Eighteenth Century Short Title Catalogue* opens the possibility of identifying the theological persuasion
of the ministers who signed conciliatory petitions. By comparing
the names of the Dissenting ministers who signed the petitions to
their pamphlets and sermons listed in *The Eighteenth Century Short
Title Catalogue*, it was possible to identify the theological persuasion
of all but six of the signing ministers. The majority (56 per cent) of
the signing Dissenting ministers were traditional in their theology,
while the heterodox comprised the clear minority.[75] Thus the crucial data for the Dissenters' decisive pro-American stance were the
beliefs and behaviours that orthodox and heterodox held in common over against the Anglican establishment, not those doctrines
that separated them. Simple statistics derived from quantitative data
refute any notion that sympathy for the colonists arose primarily
from Christological heterodoxy. The catalyst for Dissent as a body
turning against the government was not heterodoxy, but the American conflict itself, a conflict that was first drawn to their attention
by the controversy over bishops for America and the Quebec Act.

The coherence between religious Dissent and pro-American sentiment, however, goes deeper than ideology and reaches into transatlantic connections and local, structural matters as well. On the
one hand, recent work has shown just how thoroughly English Dissenters were connected with their American co-religionists through
a transatlantic exchange of correspondence, political ideas and
shared perceptions; Colin Bonwick drew out many of these connections, as did studies of the Commonwealthman school generally,
but Bartholomew Schiavo's massive dissertation has, regrettably, not
received the attention it deserves.[76] On the other hand, writings on
religion and radicalism have failed to reckon with English Dissent as
an alternative social system. Dissenters possessed separate chapels,
they engaged in separate rites of passage, and they enjoyed a separate educational system. Above all, they were habitually oppositionist
in those boroughs where they had established a long tradition of
anti-corporation practices, especially with respect to parliamentary
elections. Since Dissenters were legally hindered from holding

75. James E. Bradley, '"Religion as a cloak for worldly designs": reconciling heresy,
polity, and social inequality as preconditions to rebellion', paper presented to the
American Historical Association meeting, Chicago, Jan. 1995, pp. 10–11, based on a
sample of thirty-eight ministers from ten boroughs.

76. Bartholomew Peter Schiavo, 'The Dissenter connection: English Dissenters
and Massachusetts political culture: 1630–1774', unpub. PhD diss. (Brandeis University, 1976).

local office, in elections for members of parliament, especially in the large open boroughs, they commonly opposed the corporation candidates.[77] This pattern of opposition in the local sphere was readily transferred into opposition to any perceived form of government control or coercion.

But were the apparent religious differences merely veiled socio-economic differences? Cross tabulation of the Dissenters' occupations with all other petitioners' occupations reveals no significant difference. Occupational analysis, however, does reveal statistically significant differences between petitioners and addressers. An exploratory examination of five medium and smaller boroughs suggested marked socio-economic differences between pro-American petitioners and pro-government addressers, but six larger freeman boroughs provided even richer sources for record linkage.[78] The strong support the elite gave to the government's measures at Bristol, Newcastle and Colchester duplicates almost exactly the pattern found in the preliminary study of the smaller boroughs of Great Yarmouth, Southampton and Cambridge. The elite in the gentleman/professions and merchant categories turned out with enthusiasm to back the government. In Bristol, Newcastle and Colchester more than half of all the government supporters came from these top two categories, whereas in the electorate these two occupational groups comprised only between 10 per cent and 15 per cent of all voters. The corresponding petitioners for peace in these two highest categories made up 30 per cent of the whole at Bristol, and even less at Newcastle and Colchester.[79] Numerous signatures on the coercive addresses were those of people who belonged to the highest status groups. Fully 10 per cent of the Newcastle addressers signed their names followed by the designation 'gentleman', 'esquire' or 'baronet'. Merchants and wholesalers of all sorts at Bristol and Newcastle gave proportionately more support to coercion than to conciliation, and this is exactly the pattern that Sainsbury found in London. The earlier view that traders to America tended

77. Linda Colley locates the main centres of extra-parliamentary dissidence in London, Bristol, Norwich, Newcastle, Coventry and Colchester ('Eighteenth-century English radicalism', pp. 15–16), the very boroughs in which Dissenters formed anti-corporation parties. James E. Bradley, 'Nonconformity and the Electorate in Eighteenth-Century England' *PH* 6 (1987), pp. 252–3 and n. 96.

78. Great Yarmouth, Southampton, Cambridge, Poole and Bridgwater in Bradley, *Popular Politics and the American Revolution*, Table 7.1. Bristol, Newcastle, Liverpool, Colchester, Coventry and Nottingham in Bradley, *Religion, Revolution and English Radicalism*, Table 10.1.

79. 11.3 per cent and 14.4 per cent respectively.

to support the colonies is now thoroughly discredited: the statistics show that if anything, merchants trading to the new world were inclined to encourage the use of force.[80]

The results for the upper two occupational categories at Nottingham, Coventry and Liverpool appear, on the surface, less decisive.[81] In the case of Nottingham, the reason for the absence of polarization seems clear. When we separate the identifiable Nonconformists in the upper levels from other petitioners, the results perfectly mirror Newcastle and Colchester. The Dissenters at Nottingham had risen into the highest socio-economic levels and held posts on the corporation, and yet they maintained an oppositionist stance, and the same phenomenon may be operating at Coventry, where the Dissenters had also traditionally held many seats on the corporation.[82] It seems likely that the higher proportion of the elite support for conciliation at Nottingham and Coventry was related to the relatively high social status of the Dissenters in these boroughs.[83]

Some support for conciliation with the colonies came from the shopkeepers or retailers. At Bristol, Newcastle and Colchester the shopkeepers were disproportionately in favour of conciliation,[84] but not at Nottingham, Coventry and Liverpool.[85] The political division among shopkeepers seems to reflect some of the same ambivalence found among the merchants. John Brewer has analysed the reason why the middling ranks were involved in opposition politics, particularly the pro-American variety. Brewer showed how the growth of credit and the shortage of specie made the middling ranks especially vulnerable to trade fluctuations, particularly those produced by war. He argued that the tax structure was shifting towards commodity taxes, and these taxes were borne disproportionately by the middling and lower ranks. Finally, the growth of the importance of statute law in relation to the well-being of the local community meant that the middling ranks were likely to insist on representatives

80. Langford, *A Polite and Commercial People*, pp. 535–6, 539; Wilson, *Sense of the People*, pp. 269–70.
81. The Nottingham gentry and merchant addressers comprised 30.8 per cent of all addressers, versus 26.2 per cent of the petitioners, and these two groups at Coventry and Liverpool were also about evenly divided (Coventry 8.9 per cent versus 13.1 per cent, and Liverpool 56 per cent versus 54.3 per cent).
82. Bradley, *Religion, Revolution and English Radicalism*, pp. 346–7.
83. Of all the borough studies, only Liverpool revealed little evidence of socio-economic divisions. See n. 71 above.
84. With 26.1 per cent of the petitioners versus 16.5 per cent addressers, and 29.9 per cent versus 15.2 per cent, and 28.0 per cent versus 21.4 per cent, respectively.
85. 19.3 per cent versus 31.7 per cent; 16.7 per cent versus 26.0 per cent; 18.5 per cent versus 23.1 per cent.

in parliament who were responsive to their needs.[86] But on the whole, the support for conciliation among merchants and shopkeepers was not as strong as one might have expected.

Next to the Dissenters, the most uniform support for conciliation came from the artisans, or skilled workers.[87] In Bristol, Newcastle and Colchester, two to three times as many artisans, proportionately, supported conciliation as against coercion. These were the same artisans who loudly protested against the oppression of the magistrates at Newcastle, and they were the group most feared by the upper ranks and commonly denigrated as propertyless rabble. The battle at Newcastle was indeed what the participants claimed it was, a struggle between 'laced waistcoats and leather aprons'.[88] The Bristol artisans who insisted that 'the poor man has an *equal* right, but *more* need, to have representatives in the legislature than the rich one' were naturally sympathetic to the American colonists in their stated grievance and positive claims to representation.[89] The disproportionate involvement of artisans in Bristol, Newcastle and Colchester is mirrored in the smaller boroughs of Great Yarmouth, Southampton and Cambridge, and comparable to the results of independent work done on Manchester and London.

Dissenting and artisan support for the colonists can only be understood in light of the powerful interest groups that supported coercion. Behind the wealth of the gentry stood the clergy of the established church. Utilizing the sample of boroughs noted above, we find that only three clerics signed the petitions for peace, while seventy Anglican clergy signed the addresses for coercion.[90] The number of clergy signing the Hampshire address at Winchester was deemed almost miraculous: 30 of the 201 addressers were

86. John Brewer, 'English radicalism in the age of George III' in J.G.A. Pocock, ed., *Three British Revolutions: 1641, 1688, 1776* (Princeton, NJ, 1980), pp. 47, 334, 337–9, 341, 356.

87. Ranging from 69.8 per cent of all petitioners at Coventry to 25.9 per cent at Liverpool; the average was 51 per cent, whereas the average number of artisans who supported coercion was 31.5 per cent.

88. Knox, 'Wilkism and the Newcastle election of 1774', p. 37.

89. Quoted in Marshall, *Bristol and the American War of Independence*, p. 24. Popular agitation over the American crisis involved almost no labourers (the largest number was found at Colchester, comprising 5.5 per cent of the petitioners). Social discontent in the case of petitioning led to direct political action, but such extended only to skilled artisans, not unskilled workers. Bradley, *Religion, Revolution and English Radicalism*, pp. 38 and 85.

90. Ibid., Table 10.2, p. 390. The entire petitions and addresses at Bristol and Newcastle, rather than the letter cluster sample, were searched for clergy and attorneys. The numbers cited thus represent the full number based on the poll books, directories and registers.

clergymen.[91] Both the numbers and the unanimity of the clerical response in support of the government explain much concerning Dissenting fears about a possible resurgence of Toryism.[92] And behind the clergy stood the town corporation. In the autumn of 1775, at least thirty-three corporate bodies sent addresses to the crown appealing for submission to the supreme legislative authority of parliament.[93] The connection between insistence upon local respect for law and the corporations' concern to encourage national lawmakers is seen at Bewdley. The Bewdley corporation not only addressed the crown in favour of coercive measures, it followed this corporate act by electing Lord North a burgess of the borough, 'in consideration of his great and meritorious services in his administration of the public affairs of this country'.[94] The opponents of the government's American measures very commonly linked their perception of local oppression with the oppressions of the central government, and these conflicts were couched in terms of the need to defend liberty.

That the conflict had a strong ideological component that united local and national politics is further suggested by the uniform support attorneys gave the government. At Bristol some seventeen lawyers signed the coercive address, while only one signed the conciliatory petition.[95] Of 168 signers of the address at Newcastle, there were nine attorneys and barristers, whereas among nearly 1200 petitioners, it was possible to identify only six.[96] Moreover, these conservative interests were interlocking and mutually reinforcing. It has been estimated that in 1761 over 932 magistrates were Anglican clergymen, while in the early nineteenth century one-fourth of

91. For Lancashire, *London Gazette* 5–9 Dec. 1775; 'A freeholder of Hants', *London Evening Post* 14–16 Nov. 1775; another account in *Salisbury and Winchester Journal* 13 Nov. 1775.

92. Some index of the strength of the clerical turnout in favour of coercion is provided by comparing their response to the clergy's less enthusiastic reaction during the agitation over the Middlesex election affair (Rudé, *Wilkes and Liberty*, p. 144).

93. Table 3.4 in Bradley, *Popular Politics and the American Revolution*, for the numbers involved. The prominence of ministerial support from corporations was often noted in the press, *London Evening Post* 21–3 Sept. 1775; *Newcastle Chronicle* 14 Oct. 1775.

94. *Bristol Journal* 25 Nov. 1775.

95. At Liverpool, eight attorneys favoured coercion and two signed the petition.

96. Some attorneys, like Thomas Symonds of Bristol, who spoke against the Bristol address, had come around to pro-Americanism, but the weight of the legal profession was clearly on the side of the government. Rudé found a great number of Anglican clergymen, noblemen, JPs and gentry who signed county petitions in favour of Wilkes, but such accumulated religious authority, status, wealth and property is not to be found among those who, five years later, petitioned for peace. Rudé, *Wilkes and Liberty*, pp. 138–41.

all magistrates were clergymen.[97] The increasingly strong alliance between clergymen and lawyers in the late eighteenth century has been thought by some historians to have contributed directly to the harsher workings of the law.[98] Here J.C.D. Clark's analysis of the Anglican understanding of the established church and the unified notions of law and sovereignty is especially pertinent.[99]

Finally, in a number of larger ports a more direct form of government influence can be documented. At Bristol the collector of customs and a score of lesser custom-house and excise officers signed the coercive address. Identical patterns of response are found at Newcastle-upon-Tyne and Liverpool.[100] But the most notable example of government influence was observed in the small boroughs of Poole, Southampton and Lymington.[101] Conversely, in none of these leading ports was there any significant connection between office holding and the conciliatory petitions. Corporations and custom-houses, therefore, were almost without exception major centres of active pro-ministerial politics in the age of the American Revolution. Opposition to this power base is also readily explained; John Brewer has drawn attention to the resentment of the middling sort against revenue officers who possessed threatening powers of entry, search and seizure.[102]

The near unanimity of the Dissenters' pro-Americanism, therefore, cannot be understood apart from the support the Anglican clergy gave to coercion, and the strong backing the corporations (local nemesis of every chapel) gave to Lord North. But by the same token, the Dissenters' history of activity in the formation of

97. Norma Landau, *The Justices of the Peace, 1679–1760* (1984), p. 143; Peter Virgin, *The Church in an Age of Negligence* (Cambridge, 1989), p. 94.

98. Diana McClatchey, *Oxfordshire Clergy, 1777–1869: A Study of the Established Church and the Role of the Clergy in Local Society* (Oxford, 1960), pp. 178–201; 'The rule of law' in E.P. Thompson, *Whigs and Hunters: The Origins of the Black Act* (1975), pp. 258–69; Paul Lucas, 'A collective biography of the students and barristers of Lincoln's Inn, 1680–1804: a study in the "aristocratic resurgence" of the eighteenth century' *JMH* 46 (1974), pp. 238–9; E.J. Evans, 'Some reasons for the growth of English rural anti-clericalism c.1750–c.1830', *P&P* 66 (1975), p. 101.

99. The connections Clark draws between religion and law, and the evidence he presents for the pervasive thread of religious assumptions in legal notions of authority are valuable, because it was the Dissenters who shifted the emphasis from common law arguments and the common rights of Englishmen to natural law arguments, thereby polarizing concepts that were previously common to both parties. Clark, *Language of Liberty*, pp. 84, 93, 122.

100. For Newcastle there were at least seven in government pay and twenty-four at Liverpool. For documentation, see Bradley, *Religion, Revolution and English Radicalism*, pp. 368–9.

101. Ibid., p. 369.

102. Brewer, 'English radicalism in the age of George III', p. 339.

local anti-corporation parties does not exhaust the meaning of their sympathy for the colonists, for they were at one and the same time convinced believers in True Whig principles and the myth of George III's reign. Similarly, artisans in London, Bristol and Newcastle were avid consumers of the radical press, and in their various agitations they acted upon the principles they had assimilated, such as the rejection of virtual representation. Sympathy for America thus arose from a potent mixture of local concerns, interpreted on a broad, empire-wide canvass, and informed by vivid expressions of radical ideology and the myth of a government conspiracy.

In short, these data supply quantitative evidence for the wide dispersal of the myth of the plot to subvert the constitution. The evidence suggests that there were, indeed, social realities, not merely ideological sources, which powerfully corroborated the Whig myth of George III's reign, and these local structural patterns of behaviour provide hints for why that myth was so powerful in forming public opinion and fostering consistent political behaviour. At every level of legal jurisdiction, those with a vested interest in sound religion and law and order encouraged the use of force to compel colonial submission to parliament and the crown. At every level, people out of power – off the corporation, outside the church, fearful of the bar and quarter session – appeared to be united, aggressively united, for the defence of liberty and good government. 'It was only to be expected', wrote J.H. Plumb,

> that sympathy towards America should be rarest amongst those who were content with the fabric of British society – the aristocrats, gentry, government officers, admirals, generals, lawyers and ecclesiastics, and that it should be strongest amongst those new men – the industrial and aggressive commercial classes – to whom the future belonged. The extent of that sympathy was much wider, the identity of their interests with America much closer, than has been generally believed.[103]

But it was not the commercial possibilities alone that formed a community of interest: the myth so readily accepted by Dissenters and artisans made sense of their experience and feelings of discontent and alienation. Sympathy for the colonists, which was one form of public opinion, arose from a profound union of ideology and self-interest.

In each local setting that has received careful scrutiny, including London, Bristol, Norwich, Newcastle, Manchester and Birmingham, sympathy for the Americans and opposition to the government's

103. Plumb, 'British attitudes', p. 86.

colonial policy were expressed persistently, from the opening of the contest until its conclusion, and yet much remains to be learned about British public opinion in this period. Promising lines for further research lie in three broad areas: the study of religion, provincial opinion and urban social divisions. Because the Whig myth of the reign of George III was reinforced by religion and advanced in its most exaggerated form by the Dissenters, religious issues, as they bear on public opinion, need to be explored much further. G.M. Ditchfield has recently argued that Lord North's administration was refreshingly tolerant on religious matters and therefore the notion of a resurgence of Toryism or authoritarian ideas may need to be laid to rest, once and for all.[104] Several lines of new evidence, however, are presently converging to suggest that the Whig myth will remain an essential part of the means by which we understand public opinion, ill-informed though the myth may have been in fact.[105] For example, the benign *policy* of the North government on ecclesiastical matters had no bearing whatever on the fears and hopes of the nonconformists, because the public perception of the government remained, for the average Dissenter, highly menacing. After the government failed to support the Dissenters' appeal for removing the requirement to subscribe to the Thirty-Nine Articles, and following the passing of the Quebec Act, the issue for them was precisely whether or not the government could be trusted. Beyond the endorsement of Catholicism in Canada, however, there were other worrisome trends for the Dissenters. James J. Sack has amassed a considerable body of newspaper evidence and concluded that, 'The entire Northite press denounced the Dissenters, both of England and America, as dangerous radicals bent upon the overthrow of the constitution.' Sack finds an 'extreme anti-dissenting loyalism' well in place by 1777.[106]

Historians have not appreciated the depth of the Dissenters' anticlericalism, and further work is needed here as well. Traditionally it has been argued that the furore over Catholics during the Gordon

104. G.M. Ditchfield, 'Ecclesiastical policy under Lord North', pp. 228–46, esp. pp. 234–35, in John Walsh, Colin Haydon and Stephen Taylor, eds, *The Church of England c.1689–c.1833: From Toleration to Tractarianism* (Cambridge, 1993). Compare James E. Bradley, 'The Anglican pulpit, the social order, and the resurgence of Toryism during the American Revolution' *Albion* 21(1989), pp. 361–88.
105. Harry Dickinson rightly observed that 'when a substantial body of opinion is genuinely convinced that there is a threat to the constitution, this belief may be unfounded but the myth still has the force of reality', *Liberty and Property*, p. 206.
106. James J. Sack, *From Jacobite to Conservative: Reaction and Orthodoxy in Britain c.1760–1832* (Cambridge, 1993), pp. 200–1, 226–7.

Riots diffused radical sentiment in England,[107] but detailed work on anti-Catholicism in Scotland has shown clear links with pro-Americanism: Scottish Evangelicals were at one and the same time the most ardent friends of America and the most inveterate anti-Catholics.[108] Recent work on this subject in England has shown that 'anti-Catholicism' was often a catch-all phrase that embraced Anglican anti-clericalism, and many of the British authors whose works were reprinted in revolutionary Boston and Philadelphia, including John MacCowan, James Murray, Thomas Bradbury and Micaiah Towgood, were rabidly anti-Catholic.[109] Finally, new evidence from the poll books of parliamentary elections shows conclusively that the Anglican clergy, who were not united politically before the American Revolution, voted in favour of government candidates with a high degree of consistency during and after the revolution.[110] Thus from the viewpoint of the Dissenters and other pro-Americans, the hostility of the high-Anglican press and pulpit was reinforced by a new political consistency among the rank-and-file clergy. In terms of popular perception, Burke knew whereof he spoke, when he wrote to Charles James Fox in October 1777 about the 'manifest marks' of the resurrection of the 'Tory party'. He depicted the Tories as dedicated to crushing the colonists, and added, 'The Clergy are astonishingly warm in it – and what the Tories are when embodied, united with their natural head the Crown, and animated by their Clergy, no man knows better than yourself.'[111]

These religious and political animosities cannot be adequately explained apart from fresh research in local, and in particular, county history. Widespread divisions over America in Lancashire can now be traced largely to local religious animosities between Dissenter and Anglican.[112] Social studies of some areas, such as the west riding of Yorkshire, are yielding answers on how religion contributed to a culture of discontent. The burgeoning of Dissent in the new industrial towns of Leeds and Halifax throws considerable

107. Dickinson, *Radical Politics in the North-East*, pp. 10–11; Thomas, *Wilkes*, p. 188.

108. Robert Kent Donovan, *No Popery and Radicalism: Opposition to Roman Catholic Relief in Scotland, 1778–1782* (New York, 1987), *passim*.

109. James E. Bradley, 'English Dissent and early eighteenth-century anticlericalism', pp. 35–44, Paper presented at the Anglo-American Conference of Historians, Institute of Historical Research, University of London, July 1996.

110. James E. Bradley, 'The electoral influence of the clergy in eighteenth-century England', Paper presented at the Eighth International Congress on the Enlightenment, Bristol, July 1991, pp. 15–28. In the period of the American and French revolutions, on average eight out of ten Anglican clergy who voted, voted for government candidates.

111. *Burke's Corr.*, iii, p. 383, Burke to Fox, 8 Oct. 1777.

112. Albers, 'Seeds of contention', pp. 443–7.

light on the strong pro-American movement there (the Halifax petition for peace, for example, gathered some 1865 signatures).[113] In
the south-east of England, Dissent during the American Revolution
was found to be 'important in the development of public con-
sciousness and the spread of a more radical approach to the problems of the day'. But in addition to the leaven of Dissent, Peter L.
Humphries attributed the growing opposition to the policy of coercion to the worsening local economy and the connections between
American emigrants and their families in Kent.[114]

Conclusion

The key to public opinion outside of London remains the provincial
press, and yet opposition newspapers have been largely neglected
for the revolutionary period.[115] By the mid-1770s, in every corner of
England one could find competing papers taking an opposite stance
on the American conflict, and yet this fact has hardly been recognized, much less studied in detail. At Newcastle, it was the radical
Newcastle Chronicle and *Newcastle Journal* versus the pro-government
organ, the *Newcastle Courant*; the *Birmingham and Stafford Chronicle*
stood over against the *Birmingham Gazette*, just as *Piercy's Coventry
Gazette* vied for the attention of readers of the loyalist *Jopson's Coventry Mercury*. Every region saw this war of newspaper opinion: from
Hampshire west to Gloucester and Bristol, from the far north-west
to East Anglia, to the south-east, one can find papers that took a
consistently pro-American viewpoint, with editors regularly at odds
with the government.[116] On the strength of the provincial press
alone it could be argued that opinion in England was profoundly
divided over America, and in every locale studied to date, these
differences persisted throughout the conflict.

113. Wallace Charles Isaac, Jr., 'Religion and society in eighteenth-century England: geographic, demographic, and occupational patterns of dissent in the west
riding of Yorkshire, 1715–1801', unpub. PhD diss. (Duke University, 1975), p. 376.
  114. Peter L. Humphries, 'Public opinion and radicalism in Kentish politics,
c.1768–1784', unpub. MA thesis (University of Kent, Canterbury, 1979), pp. 177,
235, 242. The issue of consanguinity, carefully studied for Northern Ireland, should
be the subject of research in English counties.
  115. In Humphries, the press is viewed as 'the single most important source for
provincial radicalism', 'Public opinion and radicalism', p. 120. The studies of Fred
Hinkhouse, Solomon Lutnick and Robert Rea largely neglected the provincial press.
See 'Political ideology in the metropolitan and provincial press', ch. 4 of my *Popular
Politics and the American Revolution*. Grant, *Our American Brethren*, finds deep divisions
in the metropolitan press, 1775–81.
  116. The pro-American *Salisbury and Winchester Journal* versus the *Hampshire Chronicle*; the *Bath Journal* versus the *Bath Chronicle*; the *Bristol Gazette* versus *Felix Farley's*

Provincial opinion also needs to be studied in light of the pub-
lications of Dissenting booksellers, but religion and its role in shaping opinion can be well understood only through further research
on the social divisions in England. In a few of the larger boroughs,
such as Bristol, occupational data can be supplemented by estimates of wealth and status gleaned from tax records and lists of
servants. Ongoing research shows that there were statistically significant differences of wealth between the pro-American petitioners
and the addressers who favoured coercion.[117] Much further work,
however, is needed on the urban artisans. Certain parallels in interest and political orientation can be drawn between the English
artisans and the colonial artisans, particularly in Philadelphia. But
we need to understand more about the possible connections between religious Dissent and urban artisans. It may be that the link
which connects non-established religion with the lower classes and
sympathy for the colonists is, at bottom, the antipathy these groups
felt for English law and its administration. The control of property
and the exertion of political power at the local level were the key
functions of city corporations, and clearly, British pro-Americans
were interested in the use (and abuse) of that power.[118]

Different interpretations of the British public and the meaning
of pro-Americanism will undoubtedly remain, but hopefully these
differences may be adjudicated by a recognition of the complexity
of the issues and the richness of the sources. Clearly, a convincing
picture of British public opinion in the age of the American Revolution can no longer be confined to the history of parliament and the
ruling classes. But neither will an emphasis on the causative force
of religion or ideas, or a narrowing of concerns to material interests
alone, provide us with an adequately rounded picture. We now need
deeper insights into how religion and law, together with differences
in social class, and issues of power and its control, converged to
produce opinion. An integrated approach to the sources holds the
most promise for attaining this goal.

Bristol Journal, and the *Cumberland Pacquet*, the *Cambridge Chronicle*, the *Kentish Gazette*,
the *Canterbury Journal* and the *Kentish Weekly Post* all taking a pronounced position of
sympathy for the colonists.

117. Based upon all of the extant tax data for Bristol, an article entitled 'The
social sources of late-eighteenth-century English radicalism' will soon be published
by James Bradley and Elizabeth Baigent.

118. Hendrik Hartog, *Public Property and Private Power: The Corporation of the City of
New York in American Law, 1730–1870* (Chapel Hill, NC, 1983), pp. 22–5, 31–2, 42–3,
though dealing with New York throws considerable light on the conservative structures of corporations.

CHAPTER SIX

British Governments and the Conduct of the American War

STEPHEN CONWAY

On 19 April 1775 ten years of intermittent dispute between Britain and most of its mainland North American colonies finally erupted into armed conflict. For the next thirty months or so, Lord North and his ministerial colleagues devoted most of their time to the military suppression of the American insurgents. While the British forces deployed in America won some notable victories, they were unable to subdue the colonists and in October 1777 a British army was obliged to surrender to the Americans at Saratoga in New York. This changed the nature of the war dramatically. The French, who had been covertly aiding the colonists, accelerated their plans to intervene openly; in the summer of 1778 they became full belligerents. The Spanish also became enemies of the British in June 1779, and the Dutch in December 1780. What had begun as a geographically confined colonial war had become a world-wide struggle. The conflict spread to the Caribbean, Africa, India and Europe, and the British Isles themselves were threatened with invasion. In these new circumstances, the reclamation of America naturally dropped down the British government's agenda; the security of the rest of the far-flung empire, offensive operations against the possessions of the Bourbons and the Dutch, and defence of the home territory itself, became equally or more important. And with Britain and Ireland in danger, there was a mobilization of manpower and resources on a scale never seen before in the eighteenth century.

Before these developments are examined in more detail, consideration should be given to the formulation of British strategy and responsibility for the war effort. In popular mythology, George III is inextricably connected with the loss of the American colonies, even though the constitutional clashes that led to the War of Independence centred on the claims of the British parliament not those of the crown. George saw himself as 'fighting the Battle of the Legislature'.[1] Once the conflict began, the king's role was likewise less significant than has commonly been assumed. He was consulted on the conduct of the war and asked to approve plans and proposals; he gave his opinions freely and at times was certainly influential; but he was not the key decision-maker. No single person filled that position; indeed, the absence of a supreme war minister was sometimes lamented by those in government circles.[2] Lord North, the prime minister for most of the conflict, was a skilled parliamentary manager and finance minister, but was not cut out – as he himself fully appreciated – to lead the British war effort. While the cabinet collectively determined policy, and many members played a part, under North the direction of the war was in practice left to two ministers: Lord George Germain, secretary of state for the colonies from the end of 1775, and the First Lord of the Admiralty, the Earl of Sandwich. From March 1782, when North's government fell, the Earl of Shelburne, first as home and colonial secretary and then as prime minister, and the new First Lord, Admiral Keppel, became chiefly responsible.

Responsibility, however, is not the same as power. It was not possible in any meaningful sense for all military and naval operations to be *controlled* from London. The distances were too great and communications too slow to allow proper coordination of operations in America, the Caribbean and Africa, let alone in India, which was effectively six months away. Regional military and naval commanders therefore played a considerable part in determining the nature of operations in their own areas – sometimes, as we shall see, with disastrous consequences. The extent as well as the direction of Britain's war effort was also restricted by forces beyond the control of ministers. Mobilization was a complex and contested process; the number of men in uniform – in the regular army, the navy, the militia or unofficial volunteer units – depended not just on the will of the government but on the extent of resistance at the grassroots and, perhaps more important, on the often independent efforts of a whole host of local interests, many of which were antagonistic to ministerial management. Even the securing of food and other supplies for the armed forces and the raising of money to fund the war effort involved negotiations with private individuals and was

1. *Corr. of George III*, iii, p. 256.
2. The Lord Lieutenant of Ireland, for instance, wrote of the need for 'the appointment of one dictatorial minister': Hull University Library, Hotham Papers DD HO 4/19, Earl of Buckinghamshire to Sir Charles Thompson, 30 May 1778.

not simply a matter of ministerial *diktat*. So, while the focus of this chapter is the running of the war by government, we should remember the considerable limitations on the power of the eighteenth-century British state.[3]

The colonists in arms

The North ministry had hoped that a show of force would cow the colonists; hence the steady military build-up in Massachusetts in the months preceding the first clashes at Lexington and Concord. Once the fighting began, however, ministers, though in some cases less than enthusiastic about the escalation, seem to have had little doubt that the use of force was justified to compel colonial obedience. This was partly because the prize at stake was so valuable. America was widely seen as vital to British prosperity and power. The seventeenth-century Navigation Acts, which regulated colonial trade, obliged Britain's North American possessions to send their most lucrative staples to Britain and to consume British rather than other European manufactures – by 1772–3 the mainland colonies took about a quarter of all British exports.[4] The same legislation limited the transatlantic carriage to British ships, making colonial commerce a nursery for the navy as well as a wealth generator for British merchants and manufacturers and a source of significant customs revenues for the British government. Add to this the prospect that the West Indian sugar islands, dependent on the mainland colonies for their supplies, could cease to be contributors to national strength if the rebel colonies successfully broke away, and the case for fighting to keep the Americans within the system created by the Navigation Acts becomes understandable, even if not necessarily convincing.[5]

3. I owe this cautionary note to my reading of J.E. Cookson, *The British Armed Nation 1793–1815* (Oxford, 1997).

4. B.R. Mitchell, *British Historical Statistics* (Cambridge, 1988), pp. 450, 494. The statistics cited below are taken – or calculated – from this source unless otherwise stated.

5. The opposition shared the government's view that the colonies were economically, fiscally and strategically vital to Britain, but came to the opposite conclusion about the use of force. They argued that the Americans could not be coerced to stay within the Navigation system because without colonial consent the system could not work. Hence the commitment of the opposition to a negotiated solution that kept the Americans in the British empire. This remained their position until Saratoga convinced them of the need to recognize the reality of American independence. See Frank O'Gorman, *The Rise of Party in England: The Rockingham Whigs 1760–82* (1975), chs 15–17.

Nor should less obviously materialist considerations be over-looked. A visceral hostility to 'unnatural rebellion' seems to have gripped some British politicians, together with a belief that the Americans – and their British friends and abettors – were engaged in a deeply laid plot to destroy the balance of the constitution by undermining executive authority and creating an unchecked 'demo-cracy'. There was much talk among ministers and government supporters of the threat posed by 'levelling principles', and of the need to rescue innocent colonists from the 'tyranny' of Congress and restore to them the blessings of mild, well-constituted and law-ful government.[6] The sinfulness of the leaders of the rebellion, moreover, was not simply seen as bad for the Americans, but also opposed for its potentially infectious qualities. Ireland was known to be restless and many Irish Protestants were disposed to see their position as comparable to that of the Americans; both asserted their right to be treated in the same way as the king's subjects in Britain.[7] And at least one minister worried about an insurrection in the metropolis itself, so great was the sympathy for the Americans amongst extra-parliamentary radicals and even sections of the par-liamentary opposition.[8]

To will the putting down of the rebellion was one thing, to achieve it quite another. After the initial skirmishes at Lexington and Concord, General Gage's army was confined to Boston by a hastily assembled array of New England militiamen. An attempt to break the siege by clearing the Americans from high ground dom-inating the town (the battle of Bunker Hill, 17 June 1775) was successful, but at an appalling cost; about 40 per cent of the attack-ing force were killed or injured. Gage's army was now so weak that it could barely defend Boston, let alone take the offensive. Over the following months nearly all of the British posts in upper New York and Canada fell to the rebels. To recover the colonies after this unpromising start was going to be no easy task, and while Gage's troops were cooped up in Boston, various strategies were canvassed.

<hr />

6. One of the reactions of the British political elite, as Eliga Gould has recently demonstrated, was to emphasize the civilized moderation of the British state and the lawless barbarity of the Americans. See 'American independence and Britain's counter-revolution' *Past & Present* 154 (1997), pp. 107–41.

7. R.B. McDowell, *Ireland in the Age of Imperialism and Revolution 1780–1801* (Oxford, 1979), chs 4–5; J.L. McCracken, 'Protestant ascendancy and the rise of colonial nation-alism, 1714–60' in T.W. Moody and W.E. Vaughan, eds, *A New History of Ireland*, vol. iv, *Eighteenth-Century Ireland 1691–1800* (Oxford, 1986), ch. 5.

8. Shute Barrington, *The Political Life of William Wildman, Viscount Barrington* (1814), pp. 163–4.

A purely naval subjugation of the rebels was favoured by Lord Barrington, the secretary at war, and other leading political and military figures, who doubted the army's capacity to expand rapidly enough or to mount successful operations so far from home and in such a politically inhospitable environment. As the adjutant-general put it: 'attempting to Conquer A[merica] Internally by our Ld. Force, is as wild an Idea, as ever controverted Comn. Sense'.[9] Yet the government rejected proposals for a naval blockade alone, and committed itself to a major land war. The decision owed something to a desire to end the conflict quickly. The king dismissed the arguments of Barrington and other advocates of a naval solution that army augmentation would be difficult and protracted;[10] a good deal of faith seems to have been placed in Ireland's manpower potential.[11] Naval strangulation of American trade, it was assumed, would take much longer to achieve than military victory, and might therefore provide an opening for the French, who were believed to be waiting for an opportunity to avenge their defeat in the Seven Years War. Full-scale naval mobilization, furthermore, might alarm the French, encouraging them to enter the war to protect their apparently threatened Caribbean colonies. It would also, and no less important, impose a strain on public finances, which North in particular was keen to avoid.[12] Then there were the American loyalists to consider. A naval blockade would do little to help them. The government received numerous reports of the strength of 'friends to government' in the colonies, especially in the southern provinces. Whilst these reports were often based as much on wishful thinking as firm evidence, Germain was inclined to accept them as accurate. He was convinced that the majority of colonists were loyal at heart, and required only a British military presence to turn them into auxiliaries in the recovery of America. He remained unshaken in this view, despite the increasing scepticism of the army, right to the end of the war, and his faith in the potential of the loyalists was

9. PRO, War Office Papers, WO 3/5, p. 37.   10. *Corr. of George III*, iii, p. 250.
11. HMC, *Stopford Sackville MSS* 2 vols (1904–10), i, p. 137. For the use of Irish – and particularly Irish Catholic – manpower, see [Thomas Campbell,] *A Philosophical Survey of the South of Ireland* (1777), pp. 301–2; Thomas Bartlett, '"A weapon of war yet untried": Irish Catholics and the armed forces of the crown, 1760–1830' in T.G. Fraser and Keith Jeffery, eds, *Men, Women and War* (Dublin, 1993), pp. 70–1; Alan J. Guy, 'The Irish military establishment, 1660–1776' in Thomas Bartlett and Keith Jeffery, eds, *A Military History of Ireland* (Cambridge, 1996), pp. 229–30.
12. See Nicholas Tracy, *Navies, Deterrence and American Independence* (Vancouver, 1988), ch. 6; Daniel A. Baugh, 'The politics of British naval failure, 1775–1777' *American Neptune* 52 (1992), pp. 221–46.

to play a major role in shaping his recommendations to the British commanders in America.[13]

The strategy for 1776 envisaged three separate armies converging to crush the rebellion. The main force, under Gage's successor General Howe, made up of the army evacuated from Boston together with reinforcements from Europe, would operate in the lower Hudson Valley of New York. This area, it was confidently believed, would be much more well-disposed than seemingly irreconcilable New England.[14] A second army, under generals Clinton and Cornwallis, would try to tap southern loyalism by campaigning in the Carolinas. The south was thought to be a particularly promising area for military operations, not simply due to its many 'friends to government', but also as a result of its large slave population which was likely to inhibit resistance from the whites. As South Carolina's royal governor wrote in 1775: 'I leave it to any person of common sense to conceive what defence they can make in a country where their slaves are five to one.'[15] Once the southern provinces were pacified, and legitimate authority was restored, Clinton and Cornwallis would sail north to join Howe at New York. The third army, under the command of generals Carleton and Burgoyne, would clear the rebels from Canada and then push on south to rendezvous with Howe in the Hudson valley. Altogether some 50,000 troops were to be put into the field.

Yet, for all this effort, the campaigning was only partly successful. Howe defeated the main American army under Washington at the battle of Long Island (27 August 1776) and captured New York city. In December, a detachment from his command seized Newport, Rhode Island, a valuable naval anchorage. But Howe failed to press home his advantage in the New York operations – perhaps because he hoped that after a demonstration of British strength the Americans would recognize the need to come to the negotiating table[16]

13. See Paul H. Smith, *Loyalists and Redcoats* (Chapel Hill, NC, 1964).

14. General Clinton, while at Boston, wrote of the need to decamp to the 'Episcopal parts' of America – as opposed to Congregational New England – and specified lower New York: William L. Clements Library, Clinton Papers, propositions to Gage, 7 Aug. 1775.

15. K.G. Davies, ed., *Documents of the American Revolution*, 21 vols (Shannon, 1972–81), xi, p. 51. In truth the racial balance in South Carolina was changing; white migration into the back country brought the black-to-white ratio down from 2:1 in about 1750 to near parity in the 1770s. Awareness of this change, Jack P. Greene suggests, may have given South Carolina's low country elite 'the nerve to revolt'; 'Colonial South Carolina and the Caribbean connection' *South Carolina Historical Magazine* 88 (1988), pp. 209–10.

16. See Ira D. Gruber, *The Howe Brothers and the American Revolution* (New York, 1972).

– and he was unable to catch Washington's disintegrating army as it fled towards Philadelphia. Indeed, Washington boldly counter-attacked over Christmas and obliged Howe to give up much of newly conquered New Jersey. Clinton and Cornwallis did join Howe, and contributed to the successes of his campaign; but they were unable to pacify the southern provinces and suffered a morale-damaging reverse when they tried unsuccessfully to take Charleston, South Carolina. The Canadian army, while fulfilling the first part of its brief, made slow progress; and the caution of Carleton ensured that the key fortress of Ticonderoga, in upper New York, remained in rebel hands.

Despite the limited achievements of 1776, a broadly similar strategy was pursued the following year. Operations in the south – where the British had been least successful in 1776 – were this time to take place only when the campaigning in the north had finished; but, as before, two armies were to converge in the Hudson valley to cut off New England from the other rebel colonies. Burgoyne had returned to Britain during the winter of 1776–7 to lobby for command of the Canadian army, which was to launch another push south, either into New England, to co-operate with troops operating from the base at Newport, or down the Hudson valley to support Howe's army around New York. Both the king and Germain favoured the Hudson valley strategy; but no real effort was made to ensure proper coordination of the operations of the two armies. Germain, a former soldier himself, was reluctant to impose his will on commanders so far from London; it took many weeks for letters to cross the Atlantic, and in these circumstances he believed that local commanders had to be allowed a large measure of discretion: 'whatever operations he pursues', Germain wrote of Howe in August 1777, 'I have no doubt he will take those measures which are most for the publick benefit'.[17] Unfortunately for the government, Howe, increasingly obsessed with defeating Washington and capturing Philadelphia, chose, in the absence of firm direction from Germain, progressively to downgrade his commitment to Burgoyne. On 30 November 1776 he had thought in terms of 10,000 of his own troops advancing north to Albany to rendezvous with the Canadian army; by 20 December he was writing of sparing a force of only 3000 men to cover the lower Hudson, while the bulk of his army was directed towards Washington and Philadelphia. The following spring he was fully persuaded of the need for a campaign in

17. HMC, *Stopford Sackville MSS*, i, p. 139.

Pennsylvania and was very doubtful of his ability to complete it in time to help Burgoyne.[18] Yet even on 29 September 1777 Sir John Irwine, the commander-in-chief in Ireland and a close friend of Germain, could write from London: 'Not a word from Sr: Wm: Howe . . . Various opinions whether he is gone to the northward, or to Philadelphia; . . . no man on this side of the Atlantic knows.'[19] There were thus two British campaigns in 1777, carried out with only vague and intermittent references to each other, rather than the co-ordinated operation to bring the war to a close that the government had originally envisaged. Howe eventually took Philadelphia in September, after having defeated Washington's army at Brandywine Creek. In contemporary European warfare, such a double blow would usually have been sufficient to bring an end to hostilities, or at least to oblige the loser to open negotiations. This, in all probability, was Howe's expectation: at the beginning of the year he had written of 'a general action' as the only way of 'terminating the war' and described the capture of Philadelphia as 'the principal object'.[20] But the newly confederated Americans attached less significance to the capture of their notional capital than most Europeans would have done to the enemy occupation of a major urban centre, and Brandywine Creek was not a defeat to compare with Long Island in 1776. Washington demonstrated his resilience again with a bold counter-attack at Germantown in October. In the north, meantime, Burgoyne, lacking any significant support from New York, was overwhelmed and obliged to surrender at Saratoga (17 October). The defeat of a British field army naturally boosted American morale and correspondingly depressed British spirits. More important, it encouraged the French to bring forward their plans to enter the war. The conflict, as George III and his ministers fully appreciated, was about to become much more than a war for America.

Defeat in America

Even before the French and Americans formally became allies in February 1778, war with France – and probably with Spain too – was seen as inevitable by the British government. Consideration was even given to complete withdrawal from the rebel colonies to concentrate all available resources for the impending struggle with the

18. Davies, ed., *Documents of the American Revolution*, xii, pp. 265, 268; xiv, p. 66.
19. NLI, Shannon Papers, Ms. 13,301.
20. Davies, ed., *Documents of the American Revolution*, xiv, p. 33.

Bourbon powers. This drastic option was rejected, but on 8 March 1778 Germain told Clinton, the new British commander-in-chief in America, to prepare for a predominantly naval war supported from bases at New York and Nova Scotia. The evacuation of Philadelphia was recommended, together with a southern expedition to tap the loyalist strength still believed to exist in Georgia and the Carolinas. The announcement of the Franco-American alliance brought forth further instructions for Clinton. On 21 March he was informed that the main effort was now to be directed against the French possessions in the Caribbean. He was told to send 5000 troops to attack St Lucia, and another 3000 to reinforce the British posts in the Floridas. He was to withdraw his forces from Philadelphia and concentrate the remains of his army at New York. Peace commissioners, led by the Earl of Carlisle, were sent out to negotiate with the Americans, in the hopes that a settlement with the rebel colonists could be concluded before the Bourbon war began in earnest.[21]

Clinton withdrew from Philadelphia in June 1778, fighting a rearguard action against Washington's Continental Army at Monmouth Court House in New Jersey. The radically changed character of the war in America became obvious a few days after Clinton reached the safety of New York. On 11 July the comte d'Estaing and sixteen French ships of the line arrived in American waters with the aim of delivering a knock-out blow to the British headquarters and bringing the war to a rapid conclusion.[22] In the event, d'Estaing was unable to force a decisive action, or to maintain an effective blockade of New York, and the hopes of the French government were disappointed. Nevertheless, whereas General Howe had conducted land operations confident in the knowledge that the Royal Navy enjoyed almost unhindered control of the coast of the rebel colonies, Clinton was given ample reason to fear that his army could be trapped by a combination of American troops and the French navy. A further indication of this came in August 1778 when d'Estaing's fleet, working with Continental troops and New England militia, almost captured the British base at Newport, Rhode Island. On this occasion poor coordination of land and sea operations by the new allies let the garrison off the hook; but the vulnerability of the British position was only too evident to Clinton, and played an important part in inducing caution in his future operations. No less inhibiting, of course, was the loss from his command of the detachments for

21. Ibid., xv, pp. 57–62, 73–6.
22. Jonathan R. Dull, *The French Navy and American Independence* (Princeton, NJ, 1975), pp. 107–11.

the West Indies and the Floridas, which Clinton finally released in November 1778. The departure of so many troops, he told Germain, was 'fatal to the hopes of any future vigour in this army'.[23]

By this stage, the Carlisle commission's efforts to negotiate peace had been ignominiously rebuffed by Congress. Even the surrender of parliament's claim to tax the colonies was insufficient to tempt the Americans to negotiate, not least because the independent United States could not accept a return to parliamentary regulation of American trade, which for the British was their *sine qua non*. The failure of this belated attempt to settle the dispute left the government with little choice but to abandon America or continue to fight for its reclamation. The first course of action would have won the support of the opposition in parliament, most of which was by now prepared to acknowledge American independence and concentrate on the war with France. Lord North and his ministers, however, determined to carry on the struggle in the rebel colonies. As before, the reported presence of large bodies of loyalists encouraged them. Indeed, it was claimed, with some justice, that the Franco-American alliance was very unpopular in the United States and was creating new loyalists by the day.[24] But hopes of a restoration of British authority rested largely on the perceived situation of the southern colonies. 'Friends to government', as we have seen, were thought to be particularly numerous there; and the idea that the south was the 'soft underbelly' of the rebellion on account of its considerable population of plantation slaves continued to exert some influence. A complementary – and increasingly important – consideration was the potential value of a recovered south to the beleaguered West Indies. The British islands had been suffering acute difficulties since the cutting off of their food and other vital supplies from the mainland; a restoration of British control in Georgia and the Carolinas would help to solve the provision crisis in the Caribbean.[25]

Clinton remained convinced that the key to success was the destruction of Washington's main army in the north, and he was therefore reluctant to release significant resources for a southern campaign. Even so, at the end of 1778 he despatched a small force of 3000 men to take Georgia. The expedition was spectacularly

23. Davies, ed., *Documents of the American Revolution*, xv, p. 210.
24. For a report, apparently seen by Germain, see 'Dr John Berkenhout's journal' in Newton D. Mereness, ed., *Travels in the American Colonies* (New York, 1916), p. 580.
25. Davies, ed., *Documents of the American Revolution*, xv, pp. 177–8.

fruitful. Savannah was captured and local people flocked in to declare their allegiance and join a newly constituted militia. By 19 January 1779 the British commander, Lieutenant-Colonel Archibald Campbell, could boast: 'I have got the Country in arms against the Congress . . . I have taken a Stripe and Star from the Rebel flag of America.'[26] But although civil government was restored in March, the British position in Georgia in fact remained precarious. A British advance into South Carolina, which temporarily posed a threat to Charleston, led the Americans to request the assistance of the French navy. Savannah was laid under siege in September. The garrison survived, like the British force at Newport a year before, thanks to friction between the allies. A premature and unsuccessful assault in October was followed by the lifting of the siege. Once more, however, the vulnerability of British detachments to combined land and sea attack had been underscored. Clinton, recognizing the danger, evacuated the exposed base at Newport. He was criticized for his apparent timidity, and no less for his seeming inactivity; by this stage the war in the north had become nothing more than a series of manoeuvres and destructive raids. But Clinton, to do him justice, had seen his primary task as defeating Washington. The manoeuvres and raids were largely intended to entice Washington to fight.[27] Despairing of bringing the American commander to a decisive action, Clinton was now ready to give the southern strategy a proper test. Indeed, Clinton himself decided to take charge of the expedition that sailed from New York in December 1779.

The results were initially very encouraging. Clinton's army besieged Charleston and forced its surrender on 12 May 1780. Much of South Carolina seemed readily to acquiesce in the restoration of British authority. Clinton returned to New York, leaving it to Cornwallis to take charge of what it was hoped would be the final stages of operations in the south. But within a few weeks of Charleston's surrender, the frontier was embroiled in a bitter civil war between loyalists and patriots; even Cornwallis's defeat of an American army at Camden in August failed to pacify the colony. The problem, as Cornwallis's officers saw it, was that American resistance was being sustained from neighbouring North Carolina. More important, it was believed that North Carolina contained many more loyalists

26. BL, Auckland Papers, Add. MS. 34,416, fo. 246.
27. Davies, ed., *Documents of the American Revolution*, xvii, p. 146.

who could be mobilized on the appearance of British troops. 'The object of marching into North Carolina is only to raise men,' Cornwallis wrote in October, 'which from every account I have received of the number of our friends, there is great reason to hope may be done to a very considerable amount.'[28] After a false start at the end of 1780, an invasion of North Carolina was launched in January 1781. Cornwallis defeated the Americans at Guilford Court House in March, but suffered such heavy casualties that he was obliged to retire to a base established at Wilmington on the coast. Local loyalists were understandably disinclined to join so palpably weak a British army. Disappointed by the response of the people of North Carolina, Cornwallis resolved to move again to join an expeditionary force sent to Virginia by Clinton.

The folly of Cornwallis's southern peregrinations was shortly to become evident. By marching so far north, he left exposed the British bases in South Carolina and Georgia. In the spring and summer of 1781 the Americans systematically retook every fortified post, leaving only Charleston and Savannah in British hands. The gains of the last two years had nearly all been wiped out. In Virginia, meanwhile, Cornwallis destroyed a great deal of property, particularly the tobacco stocks used by the Americans to secure foreign munitions, but achieved little else. In August he started to build defensive works at Yorktown to form a base for the use of the navy. In retrospect, this was a fateful decision. On the move, his army was formidable; the Virginia militia offered scant resistance. On the defensive, in a fixed post, by contrast, he presented a tempting target. Washington's Continental Army and a French expeditionary force marched south to besiege Cornwallis. The French navy, after bettering the British in a bruising action off Chesapeake Bay, blockaded the Yorktown garrison by sea. Clinton, initially believing that the French and Americans were marshalling their forces for an assault on New York, was slow to react. At length, when a destructive attack on the coast of Connecticut failed to draw off Washington's army, Clinton assembled a relief force. He was too late. The French navy, for so long a potent threat, finally realised its true potential. On 17 October 1781 – four years to the day after Burgoyne's surrender at Saratoga – Cornwallis, his army battered by the besiegers and Yorktown's defences weakened, proposed a negotiation of terms. Two days later the British marched out of the fortifications and laid down their arms.

28. PRO, Cornwallis Papers, 30/11/81, fo. 26A.

A world-wide war

Yorktown effectively brought the war in North America to a close. Washington was unable to persuade the French to help him to attack Charleston or New York, and without the French navy he was in no position seriously to threaten these powerful bases. The British, for their part, suspended offensive operations and, like the French, devoted their resources to the war beyond America. Indeed, since the entry of the French into the war, operations in the Caribbean had been to the British government at least as important as the recovery of America. The removal of a significant portion of the army in the rebel colonies to serve in the West Indies was a clear indication of this. So was the re-deployment of the Royal Navy. In July 1778 only 8 per cent of its ships of the line were committed to the West Indies. Twelve months later, the proportion had risen to 33 per cent, by July 1780 to 41 per cent, and in April 1782 had reached 48 per cent.[29] Given the importance attached to the Caribbean colonies, this level of commitment is hardly surprising. In 1772–3 the islands purchased about 15 per cent of all Britain's exports (many of which found their way to the Spanish and other foreign colonies in the region) and they sent home sugar, cotton, indigo and coffee which freed the mother country from dependence on foreign imports and provided the government with a buoyant customs revenue.[30] But if the British had much to lose in the Caribbean, they were not thrown entirely on the defensive by the coming of the French war. The government's initial response, as we have seen, was to seek to undermine French public finances – and therefore France's capacity to wage a protracted conflict – by an attack on the French islands, which made such an important contribution to French trade and Louis XVI's revenues.

St Lucia was captured in December 1778 by the troops sent from Clinton's army. But, as in North America, the French navy was a formidable foe. In July 1779 d'Estaing's fleet enabled the French to take St Vincent, and in July Grenada surrendered. General Grant, the British commander in the Caribbean, had concentrated his forces on St Lucia and left the security of the British colonies to the

29. Dull, *French Navy*, appendices E, F, G and I.
30. There is now less certainty about the value of the islands to Britain. See, e.g., R.B. Sheridan, 'The wealth of Jamaica in the eighteenth century' *EcHR* 2nd series, 18 (1965), pp. 292–311; Philip R.P. Coelho, 'The profitability of imperialism: the British experience in the West Indies, 1768–1772' *Explorations in Economic History* 10 (1973), pp. 253–80.

Royal Navy; now he was obliged to reverse his policy and disperse his troops: 'circumstanced as we are at present', he told Germain, 'the Islands must fall if they are not defended by strong Garrisons'.[31] Dividing the British army had the obvious disadvantage of making further offensive operations much more difficult, but perhaps more important a check was provided by tropical disease and sickness. General Vaughan, Grant's successor, sent home gloomy reports of high mortality rates and the consequent impossibility of adopting a more active attitude.[32] For the rest of 1779 and all of 1780 there was effectively a stalemate in the Caribbean theatre. A number of naval engagements took place, but neither side gained a clear advantage.

The entry of Spain into the war spread the fighting further afield. The Spanish went onto the offensive against the British outposts in Central America, and began operations to recover the Floridas, which they had lost at the end of the Seven Years War. Forces led by the governor of Louisiana, Bernardo de Galvez, proceeded to seize the British bases along the Mississippi in 1779, followed by Mobile in 1780 and Pensacola in 1781. The British, however, were not confined to a defensive posture by the coming of the Spanish war, any more than they had been by the outbreak of the conflict with France the year before. The Spanish empire was seen as both rich and vulnerable and therefore ripe for attack. Omoa, in present-day Honduras, was captured by a force from Jamaica in October 1779, and in April 1780 a British expedition took San Juan Castle, near the shore of Lake Nicaragua. The aim of this incursion was to gain access to the Pacific, and from there to launch predatory raids on the Spanish settlements along the west coast of Central and South America. Plans were even drawn up to attack the Philippines, the spices and gold of which could help the British East India Company in its China trade.[33]

The British declaration of war against the Netherlands in December 1780 effectively shelved the Pacific strategy, as we shall see, but at the same time it reinvigorated the conflict in the Caribbean. The Dutch islands, and particularly St Eustatius, had been playing an important role as entrepôts in the overseas trade of the United States, much to the irritation of the British government. In February 1781 Admiral Rodney took St Eustatius and merchandise to the value of at least £2 million. The other Dutch islands were also secured. But the arrival of Admiral de Grasse with strong naval reinforcements

31. PRO, Colonial Office Papers, CO 318/5, fo. 100.
32. Ibid., CO 318/6, fo. 79.
33. Piers Mackesy, *The War for America* 2nd edn (1993), pp. 373–5.

gave the French the chance to take the initiative. A string of triumphs followed: Tobago was taken in June 1781; in November the Dutch islands were all recaptured; in February 1782 St Kitts and Montserrat fell. To crown this run of success, the French and Spanish now prepared to attack Jamaica, the biggest and most valuable of the British islands. Rodney, thanks to a timely reinforcement from Britain, was able to avert a complete Caribbean catastrophe by defeating de Grasse at the battle of the Saintes in April. Five French ships were taken, plus all the heavy artillery intended for the assault on Jamaica. The French fleet, Rodney informed Sandwich, had been given 'such a blow as they will not recover'.[34] This was a pardonable exaggeration, but the victory at the Saintes tipped the psychological balance back in Britain's favour and strengthened the hands of British representatives in the peace negotiations begun by the new government. The Saintes, a former minister wrote to Rodney, had revived the reputation of the country 'to such a Situation as will enable it to retrieve most of the Losses it has sustain'd'.[35]

The scramble to seize enemy possessions that characterized the war in the Caribbean was replicated in other areas of imperial confrontation. West Africa was the source of the slave labour that serviced the Caribbean plantations, and many of the European powers had established trading stations along the coast. With the outbreak of hostilities between Britain and France, these tiny enclaves assumed still greater importance, for it was clearly in the interests of each side to deprive its opponents of fresh supplies of slave labour in order to reduce the profitability of its West Indian colonies and therefore undermine metropolitan revenues. There was also longer-term advantage to consider; if captured enemy posts were retained after the war, a greater share of the lucrative slave trade could be secured. The French accordingly took the British bases in Senegambia in January and February 1779, and in the following May attacked and severely damaged the post in Sekondi on the Gold Coast. The British, for their part, occupied the old French base at Goree and between February and May captured nearly all the Dutch forts and factories along the Gold Coast. But a still more glittering prize, far to the south, eluded them. The colony of the Dutch East India Company at the Cape of Good Hope sat astride the sea route to India. It had been earmarked as a target by the British government as soon as the Dutch war began. Indeed,

34. G.R. Barnes and J.H. Owen, eds, *The Private Papers of John, Earl of Sandwich* 4 vols (1932–8), iv, p. 257.
35. PRO, Rodney Papers, 30/20/21/2, fo. 75.

the Cape was seen as so important that the naval and military forces assembled to take Spain's Pacific territories were diverted to the southern African expedition. The French navy again proved a bugbear. A squadron under Admiral de Suffren beat the British to the Cape and landed French troops to reinforce the Dutch garrison. The British abandoned their projected attack, and the expeditionary force proceeded to India.

The war in India was largely conducted, from a British point of view, by the forces of the East India Company. But defence and expansion of trade with Asia was also a matter of concern for the British government, which in the years immediately preceding the war was increasingly overseeing and superintending the conduct of Indian affairs. Eight British regular regiments and two Hanoverian battalions were therefore sent out to help the company's forces between 1779 and 1783, together with naval squadrons under Sir Edward Hughes and Sir Richard Bickerton. When news reached India of the start of the Anglo-French war, the East India Company's army was already engaged in a costly conflict with the Maratha confederacy of Indian princes. Even so, the company was determined to seize the opportunity to undermine its chief commercial rival, and most of the French factories were rapidly occupied. Only Pondicherry offered protracted resistance, and when it fell Mahe on the Malibar coast was the one remaining French outpost in India. The capture of Mahe in March 1779 seemed initially, then, a great triumph; but it provoked the hostility of Haidar Ali of Mysore, who regarded the French factory as under his protection. In retaliation Haidar determined to attack the territories of the Nawab of the Carnatic, his long-standing rival in southern India and an ally of the British.

The new war provided an opening for the French to regain an Indian foothold. Haidar had a formidable army, with a particularly strong cavalry arm, and he quickly overran large parts of the Carnatic. He also totally defeated a British force under Lieutenant-Colonel William Baillie in September 1780, and compelled the ignominious retreat of the main Madras army of the East India Company. Indeed, the fall of Madras itself seemed a distinct possibility and French intervention at this critical juncture might well have proved decisive. But the French, despite having naval and military resources to call on at the Isle de France (Mauritius) and Isle Bourbon (Reunion), were reluctant to commit themselves and declined to respond to Haidar's appeals for assistance. Not until February 1782 did their naval and military forces make an effective impact, and by that time the British had inflicted a series of defeats on Haidar's army and captured nearly all the Dutch bases in India, western Sumatra and the strategically vital port of Trincomalee in Ceylon. Yet belated as it was, French intervention still made a difference. Trincomalee was retaken in August 1782 and, with the landing of French reinforcements the following spring, the British position was threatened. To dislodge the French, a mixed force of royal and company troops moved south from Madras to take Cuddalore. During the siege that followed, attack and counterattack left neither side with the upper hand, but in June 1783 de Suffren's ships forced Admiral Hughes's squadron off Cuddalore to retire to Madras. This left the besiegers without naval cover and therefore vulnerable to encirclement by the French and their Indian allies. News of the signing of the peace treaties in Europe, in the view of one of the company's officers, came just in time, given the way in which the Royal Navy had been 'obliged to forsake the Army'.[36]

The war in home waters

Europe was not the scene of a major land war between Britain and its enemies; there was no great campaign in Flanders or Germany to tie down the French army as there had been in previous eighteenth-century conflicts. The British had no significant allies in Europe when the war began, and their efforts to secure alliances, which would have obliged the French to devote more resources to their army and less to their navy, were all fruitless.[37] The French, to be sure, could not build up their navy overnight; the British, with superior dockyard facilities and a larger pool of trained mariners on which they could call, retained overall naval superiority at least until the Spanish joined the contest.[38] But the absence of a land war to distract the French hardly helped the British. In 1760, at the height of the Seven Years War, the French had spent the equivalent

36. Devon RO, Kennaway Papers, 961/M/f1, Lt John Kennaway to Sir Robert Palk, 13 July 1783.

37. See H.M. Scott, *British Foreign Policy in the Age of the American Revolution* (Oxford, 1990).

38. For French difficulties in transferring resources from the army to the navy, see Daniel A. Baugh, 'Why did Britain lose command of the sea during the war for America?' in Jeremy Black and Philip Woodfine, eds, *The British Navy and the Use of Naval Power in the Eighteenth Century* (Leicester, 1988), pp. 149–69; N.A.M. Rodger, 'The continental commitment in the eighteenth century' in Lawrence Freeman, Paul Hayes and Robert O'Neill, eds, *War, Strategy and International Politics: Essays in Honour of Sir Michael Howard* (Oxford, 1992), pp. 39–55.

of £7 million on their army and only £500,000 on the navy. Between 1778 and 1782, by contrast, naval appropriations easily outstripped those for the army; by 1782 nearly £9 million was being devoted to the French navy, which in that year possessed seventy-three ships of the line, compared with only fifty-two when France entered the conflict. With seventy-three capital vessels France was the biggest contributor to the allied aggregate of 146 ships of the line. A major land war in Europe would surely have prevented such a spectacular growth in the French navy, and might therefore have brought the Royal Navy's ninety-four ships of the line significantly closer to the allied total.[39]

But if there were no military operations in Europe on a scale with those of earlier conflicts, there was still enough activity to place a further strain on British resources. Once the Spanish joined the war, the British Mediterranean outposts at Gibraltar and Minorca were targeted and besieged by Franco-Spanish military and naval forces. Minorca fell in February 1782 after a staunch defence; Gibraltar, however, held out; the defenders enduring a siege lasting more than three and a half years and repelling a grand assault in September 1782. Nearer home, war with France put the Channel Islands in danger, and Jersey, an important centre of British privateering activity against French maritime commerce,[40] was attacked in 1779 and 1781. Defending these exposed posts absorbed several regiments of British and German troops, and sustaining them required the commitment of substantial naval resources; in April 1781, for instance, Admiral Darby had to use twenty-eight ships of the line to escort a convoy of nearly 100 supply vessels to Gibraltar.

Despite the need to detach vessels for such duties, the aim of Sandwich and the Admiralty was to husband as much naval strength as possible in home waters, both to defend the country from invasion attempts and to have sufficient force available to score a decisive victory over the French and their allies. Sandwich's policy of concentration, once criticized on the grounds that it allowed the enemy, who were much more willing to divide their navies, to gain local superiority elsewhere, tends now to be viewed by experts as a sound approach to the problems confronting the British.[41] Even so,

39. Dull, *French Navy*, app. A and I.
40. Vessels operating from the Channel Islands took nearly a third of all prizes secured by British privateers in the American War. See David J. Starkey, *British Privateering Enterprise in the Eighteenth Century* (Exeter, 1990), p. 221.
41. David Syrett, 'Home waters or American? The dilemma of British naval strategy in 1778' *Mariner's Mirror* 77 (1991), pp. 365–77; N.A.M. Rodger, *The Insatiable Earl: A Life of John Montagu, 4th Earl of Sandwich* (1993), pp. 271–9.

the ships still held in home waters were not always sufficient to secure the British Isles from the threat of invasion. In March 1778 the Irish quartermaster-general drew up plans for combating a French landing. The southern and western coasts were regarded as particularly vulnerable, with Cork, Waterford, Limerick and Galway identified as likely landing places, though even the arrival of enemy troops in Ulster was thought possible. The reaction of the Catholic population to a French invasion was a cause of great concern; would they be loyal or would they, as the quartermaster-general feared, join the French?[42] Southern England was regarded as in danger too. At Plymouth it was imagined that the French troops massing across the Channel were simply waiting for their navy to gain control of the crossing routes. Admiral Keppel's engagement with d'Orvillier's fleet off Ushant in July, though less than a victory, was widely believed to have saved the country from invasion. In 1778, however, the French had no real intention of landing troops; they were merely trying to stop British naval reinforcements crossing the Atlantic at a time when d'Estaing was setting off to deliver his projected blow at New York. But in 1779 the threat was more serious. The Spanish insisted on a joint expedition to attack England as a condition of their entering the war, and the French, anxious to supplement their naval strength with that of the Spanish, readily agreed. The French and Spanish fleets, with sixty-six ships of the line, rendezvoused at Corunna and sailed north at the end of July. Admiral Hardy, with only thirty-nine ships of the line, deployed his vessels to counter an attempt on Ireland, and the combined fleet slipped into the Channel unhindered. By 16 August the French and Spanish were in sight of Plymouth. There they remained for several weeks, while on shore feverish preparations were made to meet an enemy landing. In the end, sickness on board the combined fleet, together with increasing tensions between the allies, saved the day for the British. The Royal Navy, much to the anger of many humiliated British commentators, failed to engage the Bourbon ships. There was renewed anxiety in 1781, when the Dutch were seen as a threat to the east coast – even at Lerwick in Shetland batteries were constructed 'to keep off the Dutch'[43] – and in September of that year a combined Franco-Spanish fleet took control of the western approaches, again threatening Ireland and southern England with invasion. As late as 1782 an imminent juncture of the

---

42. NLI, MS. 14,306.
43. Gilbert Goudie, ed., *The Diary of the Reverend John Mill* (Edinburgh, 1899), p. 63.

French and Dutch fleets was thought to pose considerable danger. 'The probability of . . . a landing on the eastern Coast of the Kingdom', the mayor of Hull was warned in May, 'renders it necessary to be upon our Guard.'[44]

The strains of war

To wage a world-wide war against a formidable coalition of enemies, and to defend the home territory from invasion, imposed great strain on British governments. When news arrived in March 1781 of Lieutenant-Colonel Baillie's defeat in India the previous September, the king was thrown into despair: 'I do not see what can be done . . . we certainly have neither troops nor ships that can in the present situation be taken either from hence, North America, or the West Indies.'[45] But if from 1778 there never seemed to be sufficient military or naval resources to achieve all that was required, the expansion of the armed forces was none the less spectacular.

Admittedly, not all of the men who went into uniform did so at the behest of the state. In India, as we have seen, the East India Company had its own armies, made up very largely of locally raised Indian troops. While British governments might seek to place these forces under regular commanders and regard them as instruments of the British state, the soldiers were recruited and employed by the company. Even in the British Isles themselves, government control was far from complete. When invasion seemed a distinct possibility, volunteers, largely middle-class in background, assembled in companies which were formed on local initiative and often resistant to government direction. In Ireland, where the militia could not be revived for lack of money, the Protestant population started to constitute independent or volunteer units when French attack threatened in 1778. By the middle of 1780 there were perhaps 60,000 volunteers ready to play their part in harassing any invading army. The Irish Volunteers, however, were as much a political as a military force, and in many cases they were keen to use their position to press for the dismantling of restrictions on Irish trade and then for legislative independence for the Dublin parliament. This political aspect made the Irish Volunteers, in the opinion of the

44. Hull RO, Borough Records, BRL 1386/154.
45. Ian R. Christie, ed., 'George III and the southern department: some unprinted royal correspondence' *Camden Miscellany* 30 (Camden Society, 4th series, 1990), p. 431.

British government, a doubtful asset; indeed, by January 1780 Lord North was telling the Lord Lieutenant that 'While they subsist, & correspond, the government & peace of Ireland will always be precarious'.[46] Small wonder, then, that North and his colleagues took a dim view of the volunteer corps that started to emerge in Britain itself. While in the emergency of 1779 the king was even willing to contemplate the distribution of pikes to the 'Country People',[47] volunteer corps were regarded with much suspicion and given official sanction – through the commissioning of officers and sometimes the issuing of arms – only with reluctance. Volunteer companies were nevertheless formed, with or without government approval, in the south-western counties of England, along the south coast and in the metropolis, and even in Yorkshire and the Clyde valley. The coming of the Dutch war brought forth more corps in various east-coast towns in England and Scotland, and in 1782, when the new government reversed the policy of North's ministry and actively encouraged volunteering, further units were formed in Norfolk and commercial and industrial centres such as Birmingham, Leeds, Sheffield and Liverpool.[48] Even when it came to the growth of the official armed forces, it must be recognized that the co-operation of local interests was vital if recruiting was to be successful, and that the initiative for raising some corps came from beyond the government: Highland chiefs, Irish peers, town corporations, and West Indian merchants and planters all offered to provide regiments at little or no expense to the state.

But, at least as far as the official armed forces were concerned, the process of expansion was controlled and directed by the government, with the overall numbers determined by the estimates the ministry submitted annually to parliament. And even if we confine our attention to the army, navy and militia, the growth was impressive. The navy had around 16,000 officers and men on its books in 1775. By 1783 this had increased, through a mixture of voluntary recruitment and the activities of press gangs, to 107,000. In the same period the British and Irish components of the army nearly tripled in size from 36,000 to around 100,000. As with the navy, this expansion relied to some extent on compulsion – the Recruiting Acts of 1778 and 1779 allowed for the impressment of the able-bodied unemployed – and consideration was given to more extensive

46. NLI, Heron Papers, MS. 13,039.
47. Kent RO, Amherst MSS., U1350 074/38, 41.
48. Stephen Conway, 'The politics of British military and naval mobilization, 1775–83' *EHR* 112 (1997), pp. 1179–201.

systems of conscription, on a par with those implemented in the struggle against revolutionary and Napoleonic France.[49] The government even supported limited relief for Catholics in the hope that this would help with enlistment, especially in Ireland.[50] By the end of the war there were also some sixty-six units of militia in England and Wales and several fencible regiments for home defence in England and Scotland, amounting to 46,000 men in all. The total number of Britons and Irishmen serving in the official armed forces at this time was probably in excess of a quarter of a million. If we add to these the Indian sepoys, American loyalists, Native American warriors, and Hanoverian and Hessian auxiliaries who served alongside the British army, it seems likely that by 1782–3 the British government had around 400,000 fighting men at its disposal.[51]

Sustaining these large military and naval forces required considerable effort. The army in America – the largest that a British government had ever sent abroad – had to be supplied for the most part from the British Isles. Assembling the provisions and the ships to carry food, fuel, equipment, money and men across 3000 miles of ocean was an immense logistical exercise, involving the government not just in negotiations with contractors but also in attempts to safeguard stocks and control prices, as in 1776 when an embargo was placed on the export of Irish provisions.[52] Given the scale of the task, it was hardly surprising that there were occasional crises. The army besieged in Boston was forced onto reduced rations during the winter of 1775–6; Clinton complained in November 1778 that since he had been in command his army had been 'within 3

49. See BL, Liverpool Papers, Add. MS. 38,212, fos. 29–30, 'Plan for obtaining a speedy and effectual augmentation to his Majesty's army'.
50. R. Kent Donovan, 'The military origins of the Roman Catholic relief programme of 1778' *HJ* 28 (1985), pp. 79–102.
51. There were more than 115,000 company troops in India in 1782: India Office Library, Home Misc./361, 'State of the East India Company's Forces', in —— to Henry Dundas, 25 July 1784. Jeremy Black, in *War for America* (Stroud, 1991), ch. 2, stresses the British reliance on external forces of manpower and provides further figures. The subject is explored in a wider context in P.J. Marshall, 'A nation defined by empire, 1775–1776' in Alexander Grant and Keith J. Stringer, eds, *Uniting the Kingdom? The Making of British History* (1995), pp. 208–22.
52. For the problems facing the British government, see R.A. Bowler, *Logistics and the Failure of the British Army in America* (Princeton, NJ, 1975). Historians are now less persuaded by contemporary Irish claims that the embargo was ruining farmers and destroying the provision trade generally: see Thomas M. Truxes, *Irish–American Trade, 1660–1783* (Cambridge, 1988), pp. 238–9, though it clearly had an effect on certain types of beef that had been sold to the foreign Caribbean colonies before the imposition of the embargo.

weeks of Starving' four times;[53] while in 1782 a lack of shipping greatly delayed the movement of troops from New York to the Caribbean. Yet the achievement, considered overall, was notable. In 1776, when the army in America was at its largest, Howe was delighted with his logistical support. 'The Supplies of Provisions from Europe have been so wisely planned and so well executed', he wrote, that his forces could 'be under no Apprehension of Want'.[54]

The large-scale mobilization of manpower and the provision of appropriate logistical back-up cost a great deal of money. Even though public subscriptions and other private initiatives reduced the potential charge on the state, and the East India Company paid for the troops employed in India, the British government had to take responsibility for the bulk of the necessary expenditure. Indeed, it even had to help out with the army in Ireland, which was supposed to be supported by the Dublin parliament. Augmentation of the Irish establishment meant that in 1779 the government in Dublin could only cover its immediate military spending with the aid of a grant from the British treasury.[55] Expenditure on that part of the army and ordnance for which the British parliament was constitutionally responsible, and on the navy, for which it was expected to bear the whole cost, exceeded £109 million between 1775 and 1783, compared with just under £83 million in the Seven Years War and less than £56 million in the War of the Austrian Succession.[56] In 1782 alone the British parliament approved the allocation of £20 million to the army, navy and militia. To cover such escalating costs, taxes naturally rose; government revenues went up by 30 per cent between 1774, the last full year of peace, and 1782, when the total collected was £13.7 million, or about 14 per cent of estimated national income. But borrowing provided the money to pay for almost half the expense of the war. The national debt increased from £127 million to £232 million in the course of the conflict.

Figures do not, of course, tell the full story. As the armed forces grew, and British victory began to look more and more doubtful, it became increasingly difficult to raise the necessary loans. In 1779 North told the Commons of his labours in negotiating loans 'owing to the very high terms that had been insisted upon by the monied

53. Nottingham University Library, Newcastle of Clumber MSS., NeC 2646.

54. PRO, Treasury Papers, T 64/108, fo. 73.

55. NLI, Heron Papers, MS. 13,038, North to Buckinghamshire, 17, 19, 30 July 1779.

56. John Brewer, *The Sinews of Power* (1989), p. 40 (Table 2.2). Baugh, 'Why did Britain lose command of the sea', p. 160, offers somewhat higher figures: £125 million for the American War and £105 million (including subsidies for foreign allies) for the Seven Years War.

people', while in 1781 he 'lamented exceedingly, that he should be obliged to come down and propose so large an addition to the debt of the empire, where we were obliged to borrow on such disadvantageous terms'.[57] There was also a growing mood of tax revolt with which the government had to contend. Dissatisfaction with high levels of taxation helped to inspire the nationwide protest movement calling for retrenchment and reform of public expenditure that so unsettled North's ministry in 1779–80; and in 1782 Birmingham manufacturers complained vociferously at the imposition of new duties on the carriage of goods and lobbied for relief.[58]

Yet, despite the hard bargaining and the tax resistance, successive governments, as we have just seen, raised vast sums of money – more than had ever been raised before in Britain. They did so, moreover, in a safer manner and on better terms than the governments of enemy powers. The printing of paper money by Congress and the various states in America led to hyperinflation, destroyed public confidence and almost brought the war effort of the rebel colonies to a standstill.[59] Lord North might have had to offer free stock and other inducements to attract investment in the national debt, but he was able to secure loans at a much lower rate of interest than were the Spanish and French governments. The French debt in 1783 was only 62 per cent of the British, yet French interest payments were 75 per cent of the British. Indeed, it would seem that Britain's financial capacity to pursue the war was much greater than that of the Americans, the French, the Spanish and even the Dutch.[60]

Government handling of the American conflict, in short, was not the unmitigated disaster that the loss of America might seem to imply. Considered in the round, looking at all areas of war-related responsibility, British ministers might even be regarded as having done better than the considerable strains of a world-wide struggle would lead one to expect. Strategic blunders were certainly made, particularly with regard to operations in North America, and the blame must lie in some measure with ministers for failing to ensure better coordination. But even here, too censorial a tone would be

---

57. *Parliamentary History*, xx, p. 157; xxi, p. 1330.
58. *Aris's Birmingham Gazette* 18 Mar., 13 April 1782.
59. See Peter Mathias, 'The finances of freedom: British and American public finance during the war of independence' in his *Transformation of England* (1979), pp. 286–94.
60. Stephen Conway, *The War of American Independence 1775–1783* (1995), chs 3 and 10.

inappropriate. The errors of judgement were based on an appreciation of the difficulties involved in trying to direct operations from a great distance; to allow much decision-making to devolve to regional commanders might, with the benefit of hindsight, seem a mistake, yet any attempt to centralize control of strategy further would surely have created problems of a similar or even greater magnitude. More positively, we can say that successive governments, by finding the means to pursue a world-wide struggle, achieved a great deal. Still more fighting men were no doubt needed, but larger numbers than ever before were in British pay. They were, for the most part, supplied and provisioned remarkably effectively, given the logistical difficulties involved. And, crucially, the money to fund this lengthy and stretching war for empire was forthcoming. In the end it was not lack of manpower, logistical collapse or financial exhaustion that forced Britain to the negotiating table, but a loss of political will to continue the conflict.

CHAPTER SEVEN

Britain as a European Great Power in the Age of the American Revolution

H.M. SCOTT

Britain's reputation in Europe

In 1783 Britain emerged from the War of American Independence (1775–83) with its international reputation in tatters. Defeated in America, Britain had been obliged to recognize the independence of its former colonists and had secured little by way of compensation from its European enemies: France, Spain and the Dutch Republic. The Republic ceded Negapatam (on India's south-east coast) and a vague right of commercial access to the Dutch East Indian archipelago, but this had to be set against the cession of Minorca and East and West Florida to Spain, and Tobago and Senegal to France. The European settlement thus did nothing to disguise Britain's failure to suppress the first successful colonial rebellion in modern times. The blow to its international prestige was considerable: while the negotiations were in progress, Horace Walpole had declared himself 'mortified at the fall of England' and gloomily concluded that he saw 'little or no prospect of it ever being a great nation again'.[1] During the 1780s even friendly observers were openly questioning whether Britain still was a European great power. In early 1783 the Emperor Joseph II concluded that England's power and wealth were no more, while his brother Leopold (then ruling as grand duke of Tuscany) frankly declared that Britain had been relegated to the second division of European states and now ranked alongside Denmark or Sweden.[2] In retrospect these political obituaries

---

1. W.S. Lewis, ed., *Horace Walpole's Correspondence* 48 vols (New Haven, CT, 1937–83), xxv, p. 310.
2. Alfred Ritter von Arneth, ed., *Joseph II. und Leopold von Toscana: ihr Briefwechsel von 1781 bis 1790* 2 vols (Vienna, 1872), i, pp. 149, 151–2; cf. p. 283 for Joseph II's view of 'England's weakness' in 1785.

were premature – the decade after 1783 would see a notable British recovery – but they sharply highlighted Britain's diminished international stature after the American War.

Only two decades earlier Britain's situation had been very different. Then it had emerged in triumph from another conflict – the Seven Years War of 1756–63 – with a string of territorial gains from the defeated Bourbon powers. That conflict had given Britain a dominant position in the Indian subcontinent and – following France's cession of Louisiana to Spain in 1764 – had removed the French from the mainland of North America. Britain secured from that war a position of colonial and commercial pre-eminence which was the envy of its European contemporaries, whether friend or foe. Though less severe than the draconian terms which the great war leader William Pitt the Elder (who had resigned in October 1761) would have imposed, the Peace of Paris finalized in February 1763 was still a notable triumph. It concluded the most decisive war in the long Anglo-Bourbon duel for maritime and economic supremacy during the eighteenth century. These victories had established for Britain a position as probably Europe's leading state in 1763. Only the new power of Russia could rival that pre-eminence, and then not before the 1770s. By that point Britain's commanding position as a European great power had been severely weakened, and it was apparently lost by 1783, when British decline appeared to be terminal.

This downward trajectory possessed two linked dimensions. It was, first of all, the result of Britain's own failures and weakness, at home and in the colonies, and ultimately of its defeat during the American War on the other side of the Atlantic and on the high seas. These factors undermined Britain's reputation, still the crucial basis of success in international relations, and thus weakened its foreign policy. It also resulted from London's growing concern with global issues during the second half of the eighteenth century. The problems which arose in Britain's enlarged empire, and the commercial potential of this collection of territories, dominated the minds of policy-makers in Whitehall and reduced their concern with the Continent.[3] That concern was only weakened; it was certainly not removed. Indeed, in one respect Britain was more a part

3. Daniel A. Baugh, 'Withdrawing from Europe: Anglo-French maritime geopolitics, ca. 1750–1800' *International History Review* 20 (1998), pp. 1–32. I am indebted to Professor Baugh for generously sending me a copy of his important paper in advance of its publication.

of Europe after 1763 than in earlier decades. Its own enhanced status was accompanied by a more central role within the European states-system than it had usually occupied and forced it to define its attitude to the leading Continental issues of the day. The reciprocal obligations which arose from its dominance in Europe after 1763 bound Britain more closely to the Continent at exactly the point that its own horizons were wider than ever before.

Britain's 'decline' as a great power was also relative and resulted from developments over which ministers could exercise little or no control. The third quarter of the eighteenth century saw a reorientation of the European states-system, which ultimately destroyed Britain's international position. Since the decades around 1700 the relations of the major powers had revolved around the rivalry of France with Britain and Austria, with each side aided by lesser states. The Continental Seven Years War had converted this into a five-power system through the addition of Prussia and Russia. It was the ancestor of the Pentarchy which would prevail after 1815, and was fully operational by the mid-1770s. Within this enlarged great-power system, the central issue was not – as it had been since the close of the seventeenth century – the power of France, but the interests of the three eastern powers and their territorial ambitions at the expense of their declining neighbours: Poland–Lithuania and the Ottoman Empire. Such issues were remote from British interests and London could play little part in their settlement: as Horace Walpole remarked apropos the first partition of Poland–Lithuania carried out in 1772, the British fleet could not easily sail to Warsaw.[4] The problem, however, was that Britain found itself politically marginalized exactly at the moment when the rebellion in America gave foreign policy an importance and priority it had seldom, and then only briefly, enjoyed during the first dozen years of peace.[5]

---

4. Lewis, ed., *Walpole's Correspondence*, xxiii, p. 475.
5. The best brief introduction remains Michael Roberts, *Splendid Isolation 1763–1780* (Reading, 1970). H.M. Scott, *British Foreign Policy in the Age of the American Revolution* (Cambridge, 1990) provides a comprehensive survey and is the basis of the interpretation put forward in this chapter; it contains a full bibliography of works published before the late 1980s. A longer perspective on British foreign policy is provided by Jeremy Black, *A System of Ambition?: British Foreign Policy 1660–1793* (1991) and Paul Langford, *The Eighteenth Century 1688–1815* (1976), while the essential European diplomatic background can be studied in the early chapters of the magisterial Paul W. Schroeder, *The Transformation of European Politics, 1763–1848* (Oxford, 1994), and in Derek McKay and H.M. Scott, *The Rise of the Great Powers, 1648–1815* (1983).

Weaknesses in British foreign policy

This period had one enduring legacy for the administration of British foreign policy: the establishment of the Foreign Office in 1782. It gave Britain what every other major power already possessed: a designated department headed by one individual (the foreign secretary) responsible for the conduct of diplomacy. Until then relations with the Continental states had been divided on a geographical basis. The secretary of state for the Southern Department, who was still the senior minister, handled diplomacy with France, Spain, Portugal, the Italian states and the Ottoman Empire, while his northern counterpart dealt with the Dutch Republic, the German and Scandinavian states, Prussia, Austria, Poland–Lithuania and Russia. The Northern and Southern secretaries, however, had far wider responsibilities than Britain's diplomacy. They were the principal executors of all government policy. Assisted only by a handful of secretaries and clerks, they were responsible for maintaining the regular correspondence and implementing official policy in all the areas of government activity with the single and partial exception of military affairs. All domestic and colonial affairs as well as diplomacy came within their remit.

There were two principal consequences of this geographical division of responsibility. In the first place there was the problem of ensuring that British foreign policy was coherent and unified. Periodically the two secretaries adopted policies that were not fully synchronized and sometimes actually opposed. Foreign diplomats could be startled to receive two different and even contradictory accounts of the British attitude to a particular problem from the Southern secretary and his Northern counterpart. The number of occasions when opposite policies were pursued simultaneously were relatively few, though it did happen. One of the best examples came in 1768, when the cabinet was split over whether or not the French annexation of the strategic Mediterranean island of Corsica should be actively opposed. The Earl of Shelburne, then the Southern secretary, favoured firmness and was prepared to fight to resist France's striking territorial gain. His Northern counterpart, Viscount Weymouth, advocated peace at almost any price. This stark division, and the resulting fault lines within the Chatham administration, were well known to the French ambassador and his superiors, and did much both to paralyse Britain's response and encourage France's action, thus making possible this important yet highly risky gain.

The extent of disagreement in 1768 was unusual, though not unique. For much of the period the problems inherent in the geographical division of responsibility were reduced, if not removed entirely, in one of two ways. One secretary might take the lead and act in effect as a sole foreign minister, conducting all diplomacy himself, even if it fell technically within the other department: as the Earl of Sandwich did during the Grenville ministry (1763–5) and Lord Stormont during the American War (1779–82), when in each case their brother secretary was a nonentity. Alternatively, the two secretaries could co-operate closely and in this way impart unity to Britain's diplomatic strategy. The best example of this occurred during the first half of the 1770s when harmonious co-operation between the Earl of Rochford and the Earl of Suffolk imparted considerable purpose and direction to foreign policy, and made possible the recovery apparent at that time. Though this partnership broke down under the strain of the new situation created by the American rebellion, for several years it had enabled Britain to adapt to a new and puzzling situation on the Continent, with France's decline and the ascendancy of the Eastern Powers.

The problems which the geographical division of foreign policy caused were less serious than those which resulted from the extensive other responsibilities which the two secretaries shouldered. The fact that in Britain the same minister was responsible for domestic and colonial policy as well as diplomacy was not in itself unique: purely functional departments of state were only slowly emerging in later-eighteenth-century Europe. On the Continent foreign ministers were often involved, formally or informally, in domestic affairs. But Britain's situation was unusual in the degree of responsibility which the two secretaries of state had over other areas of policy. They frequently found that foreign issues were less important, or simply less urgent, than the other business which passed through their offices, and in this way the two ministers were diverted from giving their full attention to Britain's international position. This was especially so for the Southern secretary, who handled American and other colonial matters during a period when imperial problems loomed large in the eyes of British governments. The establishment of a separate American Department in 1768 gave some relief to the hard-pressed Southern secretary, but the fundamental problem remained. One of the clearest examples of such distractions was provided when Sandwich was Northern secretary in the early years of peace. He was also the leader of the House of Lords, which made him responsible for the measures taken against John Wilkes.

During 1763–4, when Continental alignments were taking shape, Sandwich's preoccupation with the first stage of the Wilkes' affair contributed to the shortcomings of British diplomacy. In a similar way, in the summer of 1780 Lord Stormont was forced to deal with the aftermath of the Gordon riots, and for several weeks this led him to neglect Britain's diplomacy.

This exemplified a wider problem. The Russian minister in London, A.R. Vorontsov, spoke for a whole generation of foreign diplomats when he sourly remarked shortly after 1763 that British ministers were more interested in the election in Essex than that in Warsaw, where Russian control over Poland–Lithuania was being perpetuated through the imposition of Stanislas Poniatowski.[6] Vorontsov's general point was that ministers were preoccupied with their own domestic and colonial problems rather than with the key issues of Continental diplomacy. A generation of foreign diplomats in London proclaimed, with mounting exasperation, that British ministers were introspective and insular, and could only slowly and with extreme reluctance be brought to give their attention to Continental issues. The view of Britain's priorities which they transmitted to their governments in their despatches further weakened its international position.

This was partly the consequence of the distinctive British political system. All the other great powers were absolute monarchies governed by their rulers, perhaps aided by an all-powerful minister, who took little or no account of the views of their subjects. This inevitably shaped their attitudes to Britain as a political system and as a great power. These decades saw a noted expansion of newspapers and journals in many Continental countries, at least in western Europe, and the emergence of something approaching public opinion, particularly in France, but Britain remained unique among the major states in the degree of participation in political life which George III's subjects enjoyed. Foreign diplomats and their superiors struggled to understand the mysteries of the British constitution and only with difficulty comprehended the problems which the existence of parliament could cause for the government of the day.

Foreign observers were also used to considerable stability in government and to ministries which survived for an extended period of time because they depended only upon the continuing support of the ruler. The four decades after 1753 during which Wenzel Anton von Kaunitz was responsible for Austrian diplomacy, and

---

6. Michael Roberts, *Macartney in Russia* (*EHR*, Supplement 7; 1974), p. 38.

played a leading role in the formulation of domestic policy, might be unique; more usual were the dozen years (1758–70) during which the duc de Choiseul controlled French foreign policy and was Louis XV's leading minister, or the thirteen years (1774–87) during which the comte de Vergennes served his successor on the French throne. To observers accustomed to continuity, the frequent changes of ministries and ministers in London diminished the regard in which Britain was held. This was particularly so during the first decade of George III's reign, when there was a series of short-lived governments. Prussia's Frederick the Great was quick to sneer: the British king, he declared, changed his ministers as frequently as he changed his shirts.[7] Yet behind this malevolent sally lay an important point. The men who passed through the revolving doors of the two secretaries' offices during the 1760s were usually preoccupied with strengthening their own political position and that of the government in which they served, rather than buttressing Britain's international standing, which was frequently neglected. Often fresh to office, younger and less experienced than their counterparts at other points in the eighteenth century, they brought little knowledge and less understanding of Continental issues to their period as a secretary, which was in any case usually brief. No less than eight changes of minister took place at the Northern Department between 1763 and 1772.[8] There were exceptions to this dismal trend: Sandwich was conscientious and competent, and Rochford, in spite of his personal failings, was a minister of intelligence and imagination, while the situation was noticeably improved after 1770.

The consolidation of Lord North's ministry in that year represented a turning point in a second respect. It inaugurated a decade during which political stability returned and with it more direction to official policy, foreign as well as domestic. This improvement was threatened by the outbreak of the American rebellion in 1775, and was breaking down altogether by the end of that decade. Yet it remains true that British government wore a better face during the 1770s than it had during the previous decade, as foreign diplomats and their superiors clearly appreciated. The problem was that by then Britain's European position had been undermined by its own apparent indifference to the major issues of the day and by a more fundamental transformation within the international system.

7. J.G. Droysen et al., eds, *Politische Correspondenz Friedrichs des Grossen* 46 vols (Berlin, etc., 1879–1939), xxv, p. 353.
8. Roberts, *Splendid Isolation*, p. 5.

Britain and the great powers of Europe

During the two decades after 1763, Britain's foreign policy was dominated by relations with its traditional enemy, France, now closely allied with the other major Bourbon power, Spain.[9] The Third Family Compact, signed in August 1761, had brought Madrid into the Seven Years War belatedly and unsuccessfully. Nevertheless, the Bourbon alliance had survived Spain's defeats and, during the generation after 1763, the Franco-Spanish axis was a fixed point of European international relations, except for the first half of the 1770s. Though France was normally the dominant partner, particularly during the ministry of the energetic Choiseul, who remained in power until the very end of 1770, Spain came to play an enlarged and more important role in Anglo-Bourbon relations during the age of the American Revolution. This was primarily because of its wide-ranging and vulnerable empire, which was an enticing target for British commercial and naval power. The peace settlement at the end of the Seven Years War and the subsequent cession of the French colony of Louisiana to Spain (as compensation for Madrid's losses in 1762–3) had deprived France of a foothold on the North American mainland and weakened its position in the colonial sphere, perhaps deliberately. The vulnerability of the far-flung Spanish empire had been revealed by the recent fighting, but it was now in the front line against the confident and even aggressive British imperial interests; this explains why so many of the Anglo-Bourbon disputes during the 1760s originated in clashes between the colonial representatives of Britain and Spain.

During the age of the American Revolution, as throughout the eighteenth century, relations with the two Bourbon powers shaped British foreign policy. Both sides assumed that their rivalry was permanent and probably ineradicable, that the peace established in 1763 would be short-lived, and that clashes and perhaps open fighting would soon be resumed. Britain and the Bourbon powers had both been exhausted by the recent conflict: in London and at Versailles there was real concern at the state of the national finances, while Madrid contemplated an imperial structure visibly in decay, with administration and defence greatly in need of regeneration. A

---

9. Nicholas Tracy, *Navies, Deterrence and American Independence: Britain and Seapower in the 1760s and 1770s* (Vancouver, 1988) provides a naval perspective on Anglo-Bourbon relations after 1763 and consolidates an important series of detailed articles which are referred to in his bibliography; while there is a useful article by Jeremy Black, 'Anglo-French relations, 1763–1775', *Francia* 18 (1991), pp. 89–114.

shared desire to tackle the financial and colonial problems created, or simply exposed, by the Seven Years War meant that neither side was anxious for a rapid renewal of warfare and this ensured a period of peace. But there was no expectation that this would last very long. From Britain's perspective there appeared to be considerable evidence of continuing Bourbon ill-will immediately after 1763. The efforts by France and Spain to rebuild their navies caused particular concern, as did a series of relatively small-scale colonial disputes in the early years of peace.

The Seven Years War had demonstrated Britain's supremacy at sea, and this continued after 1763. The British navy had reached a new peak of size and relative effectiveness during that conflict, while the navies of both Bourbon monarchies were in poor condition and had suffered defeats at Britain's hands. Naval reconstruction was Choiseul's main aim, and he himself took the all-important naval portfolio from 1761 until 1766.[10] He sought to rebuild the shattered French fleet, while simultaneously urging naval reconstruction upon his Spanish ally. His efforts were not without success: the real challenge which Britain would face from the combined Bourbon fleets during the American War was largely made possible by the building and repair programmes launched at this time. In the short term, however, Bourbon naval reconstruction fell appreciably short of the unrealistic targets set at the close of the Seven Years War. France and Spain lacked the men and *matériel*, the infrastructure and, above all, the financial resources to rebuild their fleets with the speed which Choiseul had initially hoped, while Britain's superiority at sea – though weakened by economies and partial neglect – could not quickly be challenged. Recognizing this, Choiseul abandoned the naval portfolio in the spring of 1766, returning to the foreign office, and though naval reconstruction continued on both sides of the Pyrenees, in France it proceeded at a slower pace than had been anticipated immediately after the Peace of Paris.

10. H.M. Scott, 'The importance of Bourbon naval reconstruction to the strategy of Choiseul after the Seven Years War' *International History Review* 1 (1979), pp. 17–35. It has recently been argued by Jan Glete, using a different system of measurement ('displacement tonnage') that Bourbon reconstruction was even more successful and that, by 1770, the Bourbon navies were stronger than that of Britain. But he does not fully take into account that French ships at least were generally larger than their British counterparts and also fails to consider the condition of these vessels, some of which were awaiting rebuilding and were in a poor condition: see Jan Glete, *Navies and Nations: Warships, Navies and State Building in Europe and America, 1500–1860* 2 vols (Stockholm, 1993), ii, pp. 271, 273.

Britain's continuing lead at sea was known in some detail to ministers both in London and at Versailles. The enlarged importance which naval power now possessed within the overall framework of Anglo-Bourbon relations was apparent in the attention and resources devoted to the gathering of naval intelligence. France maintained a spy-ring in Britain, run from the embassy in London, and picked up scraps of information in a wide variety of other ways. This was the basis of detailed tables of British naval strength, together with the exact location of the ships, maintained by the French ministry throughout the 1760s and 1770s. For its part, Britain secured naval intelligence both indirectly, through an agency run from the Dutch Republic, and directly through the reports of strategically placed diplomats and captains in both the merchant navy and the fighting fleet. The result was that each side knew with surprising accuracy the state of its enemy's naval power and its own superiority or inferiority at sea. Detailed knowledge of French and Spanish rebuilding confirmed British ministers in their assumptions of enduring Bourbon enmity, though they did realize that they retained the advantage at sea. This made them more willing to use their naval supremacy in the disputes which arose during the first decade of peace.

The Seven Years War and the treaty which ended it had created a series of relatively small problems to be resolved by Anglo-Bourbon diplomacy: the fortifications at Dunkirk, the Canada Bills and in particular the question of the so-called Manila Ransom. None of these disputes was particularly serious, nor likely to lead to a renewed war, but they provided a barometer of the state of relations between the three countries. They both contributed to and were exacerbated by the poor state of Anglo-Bourbon diplomacy immediately after 1763, caused friction and bad-feeling, consumed the time and filled the despatches of diplomats, but were in the end all settled by negotiation. A much more serious threat to peace were the unpredictable clashes which arose at the imperial periphery between agents of the British state and of the Bourbon monarchies, over which metropolitan governments could exercise little control. Immediately after the Peace of Paris there were disputes over Turks Island, then the Gambia, and finally and most seriously (in 1766) the Falkland Islands. Each had its origins in the actions of an enthusiastic subordinate probably exceeding the instructions, or at least the intentions, of his superiors; each threatened for a time to lead to a wider conflict; and each was eventually resolved by Bourbon concessions in the face of an immediate British naval mobilization.

Choiseul, who effectively controlled Bourbon policy at this period, recognized that French and Spanish inferiority at sea forced them to accede to British pressure, since they were unable to fight with any chance of success. Successive British governments, realizing the potential for successful naval blackmail, used the threat of force rather than the path of diplomacy to bring about a settlement favourable to their view of events.

The most serious of these clashes was that over the Falklands, and it was shelved rather than solved in 1766. Lying as they did to the east of the Straits of Magellan, these islands were strategically important for any British attempt to break into the Pacific Ocean, which Madrid was determined to maintain as a Spanish *mare clausum*, a status which the terms of the Treaty of Utrecht appeared to uphold. At issue in the first clash over the islands in 1766 had been the blockhouse established at Port Egmont on West Falkland by a British expedition, and in the later 1760s the Spanish government determined to remove this by force. Calculating that in any war France would have no alternative but to support Spain, Madrid evicted the small British garrison in the late spring of 1770. The arrival in Europe of news of this expulsion in the summer of that year set in motion a crisis which brought war closer than at any point since the conclusion of the Peace of Paris.

At first this dispute assumed a predictable form. Britain mobilized its fleet, the Bourbons followed suit, and the government in London then brought forward more ships of the line. The mechanisms which had preserved peace since 1763 now seemed likely to lead to a war over Spain's actions in the distant South Atlantic. The fundamental source of the dispute was intrinsically more serious than previous clashes: force had been used against the British flag. War almost broke out in 1770–1 because of three factors which had not been present in earlier colonial disputes. Britain's response was handled by the then Southern secretary, Weymouth, who adopted a much more hard-line approach than most of his colleagues and certainly than the king, George III. This was because the earl was prepared to risk open conflict and may even have been anxious for fighting to begin, in order to further his own political career. Weymouth hoped than any war might bring the Earl of Chatham (as Pitt had become in 1766) back to power and that he himself would dominate any ministry which replaced North's government. In the second place, Madrid was determined to expel British forces from West Falkland and was prepared to exploit the Family Compact to bring this about: the second Falklands' crisis was, until its final stages, much more of a purely Anglo-Spanish dispute than previous clashes. In the critical final months of 1770, Choiseul – who had hitherto been an advocate of moderation and a negotiated settlement – accepted and perhaps encouraged the risk of war. This was because his own ministry was being undermined at Louis XV's court, and he believed that a war with Britain might be the only way in which his power could be perpetuated. In the end peace was preserved. Choiseul was dismissed by the pacific Louis XV on Christmas Eve 1770, while Weymouth found himself increasingly opposed by his cabinet colleagues and finally resigned. Spain, deserted by its Bourbon ally, backed down in the face of Britain's evident naval supremacy and a negotiated settlement was patched together. War was averted, while France's desertion of its ally created a period of tension with Madrid and weakened the Family Compact, which had been far stronger and more unified under Choiseul then during the decade which followed his fall.

Colonial rivalry had been intensified by the Seven Years War and this ensured that the main focus of Anglo-Bourbon relations after 1763 lay outside Europe. Yet the first decade of peace saw two serious clashes over purely European issues, first over Corsica and then over the Swedish *coup* in 1772–3. In 1768 the ailing Chatham administration was paralysed by divisions within the cabinet and confronted by serious unrest on the streets of London, and this ensured that Britain did nothing to prevent France securing the most important political success of Choiseul's ministry. Five years later, in the crisis which followed the French-backed restoration of the powers of the Swedish monarchy by Gustav III in August 1772, continuing British mastery at sea and the North ministry's willingness to mobilize the fleet forced France to back down rather than support its ally, Sweden. These episodes were unusual in that their origins lay in Europe rather than overseas. In all these clashes – with the single exception of that over Corsica – France and Spain retreated, conscious of their own relative weakness, when confronted by Britain's willingness to deploy its naval superiority.

Continuing rivalry with the Bourbons confirmed ministers in their view that Britain needed a European ally, the traditional goal of London's eighteenth-century foreign policy. This quest provided the second strand in British foreign policy during the decade after the Peace of Paris. It was pursued intermittently, and was to end in failure: by the early 1770s the search had been abandoned, at least for the present. Since the close of the seventeenth century, opposition to France and its satellites had been achieved by means of war-time alliances with other enemies of the powerful French monarchy. Memories of past rivalry with the leading Bourbon power convinced ministers that such alliances were still the best way of countering France's deep-rooted hostility. If Continental states could be persuaded to put their armies at Britain's disposal, the resources of the French king could be tied down within Europe while Britain concentrated its effort against the vulnerable French empire overseas. This had in essence been the strategy adopted during the Seven Years War, when a subsidy to Prussia, and rather larger payments to finance the so-called 'Army of Observation' in western Germany, had helped to occupy France in an indecisive Continental struggle and thus contributed to its defeat in the North American and Indian subcontinents. Past history and recent successful experience thus combined to suggest the importance of allies to the next generation of British statesmen, who had grown up during the Anglo-Bourbon warfare of 1739–63, in which some of them had actually fought. In fact the search for peacetime alliances after the Peace of Paris was less well rooted in Hanoverian precedent than contemporaries assumed: Britain concluded relatively few alliances except during war-time in the eighteenth century. George III and his ministers believed the contrary and this was reflected in British diplomacy down to the early 1770s.

The first ally to be sought was Britain's traditional partner, Austria, who had been allied to France since the Diplomatic Revolution of 1756. Immediately after 1763 an unrealistic attempt was made by the Grenville ministry to recover the alliance with Vienna, but it was rejected out of hand by the Austrian state chancellor, Kaunitz, who believed that the Habsburg Monarchy's future security and political success depended upon the maintenance of the treaty with Versailles. The other major German power, Prussia, had been aligned with Britain during the Seven Years War. That partnership had been formed by accident, had been marked by strain and distrust, and had ended in an acrimonious split in 1762 which poisoned relations for a generation. Prussia's king, Frederick the Great, was determined to avoid alliance with either of the western powers, resenting the way he had been 'deserted' (as he believed) in 1762 and assuming that such links would involve his exhausted state in the new round of Anglo-French warfare which he regarded as inevitable. Advocates of a Prussian alliance within British public life were few and far between. Principal among them was William Pitt, the architect of the war-time alliance, and renewed links with Prussia were his first political objective when he finally consented to return to office in the summer of 1766. It was hoped that this would be the basis of a new northern league. Since 1764 Frederick the Great had been the ally of Russia, with whom Pitt also intended to align Britain. The initiative ran aground almost before it had been launched: Frederick the Great rejected the British overtures out of hand, and relations remained cool and distant until the 1780s.

The prospects for the signature of a formal treaty with Russia appeared brightest for several years after 1763.[11] Contemporaries believed that the two states were, in the parlance of the times, 'natural allies'. They were united by a mutually profitable trading connection, had been allies in the past, and were both declared rivals of France, and at many points their interests seemed to overlap. Britain's naval and commercial strength was thought to complement Russia's military might. In 1763 the conclusion of an alliance appeared to be only a question of time and terms. Britain's wealth and enhanced international standing, at the end of the triumphant Seven Years War, were powerful attractions to an impoverished and backward state such as Russia. Its power and standing had also been much enhanced by the recent conflict, though Russia was not yet able to support this new position with its exiguous resources and fragmentary infrastructure. The Russian empress, Catherine II, was personally Anglophile, and she and Nikita Panin (her leading adviser on foreign policy) were initially anxious to conclude a political alliance to set alongside the commercial treaty dating from 1734 which was renewed – not without difficulty – in 1766.

Despite these promising beginnings no alliance was concluded. Negotiations had begun even before the Peace of Paris was signed and continued intermittently for almost a decade, but did not produce the treaty which both sides genuinely desired. The problem was that Britain would never make the kind of concession which St Petersburg demanded as the price of a formal treaty: whether in the form of a subsidy (for a decade after 1763 British ministers repeated *ad nauseam* that they would never pay subsidies in peacetime), or in the acceptance of the 'Turkish clause', which meant the inclusion in any defensive alliance of the event of an attack by

11. A series of detailed studies by Michael Roberts explores Anglo-Russian relations during the decade after 1763: see in particular, *British Diplomacy and Swedish Politics 1758–73* (1980); *Macartney in Russia* [this was reprinted, in an abbreviated form, in Peter Roebuck, ed., *Public Service and Private Fortune: The Life of Lord Macartney 1737–1806* (Belfast, 1983)]; 'Great Britain, Denmark and Russia, 1763–1770' in R.M. Hatton and M.S. Anderson, eds, *Studies in Diplomatic History: Essays in Memory of David Bayne Horn* (1970), pp. 236–67; 'Great Britain and the Swedish Revolution, 1772–73' in idem, *Essays in Swedish History* (1967), pp. 286–347.

the Ottoman Empire upon Russia. Britain always refused to promise aid against the Turks and instead hoped, by minor concessions over apparently insignificant matters, to avoid a major concession over either of these two crucial issues. Such an attitude ensured that the negotiations would fail. As the years passed, the balance of advantage in Anglo-Russian diplomacy moved away from London and towards St Petersburg. In 1763 Catherine and Panin, aware of their vulnerability, had been anxious to conclude an early alliance. By the end of that decade, Russia's international position was stronger, being buttressed by alliances with Prussia (1764) and Denmark (1765). Britain, by contrast, was beset by problems at home and in the colonies, and was a less attractive partner than it had been when the discussions had first begun. These developments were reflected in Anglo-Russian diplomacy. By the end of the 1760s both sides were coming to accept that the *entente* which existed was probably preferable to the elusive alliance.

Britain's search for an ally had been undermined in part by its own failures. Political instability, urban and radical unrest, and mounting colonial problems during the 1760s damaged Britain's standing in Europe and thus its search for security in the shape of an alliance. The triumphant peacemaker of 1763 had become, within a few short years, a divided and troubled realm, with resulting damage to its prestige and international reputation. This was intensified by the publicity which surrounded its misfortunes. Newspapers carried word of the shortcomings and failures of successive British governments around Europe. The British ambassador in Russia, Lord Cathcart, commented significantly that, with regard to British politics, Catherine II and her ministers were '*in the Opposition*'. He thought that they were strongly influenced by the propaganda launched across the Continent by the critics, parliamentary, domestic and foreign, of Britain's government.[12]

In a more fundamental manner London's failure was due to a reorientation of the European states-system, which within a decade had the unexpected effect of marginalizing the victor of the Seven Years War. The emerging pattern, and the consequent problems for London, had first become apparent in the failure of the British negotiations with Austria, Prussia and Russia in 1763–6. The conclusion of a Russo-Prussian alliance in April 1764, an axis which was to prove remarkably stable throughout the 1760s and 1770s,

12. *Sbornik imperatorskogo russkogo istorischeskogo russkogo obshchestva* 148 vols (St Petersburg, 1867–1916), xix, p. 228.

reduced Russia's need for a British alliance as well as ensuring that Frederick the Great's considerable influence at St Petersburg would be employed against Britain. While there was no Prussian veto at the Russian court, the king's opposition did nothing to improve British prospects for an alliance. The powerful Russo-Prussian axis, uniting the two strongest Continental military states, paralysed Austrian policy for a decade to come. In the face of this overwhelming military threat from north and east, Kaunitz consolidated the French alliance and adopted a policy of peace at almost any price.

The division of the Continent into two rival blocks, without any obvious entry-point into the alliance system for Britain, underwent a further transformation in the later 1760s and early 1770s. The outbreak of a Russo-Turkish War in 1768, the scale of the victories which Russia eventually won in that conflict, and the First Polish Partition to which it led in 1772, combined to bring about a further and decisive reorientation of the European states-system. Austria, while maintaining its established alliance with France at least in form, moved into the orbit of Russia and Prussia: as contemporaries appreciated, the First Partition was at one level a triple alliance of the three Eastern Powers. By the early 1770s the fault lines which had been present in Continental diplomacy since the Seven Years War had been revealed for all to see. The major diplomatic issues were now to be found in the eastern half of the Continent – above all the fates of the declining Polish kingdom and the militarily feeble Ottoman Empire – and in their solution Britain, like France, played little or no part. The Eastern Powers had come to dominate the states-system and give the law to Europe.

By the first half of the 1770s this development was appreciated, at least in outline, by observers in London. The breakdown of the latest round of negotiations with Russia in 1771 was the last occasion upon which an alliance was sought before the outbreak of the American rebellion. Instead Britain's security was to be upheld by the navy, expenditure upon which was increased in the aftermath of the second Falklands' crisis, which had revealed flaws in the mobilization of the British fleet. The problem was that the only possible alliance open to Britain – at least among the major powers – was now France: France the national enemy, the object of British anxieties and the ultimate target of the recent failed alliance negotiations.

This was understood by a handful of far-sighted statesmen at Versailles and in London, and in 1772–3 there were some shadowy moves towards a political *rapprochement* intended to check the ascendancy of the Eastern Powers. The prospects of success were always remote, because the weight of traditional rivalry and the ingrained assumptions of mutual hostility were simply too great for these discussions to make any real progress. The French foreign minister, the duc d'Aiguillon (1771–4), sought to interest Britain in political co-operation. His hints were taken up in London by a group headed by the king and including the prime minister, Lord North, and especially the Southern secretary, Rochford. But fear of parliamentary censure and political oblivion prevented Rochford from pursuing the discussions, and they petered out before they led anywhere. Their principal interest lies in the clear demonstration of the central problem for British foreign policy: that the ally made available by the workings of the European states-system was none other than the national enemy, France. In the apparently untroubled early 1770s it was easy to underestimate the importance of an alliance and instead to entrust Britain's security to a strengthened navy: a strategy which implied the acceptance of British diplomatic isolation. It was to be a very different matter once the rebellion in North America had broken out.

War and peace with America

A principal motive for the decision to confront American resistance by an immediate show of force was the recognition that Britain's position as a great power depended upon the suppression of any colonial rebellion.[13] As George III expressed it, 'We must get the colonies into order before we engage with our neighbours.'[14] The American War, however, was to deal a further severe blow to Britain's declining reputation in Europe. It would demonstrate the truth of Edmund Burke's observation, made shortly before fighting began, that Britain was now 'at the Circumference' of European politics and that in the new pattern of alliances there was no obvious niche for it.[15]

The most immediate effect of the fighting at Concord and Lexington was to draw foreign policy out of the deep freeze into which it had been consigned immediately before 1775.[16] Relations

13. R.W. Tucker and D.C. Hendrickson, *The Fall of the First British Empire: Origins of the War of American Independence* (Baltimore, MD, 1982), p. 356.
14. *Corr. of George III*, ii, p. 372, for the view of the king in 1774. (This letter is misdated by the editor.)
15. *Burke's Corr.*, ii, p. 513.
16. The most important study of British diplomacy during the American War is Isabel de Madariaga's authoritative *Britain, Russia and the Armed Neutrality of 1780*

with France were moved back to the top of the cabinet's diplomatic agenda, as old anxieties re-emerged and it was recognized that the colonial revolt might provide an opportunity for Louis XVI's monarchy to take the revenge upon Britain of which it had long dreamed. The improved relations with Versailles evident during the previous two years were supplanted by the more familiar watchful concern, and close attention was particularly paid to the French navy. The leading Bourbon state was drawn into the rebellion by the actions of the Americans. As they scoured Europe for aid in their struggle, they naturally focused upon France, both as an outlet for their trade and a source of the material assistance which was so essential. Maritime America was already trading with the French West Indian islands and this commerce increased in volume and importance after 1775. Before long, France was covertly providing aid, with the scale increasing as the months passed.

Britain's initial reaction was to ignore the development of Franco-American trade. Ministers turned a blind eye to its expansion, though they were well aware of it, from mid-1775 until mid-1776. The pretence of good relations with Versailles was maintained even as they began to crumble. By the second summer of the war, however, the façade was slipping. Britain was determined to do everything possible to delay or prevent French intervention on the side of the Americans, but ministers could do nothing to determine France's policy.[17] The question of intervention was settled at Versailles, being debated at length at Louis XVI's court in spring 1776. By May the decision to fight had been taken and funds provided for a swift build-up of the French fleet, supervised by the energetic naval minister, Sartine. The consequent activity in France's dockyards and the expansion of trade with the Americans was apparent to ministers in London by the summer. This transformed British policy, bringing a resumption of the strategy pursued with considerable success between 1763 and 1773: that of naval blackmail and intimidation. The timing of France's intervention – like the decision to fight – was

---

(1962). Nicholas Rodger's outstanding *The Insatiable Earl: A Life of John Montagu, 4th Earl of Sandwich* contains important material upon the navy and relations with France and Spain. The wider diplomatic context can be studied in Jonathan R. Dull, *A Diplomatic History of the American Revolution* (New Haven, CT, 1985) and in R.W. Van Alstyne, *Empire and Independence: The International History of the American Revolution* (New York, 1965); the same author's 'Great Britain, the war for independence and the "gathering storm" in Europe 1775–1778' *HLQ* 27 (1964), pp. 311–46, is important for the early years of the war.

17. The best guide to this is Jonathan R. Dull, *The French Navy and American Independence: A Study of Arms and Diplomacy, 1774–87* (Princeton, NJ, 1975).

beyond the control of the North government. Sartine's build-up of the navy was decisive when combined with the increasingly blatant aid provided to the Americans, especially the use of France's ports by American privateers (as the war spread to European waters). Consequently relations worsened sharply in 1776–7.

By mid-1777 Anglo-French diplomacy was in a state of 'half war', and thereafter France's intervention could not be deflected.[18] The outbreak of open hostilities was principally determined by the pace of the French naval build-up. Throwing off the mask of neutrality, Louis XVI's ministers began negotiations with the American representatives in Paris. By February 1778 Franco-American treaties of friendship and alliance had been signed, and Anglo-French diplomacy formally ended in the next month when the respective ambassadors were withdrawn. In July 1778, after naval clashes in the Channel, France formally declared war.

The mounting tension and eventual hostilities with France were transferred to Anglo-Spanish relations. These had improved noticeably during the 1770s, when Britain had come to treat the two Bourbon powers as separate states rather than a single hostile block. Under the pressures of the American revolt, as British ministers once more assumed Madrid's hostility, relations with both monarchies again coalesced. Spain, as a major colonial power, was always ambivalent about the American revolt – fearing possible repercussions within its own empire – and vigorously defended its own interests within the framework of the Family Compact. Spain was slowly drawn into the American struggle. French war-planning depended – as it had done since the close of the Seven Years War – upon the availability of Spanish naval power, while Spain's territories in the new world and ports in Europe became the target of American traders and privateers. Ministers in Madrid were eventually won over to the cause of intervention, though it was to be 1779 before they committed Spain openly to the Franco-American alliance.

The American rebellion, and especially the intervention of the Bourbon powers, highlighted Britain's diplomatic isolation. The need for a European ally became a mantra, intoned by ministers with little regard to the likely benefits which would accrue. There was no obvious French threat to Hanover during the American War. France's policy, which had learned the strategic lessons of earlier unsuccessful conflicts against Britain, especially in the Seven

18. The phrase was that of the shrewd and well-informed Swedish minister in London, Baron Nolcken: Scott, *British Foreign Policy*, p. 252.

Years War, aimed solely at the neutralization of Europe: something that was apparent to ministers in London. Britain was not defeated in America and, after 1778, on the high seas and in the colonies simply because it lacked a Continental ally. At most an alliance might have provided useful assistance, such as military forces, and altered the strategic complexion of the war. Britain's lack of a 'Continental sword' reversed the strategic position in earlier eighteenth-century conflicts. France, lacking the distraction of a German war, was able to concentrate financial resources and attention upon the struggle with Britain and in particular to spend more upon its navy, thereby exacerbating London's difficulties.

This search for Continental allies, however, proved unsuccessful. Austria (in 1780–1) and Prussia (in 1778 and again in 1782) were unsuccessfully courted by Britain, while several approaches were made to Russia throughout the war. In 1778 Catherine II was finally offered a subsidy – though ministers still insisted upon the 'Turkish clause' – and three years later the empress was even promised the Mediterranean island of Minorca in return for an immediate treaty. None of these initiatives was successful, despite the fact that there was considerable sympathy for the British cause at least in Vienna and St Petersburg. In part the search for an ally was undermined by its timing. Britain was trying to conclude a treaty during war-time, and any ally would immediately become involved in the hostilities. More fundamentally, the failure to secure an alliance revealed the new pattern of alignments and Britain's own political marginalization. The military threat from France upon which earlier generations had relied in their creation of alliance-systems had disappeared. European diplomacy was dominated by the Eastern Powers, who during the American War were preoccupied with the Balkans and, in 1778–9, with the War of the Bavarian Succession between Austria and Prussia, a short-lived conflict in which Versailles remained neutral, despite being Vienna's ally. The obstacles to Britain securing an alliance were insurmountable.

In an attempt to close the western European states' ports and colonial harbours in the new world to American shipping and privateers, the American War involved Britain in a diplomatic offensive against the neutral commercial powers. Diplomacy was intended to support the military and naval effort directed against the former colonists. This campaign enjoyed a measure of success, though by its nature this was bound to be incomplete. Portugal, Denmark and Sweden were all co-operative and took steps to place obstacles in the way of American trade with their possessions in the western hemisphere and in Europe. Most problems arose with the Dutch Republic, both because – as Europe's leading commercial power among the neutrals – it was an obvious target for American traders and because British expectations proved to be at variance with Dutch practices. As a result of previous commercial treaties with Britain, the republic enjoyed a particularly favourable position over trade in war-time. Technically it remained London's ally because of a treaty signed in the seventeenth century which had never been formally abrogated. As a result of Britain's behaviour, however, there was a sharp deterioration in relations and by the end of 1780 the two countries were at war.

From the very beginning of the American War, the Dutch Republic had been a major American target, particularly for munitions and especially the all-important gunpowder. Its colonial empire in the western hemisphere, particularly the Caribbean island of St Eustatius, was soon trading extensively with the rebels. This produced an immediate deterioration in Anglo-Dutch diplomacy, which was exacerbated by the rough treatment of the republic's ministers and even the Stadtholder, William V, by Britain's long-serving minister at The Hague, the outspoken Sir Joseph Yorke. By 1779–80 relations had been reduced to a very low ebb by the escalating maritime disputes. At the end of December 1780 Britain declared war. The final breach between the two countries was created by two British decisions. First, ministers became convinced that the Dutch and their trade would be less of a problem for Britain if they were enemies rather than neutrals: this would deprive them of the protection of maritime law. In the second place, the war was linked to the republic's domestic politics.[19] The feeble regime of William V and the Orangists was increasingly under attack by the Patriots. Britain was a traditional supporter of the House of Orange and of the Stadtholder. In the final months of peace ministers, especially Stormont (encouraged and in part directed by Yorke), became convinced that war might revive the power of the Stadtholderate.

Another element which encouraged war was the emergence, under the patronage of Catherine II's Russia, of a league of neutral powers who opposed Britain's severity in curtailing war-time trade. The formation of this Armed Neutrality (which came to be joined by Austria, Prussia and even the Kingdom of the Two Sicilies, as well as Denmark, Sweden, the Dutch Republic and Russia), together with the outbreak of the Anglo-Dutch War at the end of December 1780,

19. For this dimension, see H.M. Scott, 'Sir Joseph Yorke, Dutch politics and the origins of the fourth Anglo-Dutch war' *HJ* 31 (1988), pp. 571–89.

appeared to complete Britain's eclipse as a European power. The Continent had united against Britain; it was at war with its traditional friend and ally the Dutch Republic; and it was suffering mounting defeats by the Americans and the Franco-Spanish forces. In this context the peace settlements concluded three years later were less onerous than might have been anticipated, or many British contemporaries expected.

Throughout the war peace-feelers had been made, first to the Americans and then to the Franco-Spanish alliance. This was a normal way of testing the will to fight of one's enemies rather than a genuine attempt to find a settlement, and they had led nowhere. The diplomatic stalemate was only broken by a series of British reverses during the second half of 1781, climaxed by Cornwallis's celebrated surrender at Yorktown in October. This convinced most British observers that the former colonies could not be reconquered and that American independence would have to be recognized. By the winter of 1781–2 war-weariness and particularly financial exhaustion were affecting all the participants, and this quickly became apparent when serious peace negotiations began in the following spring.

The peace settlements secured by Britain at the end of the American war were the work of one man: the Earl of Shelburne, probably the most disliked and least understood figure in eighteenth-century British politics.[20] Aided only by the king, whose role in the negotiations of 1782–3 was considerable, Shelburne handled all the detailed discussions himself, usually behind the back of his colleagues, and personally negotiated the settlement with France with an emissary sent to England by Vergennes. The final settlement constituted the one positive if flawed achievement of the earl's political career. Though he had held office during the 1760s, he had been in the political wilderness for over a decade when the vagaries of party strife brought him back into power in 1782, first as part of a short-lived government headed by Rockingham and then from early July as leader of the ministry of the day. The lieutenant and political executor of Chatham, an association which did nothing to recommend him to his contemporaries, Shelburne was widely distrusted – legitimately, in the light of the way in which he deceived his ministerial

---

20. The most important study of the peace negotiations is the regrettably unpublished thesis by Andrew P. Stockley, 'Britain, France and the peace of 1783', unpub. PhD thesis (University of Cambridge, 1994); until it appears in print the best accounts are Vincent T. Harlow, *The Founding of the Second British Empire 1763–1793* 2 vols (1952–64), i, pp. 223–447, and C.R. Ritcheson, 'The Earl of Shelburne and peace with America, 1782–1783' *International History Review* 5 (1983), pp. 322–45.

colleagues and excluded them from any detailed scrutiny of the peace negotiations – and even more widely hated. To contemporaries he was the 'Jesuit of Berkeley Square' (where his London house was located), an epithet coined by George III in the 1760s which had stuck fast to the earl. In private Shelburne could be charming and entertaining, but in public he displayed an aloof sarcasm which alienated friend and foe alike. The ease with which he had discarded his earlier political ideas – the Chathamite Francophobe had become the advocate of political reconciliation with Versailles – together with a pronounced evasiveness in personal relations intensified the general suspicion and dislike which the earl aroused.

Yet Shelburne was a statesman of unusual vision and real originality, open to the ideas of the European Enlightenment and strongly influenced by *philosophe* ideas of trade liberalization. He brought to the task of peace-making an appreciation that the process was more than a negative surrender, though his ideas often went beyond what was possible in the circumstances which confronted Britain at the end of the American War. The earl's broad approach shaped the settlements concluded in 1783–4, though many of his detailed ideas had to be abandoned during the negotiations. Shelburne also demonstrated considerable tactical skill during the detailed discussions, while the relationship of trust he eventually established with Vergennes – who had at first been suspicious of the earl because of his previous hostility towards France – paved the way to the final settlement.

The crucial importance of American independence in the modern history of the western world has encouraged historians to conclude that the Anglo-American peace negotiations were the most significant dimension of the settlement. In fact, with the passing of the Conway motion against 'offensive war' in America by the House of Commons at the very end of February 1782, the fact of independence had already been accepted in Britain. Shelburne's principal contribution to the American settlement was his attempt to dress up military and political necessity – the reconquest of the former colonists was recognized to be impossible – in the guise of magnanimous statesmanship. The earl dreamed of an Anglo-American political community being born of a future reconciliation, though this aim was soon revealed to be unrealistic at the end of a bitter Anglo-American civil war which had already lasted for seven years and shed much blood. He also hoped that the new American Republic would remain a British economic colony, providing raw materials and a captive – and growing – market for Britain's protean industrial revolution.

These aims were apparent in the actual terms agreed with the American negotiators during detailed discussions which took place in Paris. Shelburne was prepared to grant generous terms, particularly where the territorial extent of the new republic was concerned. Though Britain retained Canada, the Americans secured a more favourable north-western frontier than they anticipated and thus no obstacles were placed in the way of future expansion westwards. They were also admitted to the Newfoundland fisheries, and secured less unfavourable terms than they expected over two difficult issues: those of the loyalists (those colonists who had continued to support Britain and had suffered material losses as a consequence) and the Americans' responsibility for debts to British subjects contracted before the war began. The peace preliminaries signed in November 1782 and subsequently confirmed in the final Treaty of Versailles (September 1783) were more generous than the Americans had anticipated, and certainly than their Bourbon allies had intended.

The key dimension of the settlement was the Anglo-French peace. Shelburne's ideas once again went beyond the simple search for a negotiated settlement. Recognizing that the dominance of the Eastern Powers had undermined the place in Europe not merely of Britain but of France as well, he set out to shape a treaty which laid the ground for reconciliation and future diplomatic co-operation against the Leviathans who now dominated Continental politics. This was to be buttressed by a trade agreement, which would benefit the economies of both Britain and France and was eventually to be signed in 1786. Concluding a peace treaty proved rather easier than might have been anticipated: France, close to bankruptcy, needed a settlement even more than Britain, and Vergennes had long shared Shelburne's anxieties about the dominance of the Eastern Powers. The speed with which peace was negotiated, and the actual terms accepted by each party, were influenced by a revival of British fortunes during the final campaigns of the war, especially Admiral Rodney's famous victory at the Saintes in April 1782. It was followed in the autumn of the same year by the relief of Gibraltar, whose garrison had heroically survived a prolonged Spanish siege. Yet while these exigencies produced a peace, diplomatic co-operation was to prove elusive. The close political understanding demanded by the earl's ideas was a difficult and perhaps impossible goal at the end of an extended and highly destructive war in which Britain and France had fought on different sides. Shelburne was swept from power in March 1783 – his was the only eighteenth-century ministry to be defeated in parliament over the terms of a peace settlement – though the Fox–North ministry which succeeded him did endorse the terms he had negotiated and signed the definitive treaties.

The final settlement with the Bourbon powers, signed at Versailles on 3 September 1783, gave France some minor gains at British expense: the West Indian island of Tobago, Senegal in Africa and small concessions in India, along with a more secure position in the Newfoundland fisheries and the right to fortify Dunkirk. Madrid's territorial gains were more substantial, although these did not include the cherished war-aim of Gibraltar. Spain secured Minorca and the two Floridas. Though the two Bourbon powers had some territorial trophies to show for the high costs of their intervention in the American War, they had not overturned the commanding position secured by Britain two decades before. This was apparent to George III. In 1781 the king had feared Britain's extinction as a great power if the struggle ended in defeat, but his view of the eventual peace terms was much more positive. 'The more I reflect', he wrote in the same month that the peace preliminaries with the Bourbons were signed, '. . . the more I thank Providence for having through so many difficulties . . . enabled so good a peace . . . to be concluded.'[21]

In a more fundamental sense, however, Shelburne's failure in 1782–3 expressed the fundamental problem of Britain's diplomacy throughout the age of the American Revolution. The earl had correctly identified the principal cause of British decline as a great power: a new pattern of European alliances in which there was no obvious place for Britain except through a *rapprochement* with France. Yet France remained the traditional enemy and rival of British power, and had recently fought a wide-ranging and costly war in an attempt to reduce this dominance. The American War thus demonstrated what had been recognized by a few perceptive observers before 1775: that Britain was driven, by past tradition and present rivalry, to pursue an anti-Bourbon foreign policy at exactly the moment when that rivalry was becoming insignificant for the relations of the major Continental powers. This weakened its ability to resist the new dominance of the Eastern Powers, and ultimately condemned its foreign policy to failure and to the apparent, though temporary, decline of Britain's great-power status.

21. *Corr. of George III*, v, pp. 247, 297; vi, p. 222.

CHAPTER EIGHT

The Impact of the American
Revolution on Ireland

NEIL LONGLEY YORK

In February 1772 Governor Thomas Hutchinson of Massachusetts finally responded to a letter sent to him two and a half years before. That letter came from John Hely-Hutchinson, MP for Cork in the Irish House of Commons. Hely-Hutchinson had read Hutchinson's history of Massachusetts and wondered if he and the governor might be related. Hutchinson noted that there were indeed distant familial ties, but before doing so he made observations about what he thought linked Ireland with Massachusetts.

> I am a native of the Colonies[;] my bias naturally is in favour of them. I verily think notwithstanding the Subjects in the Colonies are as happy upon the whole as those in the Kingdom [of Britain]. Ireland is a subordinate Kingdom. Are not the people of Ireland upon the whole under as easy a Government as the people of Great Britain? Is not an unwarrantable desire of Independence at the bottom of all the discontents both in Ireland and in the Colonies? In a Government which has any thing popular in its form or constitution the remote parts will grow more dissatisfied with any unfavourable distinction in proportion as those parts increase and become considerable. A doubt or scruple in the Supreme authority of its absolute uncontrollable power and a relaxation in consequence will encrease the dissatisfaction and endanger a disunion or total separation.[1]

Hutchinson's long-delayed response hinted at the troubles burdening him. His critics within the province had become legion. As far as they were concerned his 'bias' was not in their 'favour'; on the contrary, it was wholly against them. They condemned him not only for his present policies, but for his understanding – misunderstanding, as they saw it – of Massachusetts' past. Hutchinson had

---

1. Massachusetts Archives xxvii:297, Massachusetts Historical Society typescript, pp. 523–4. Thomas Hutchinson to John Hely-Hutchinson, 14 Feb. 1772.

written in his history that Massachusetts was a subordinate part of
the British empire, and as such was also subordinate to the British
parliament. Residents of the province who did not comprehend
that relationship, he contended, were as mistaken in their notions
as those Irish who failed to see that they were in the same sort of
political position. To which 'Valerius Poplicola' – apparently Samuel
Adams writing under one of his many pen names – retorted, in
defence of the Irish in question as well as his colleagues in Massachusetts, 'such arguments may serve to evince the power of the
parent state, but neither its wisdom nor justice appears from them'.[2]

That Hely-Hutchinson read Hutchinson's book and attempted
to strike up a correspondence attests to the existence of what can
be called an 'Atlantic community'. The former ocean barrier now
acted as a highway, carrying passengers, goods and ideas from one
side to the other in a steady stream of traffic. More important,
Hutchinson's letter demonstrated the tendency for people in one
part of the empire to think about those in other parts of the empire,
if only to draw analogies. In making those analogies – some of them
appropriate, some of them not – they revealed the *ad hoc* nature of
empire-building and the difficulty, even the impossibility, of using
the past to clarify the present. Moreover, in their quest to use the
past can be seen both the similarities and the differences in the Irish
and colonial American experiences within the British empire.

The case for Irish rights

When Hutchinson at last replied to Hely-Hutchinson, Irish politics
were, for the moment, comparatively placid. That had not been the
case in 1769, at the time of Hely-Hutchinson's original query. Dublin Castle, home of executive authority in the person of the lord
lieutenant, was locked in a bitter struggle with opposition leaders
down the hill in Parliament House. Styling themselves 'Patriots',
these members of the Houses of Lords and Commons were a throw-
back to politicians of the previous decade who had taken on Dublin
Castle. Upholding what they venerated as fundamental rights, they
protested against the imperial arrangement that they believed gave
Whitehall and Westminster too much power in Ireland. Dublin
Castle, they complained, was a willing accomplice in that unconstitutional usurpation. Doling out places, pensions and the promise of

2. 'Valerius Poplicola', *The Boston-Gazette and Country Journal*, 28 Oct. 1771.

peerages, a lord lieutenant could often undermine his opponents, some self-proclaimed 'Patriots' included.

It was no coincidence that a new edition of William Molyneux's *Case* for Irish rights appeared in the middle of this latest controversy. Molyneux's 1698 tract, itself the result of a previous imperial dispute, had become a primary source for parliamentary Patriot arguments, a constitutionalist's equivalent of a theologian's sacred text. Molyneux had sat in the Irish Commons as a representative for Trinity College. He built his *Case* on a philosophical foundation laid by his friend John Locke. He also borrowed historical and legal arguments made by constitutionalist predecessors, and drew on his own reading of English and Irish statutes. 'That the Right of being subject Only to such Laws to which Men give their own *Consent*, is so inherent to all Mankind, and founded on such Immutable Laws of Nature and Reason,' Molyneux declared, 'that 'tis not to be *Alien 'd*, or *Given up*, by any Body of Men whatsoever'.[3] The Irish, he contended, had certainly not made any such surrender. Plumbing the depths of the Irish past, he attempted to reconstruct the original ties that bound England and Ireland together. According to him, although Henry II joined the two islands under a single 'imperial crown' in 1172, they nevertheless remained two distinct kingdoms. The Irish had consented to that relationship in a voluntary compact. They were not compelled, as some would have it, by conquest. Henry II soon after extended English common law to Ireland and he provided for the creation of an Irish parliament modelled on that at Westminster, with its own House of Commons and House of Lords. It would legislate as a sovereign body for Ireland, just as its counterpart at Westminster did for England. That the crown appointed a lord deputy or lord lieutenant to act in his stead, with authority to form his own Irish privy council, was only logical. This, then, was Ireland's 'ancient constitution', a guarantee of fundamental rights dating from the twelfth century.

The English parliament had nothing to do with creating this arrangement, Molyneux emphasized, and could therefore make no historical or legal claim to govern Ireland. 'It is manifest that there were no Laws Imposed on the People of *Ireland*, by any Authority of the Parliament of *England*', rather, the only statutes valid in Ireland were those passed 'by the *Consent* and *Allowance* of the People of Ireland'[4] through their representatives in the Irish parliament. True,

3. William Molyneux, *The Case of Ireland's Being Bound by Acts of Parliament in England Stated* (Dublin, 1698; repr. 1977), p. 93.

4. Ibid., p. 46.

Molyneux conceded, Poynings' Law, introduced in 1494 during the reign of Henry VII, set limits on what the Irish parliament could do. None the less, he added, that law had been passed by the Irish, not the English, parliament, and it dealt with relations between the Irish parliament on the one hand and the king, the lord lieutenant and their privy councils on the other. 'We know not an single Instance of an English Act of Parliament *Expressly Claiming* this Right of binding us', whereas 'we have several Instances of Irish Acts of Parliament, *Expressly Denying this Subordination*'. Poynings' Law, as he read it, made it clear that from that point on no law passed in the English parliament regarding Ireland should be binding there until it was also passed in the Irish parliament. '*That Ireland should be Bound by Acts of Parliament made* in England, *is against Reason, and the Common Rights of all Mankind*', Molyneux claimed emphatically and, he hoped, conclusively.[5]

Molyneux was no fool. He styled himself a loyal citizen of the empire and dutiful subject of his king, William III. He was even deferential in his references to the English parliament. Still, his arguments carried no weight at Whitehall and offended many at Westminster who moved, successfully, that the *Case* be condemned. Molyneux was faulted for what critics ridiculed as flawed logic, specious assumptions about natural rights, and a wild ramble through the Irish past. In short, they rejected all of his most basic contentions, which struck them as a politically dangerous form of special pleading.[6] Molyneux had tried manfully to explain away English and Irish actions that did not conform to his reordering of what, with hindsight, could appear to be a chaotic past. But the English parliament had in fact legislated for Ireland at various times, before and after passage of Poynings' Law, and the Irish parliament had effectively ceased to exist at one point during the Interregnum (1649–60) and went through most of the reigns of Charles II and James II without ever being called into session. If Molyneux occasionally became lost when he wandered through the distant past, the more recent past proved even more problematical. Politically and constitutionally, much had changed in England as well as Ireland since the days of Henry II. Indeed, if the English parliament, which began as the king's council, scarcely even existed then, Lords and Commons had now achieved legislative dominance and after the Glorious Revolution of 1688–9 it became increasingly common

5. Ibid., pp. 65, 116.
6. See, e.g., *An Answer to Mr Molyneux* (1698); William Atwood, *The History, Reasons, of the Dependency of Ireland upon the Imperial Crown of England* (1698).

to speak of the 'crown in parliament', as if the two had no separate existence. What sounded correct to Molyneux did not ring true in London, and Molyneux's opponents there seized upon his apparent inaccuracies and inconsistencies. To them he was wrong in his facts, wrong in his interpretations, and wrong in the cause he championed.

The constitution in dispute

Thomas Hutchinson shared their sentiments. When he wrote of erroneous ideas held by the Irish, he had Molyneux in mind and said as much in his history of Massachusetts.[7] Many of Molyneux's Irish contemporaries may have privately agreed with the position taken in the *Case* but they were not willing to force a public showdown with Dublin Castle or London. Westminster underscored its rejection of Molyneux's brand of 'constitutional nationalism' in the Declaratory Act of 1720 which stripped the Irish Lords of their appellate jurisdiction and shattered any pretensions of parliamentary legislative primacy by stipulating:

> That the said kingdom of *Ireland* hath been, is, and of right ought to be subordinate unto and dependent upon the imperial crown of *Great Britain*, as being inseparably united and annexed thereunto; and that the King's majesty, by and with the advice and consent of the lords spiritual and temporal and commons of *Great Britain* in parliament assembled, had, hath, and of right ought to have full power and authority to make laws and statutes of sufficient force and validity, to bind the kingdom and people of *Ireland*.[8]

The Declaratory Act repeated the sentiments, even the words, of the English Commons in its reaction to Molyneux's *Case* a generation before. Though it thereby clarified the issues, it did not resolve them. By specifying Westminster's interpretation of what had been, or, as Westminster saw it, should have been, the imperial relationship all along, it imposed one view over another, a view that was perhaps as impaired as the one it attempted to displace. But, like the American colonies in their periodic disputes with Britain, constitutional issues arising in Ireland could be papered over unless there were more tangible, immediately pressing issues crying to be

7. Thomas Hutchinson, *The History of the Colony and Province of Massachusetts Bay* 3 vols (Boston, 1784; rep. Cambridge, MA, 1936), i, pp. 272–3.
8. [Great Britain,] *The Statutes at Large* 47 vols (1769–1809), at *6 George I, c.5.*

resolved. The complications and contradictions in British–Irish relations were often veiled because of the desire for accommodation
and compromise. Poynings' Law had been revised during Mary's
reign to make relations between London and Dublin more work-
able, but the informal constitutional alterations were even more
important.[9] By the era of the American Revolution the Irish parliament had grown accustomed to drafting legislation originating
within its own chambers instead of being sent down by the lord
lieutenant through his privy council. Passing the 'heads' of a proposed statute rather than a true bill, the Irish parliament could see
its action result in a new law, provided the proposed legislation
survived review by the lord lieutenant and privy council in Dublin,
and the crown in council in London. Technically, the Irish parliament could still not exercise any legislative initiative; in more practical terms, it routinely did – a system that resulted from informal
arrangements, not formal constitutional amendments. During peaceful times this hardly mattered; in times of imperial crisis it could
matter a great deal.

By the 1760s growing numbers of disgruntled Americans had
begun to complain that Britain's regulation of the colonial trade
was oppressive and that Westminster, in choosing to tax them directly, had become tyrannical. Their protests about 'no taxation
without representation' were reminiscent of Molyneux, who, anti-
cipating the Woollens Act about to come out of Westminster, exclaimed that to 'Tax me without Consent, is little better, if at all,
than *down-right Robbing me*'.[10] When, in 1766, Westminster coupled
repeal of the hated Stamp Act with the passage of a Declaratory Act
for the colonies, the tendency of Americans and Irish to compare
their plight became even more pronounced. The Act stated:

> That the said colonies and plantations in *America* have been, are, and
> of right ought to be, subordinate unto, and dependent upon the
> imperial crown and parliament of *Great Britain*; and that the King's
> majesty, by and with the advice and consent of the lords spiritual and
> temporal, and commons of *Great Britain*, in parliament assembled,
> had, hath, and of right ought to have, full power and authority to
> make laws and statutes of sufficient force and validity to bind the
> colonies and people of *America*, subjects of the crown of *Great Britain*,
> in all cases whatsoever.[11]

9. [Ireland,] *The Statutes at Large* 20 vols (Dublin, 1786–1801) at *10 Henry VII c.4*
for Poynings' Law and *3 and 4 Philip and Mary c.4* for the revision.
10. Molyneux, *Case*, p. 130.
11. [Great Britain,] *Statutes at Large, 16 George III c.12.*

This latest Declaratory Act was more emphatic than the first. In 1720 Ireland's subordination was to the 'imperial crown', with the 'advice and consent' of parliament. In 1766 the Americans found themselves 'subordinate unto, and dependent upon' the 'imperial crown' *and* parliament. None the less, in both instances Westminster had attempted to evade as well as to confront. In 1720 it was careful to call Ireland a 'kingdom', thus preserving the title as it had been passed down from the twelfth century and the dignity of those who believed that the distinction between a subordinate kingdom and colony was not merely rhetorical. Nor did it specify how the 'imperial crown' as understood at Westminster differed from the characterization offered in Molyneux's *Case*. In 1766 it avoided use of the word 'tax' even as it claimed 'full power and authority' to make laws for the colonies 'in all cases whatsoever'. Admittedly, there was a strong constitutional tradition in England that distinguished between taxation and the general run of legislation. But what seems to have been most important to the Rockingham ministry was, paradoxically, placating the Americans at the same moment that it sought to subdue them. So too with the Irish in 1720. Whitehall and Westminster realized that constitutional questions arose as a sense of community within the empire declined. A carrot-and-stick approach would help restore order, soothe hurt feelings, and, with that, they hoped, questions of right and prerogative would cease to have their appeal.

They were wrong. Constitutional disputes and the frictions of imperial regulation that generated them did not go away. Concerned Irishmen knew that when the Stamp Act for Americans was being shaped, George Grenville had asserted Westminster's right to tax Ireland as well as the colonies. Like a growing number of Americans, concerned Irishmen began to impute the worst motives to British policy-makers, and lords lieutenant could find themselves facing the same sort of opposition that confounded royal governors in the colonies such as Thomas Hutchinson.

This was the situation when Hely-Hutchinson penned his 1769 letter. George Townshend, the lord lieutenant of Ireland, had put himself under political siege. He came to Dublin in 1767 intending to improve the management of Ireland and its parliament by residing on the island virtually full-time, unlike previous lords lieutenant. The Irish political managers known as 'undertakers', who were supposed to handle affairs between parliamentary sessions, could not always be relied on to be good government men, especially when the lord lieutenant was absent – as the political crises of the

1750s had demonstrated. The Irish also had their own version of the Court and Country divisions seen in British politics, and struggles in the Irish parliament could have as much to do with the control of parliamentary constituencies by powerful families as they did with public policy. Townshend, the sixth lord lieutenant appointed by George III since he took the throne in 1760, expected his presence to strengthen the executive at Dublin Castle and to insulate Irish affairs from the contentions that were becoming endemic at Westminster. In this he acted as George III and his ministers expected. Hely-Hutchinson, attached to the government as prime sergeant and privy councillor, was worried that Townshend's personality and policies would lead to a resurrection of the Patriots as an opposition force, and he was right. He nearly joined them himself. Townshend's augmentation of the military and money bill plans both encountered heated opposition. They were passed by parliament, but they cost him dearly. He left Dublin under a cloud in 1772, no longer lord lieutenant.

Even though the ranks of his political opponents swelled, they never outnumbered those who backed him. The Patriots clamoured for general elections to be held at regular intervals, for more control over Ireland's budget, and for a reduction in crown patronage. They did succeed in pushing through an act to ensure more frequent general elections but, of course, they only did so with the co-operation of Dublin Castle and the king in council, and only after accepting a change (from septennial to octennial elections) effected in London. If in this particular instance they let their desire to obtain a guarantee of regular elections override their scruples about accepting an altered bill, they later refused to accept a money bill amended in London and they still fretted about political conditions in Ireland overall. Not content to confine their arguments to parliamentary debates, they used the press to take their case to the public, a public that they hoped to create, influence and then shape ideologically.

Opposition writers, parliamentary Patriots foremost among them, planted pseudonymous political pieces in Dublin newspapers. Many of those printed in the *Freeman's Journal* were collected and reprinted under separate cover as *Baratariana*. In these Townshend was castigated for endangering Irish liberties, whereas Patriots were applauded for holding 'their shields against the stab made at our constitution'. Appealing to parliamentary Patriots to stand firm and for the public to support them, one essayist in the series declared 'let us cast off the yoke of slavery, and vindicate our freedom and independence. Let us no longer be rid, rather than ruled, as we have too long been, by men who have neither heads nor hearts.'[12] Polemicists of this ilk cast their net wide. They not only belittled Townshend and his supporters in Ireland, they attacked those in London who, they claimed, were behind the unsound policies being implemented by Dublin Castle. They warned of conspiracies against their liberties hatched at Westminster and Whitehall, conspiracies that involved the king's own ministers – though not, they were careful to note, the king himself.

In doing this they showed the same tendencies as American critics of Britain's attitude to empire. They juxtaposed freedom with slavery and justice with tyranny in their lamentations about the potential loss of liberty. And like their American counterparts they sought to form a larger, transatlantic community of protest that linked the situation in the British Isles to that in the colonies. 'The same arts which may be capable of destroying our liberties', one Irishman admonished Americans, 'must certainly operate more strongly against yours.'[13] The people of Ireland, warned another, must expect the worst unless they exerted themselves 'with the same spirit as the *brave* Americans have done'.[14]

The lower houses of colonial assemblies often led the protests on the American side of the Atlantic; so did the Irish House of Commons on the other side of the ocean. Words spoken in parliamentary debates and written in newspaper essays and pamphlets in Ireland were widely reported. The *Pennsylvania Chronicle*, for example, in reprinting one of the *Baratariana* pieces, congratulated the 'supposed' author, the MP and leading Patriot Henry Flood, as 'a Gentleman of great erudition, an eloquent speaker, an excellent writer and one of the truest and most inflexible patriots that was ever produced in that kingdom'.[15] Irishmen who sympathized with the Americans could in effect return the compliment by reprinting American protest literature – such as John Dickinson's influential *Letters* of a Pennsylvania farmer. In these Dickinson dropped just enough references to Ireland to make his arguments attractive to opposition leaders there. Using the political distribution of pensions and places in 'that poor kingdom' to his advantage, he painted a grim political future for the colonies if the increased

---

12. *Baratariana: A Select Collection of Fugitive Pieces, Published during the Administration of Lord Townshend in Ireland* 2nd edn (Dublin, 1773), Letter iv, pp. 32, 39.
13. Ibid., p. 39.
14. 'Brutus', in *The Public Register: Or, Freeman's Journal*, 24 Mar. 1774.
15. *Pennsylvania Chronicle*, 8 Nov. 1773.

crown civil list rumoured to be planned in London actually came into being.[16]

In a sense, the ideas expressed in Granville Sharp's *Declaration* can be read as the logical culmination of all this transatlantic analogizing. Sharp, an Englishman, coupled a reformer's zeal with a catholicity of interests. Largely self-taught, he entered the rhetorical fray over rights in the empire before he had completed his studies – as evidenced by the first edition of the *Declaration*, written in 1774 before he knew much about Ireland or the significance of the 1720 Declaratory Act. By the next year he knew a good deal more and became decidedly more critical in his new edition. Treating all legitimate government as a compact between ruler and ruled, he invoked natural rights and a reified English constitution as the sources of fundamental law within the empire: 'And as all British subjects, whether in Great-Britain, Ireland, or the Colonies, are *equally free* by the law of *Nature*, they certainly are *equally* entitled to the same *Natural* Rights that are *essential* for their own preservation.' For Ireland this meant that the Declaratory Act could not be binding because the Irish had not been represented in the legislature that passed it. Noting and accepting the arguments set forth in Molyneux's *Case*, he called for Irish parliamentary independence because 'the King and the People of Ireland are the natural and constitutional legislature or State of that kingdom'.[17]

Sharp did not argue that the American and Irish cases were exactly alike in every detail, nor did Americans like Dickinson when drawing their analogies. Rather, what joined them were their assumptions about fundamental law and the questions they raised about the locus of sovereignty and the nature of representation. Their notions about a separable crown and parliament in Britain and their defence of local legislatures – assemblies in America and a parliament in Ireland – as the equivalent, in their respective lands, of the Westminster parliament in Britain, flew in the face of the prevailing London view. By contending that they could not be effectively represented at Westminster, they made some sort of federal arrangement on the legislative level the only solution to the problem of imperial administration, a solution that was indeed

16. Dickinson's *Letters from a Farmer in Pennsylvania* (1767–8) are most accessible in Paul Leicester Ford, ed., *The Writings of John Dickinson* (Philadelphia, PA, 1895). See Letter 10, p. 378 for the reference to Ireland.

17. Granville Sharp, *A Declaration of the People's Natural Right to a Share in the Legislature* 2nd edn (1775), pp. 21, 25.

recommended by a handful of reformers, but a solution that proved impossibly elusive.[18]

Responses to the rebellion in America

The fighting that erupted in the colonies in April 1775 made discussions of imperial reform moot. The *Freeman's Journal* had anticipated that confrontation months before it actually occurred in Massachusetts and it did not condemn the Americans as rebels once it did. 'Whatever step they take is critical', the paper sighed before war broke out, because 'they have no choice but of *freedom* and *slavery*'.[19] This echoed the same emotionally charged language that colonial newspapers used in supporting resistance. 'The innocent *blood* of our suffering brethren in *America* which has been shed in the *defence* of their *rights* and freedom, calls aloud to *us* for revenge', urged the editors after word of the skirmishing at Lexington and Concord reached Dublin.[20]

The Continental Congress in Philadelphia did what it could to encourage friends abroad to pledge more than just moral support. One of the appeals that it sent out to other parts of the empire in the summer of 1775 was addressed to the people of Ireland. It accused Westminster and the North ministry – though not George III himself – of a conspiracy to subvert American liberties. Speaking to the Irish as 'friends and fellow-subjects', Congress ticked off a litany of grievances as it derided Westminster while carefully excluding Irish politicians from any criticism. 'Your parliament had done us no wrong'; just the opposite, the address continued flatteringly, 'you had ever been friendly to the rights of mankind, and we acknowledge, with pleasure and gratitude, that y*our* nation has produced patriots, who have nobly distinguished themselves in the cause of humanity and America'.[21]

But if members of the Continental Congress were hoping for formal recognition by the Irish parliament, they were soon enough

---

18. See, e.g., Thomas Pownall, *The Administration of the British Colonies* 5th edn, 2 vols (1774), the last revised edition and the culmination of tortuous arguments Pownall had been making for more than a decade. G.H. Guttridge, 'Thomas Pownall's *The Administration of the British Colonies*: the six editions' *WMQ* 3rd series, 26 (1969), pp. 31–46.
19. *Freeman's Journal*, 18 Aug. 1774.   20. Ibid., 17 June 1775.
21. Worthington C. Ford, ed., *The Journals of the Continental Congress* 34 vols (Washington, DC, 1904–37), ii, p. 214. 28 July 1775.

disappointed. Townshend's replacement as lord lieutenant, Simon, Earl Harcourt, had painstakingly rebuilt Castle power, including comfortable majorities in both Lords and Commons. He realized that the Patriots in both houses were sympathetic to the American cause and were awaiting their chance to condemn Britain's use of force in the colonies. Concern over what the Patriots would do must have weighed heavily on him as he prepared to open a new parliamentary session in October 1775 with the traditional speech from the throne, when he spoke as if he were the king himself. Knowing that he was taking a political risk, he delivered an address affirming efforts to quell the American 'rebellion'. Opposition leaders tried to push through a response to his message that registered their disapproval. Using language similar to that of their colleagues in the House of Commons, the Patriots in the Lords expressed their 'utmost concern' over 'the unhappy differences' between the Westminster parliament and the American colonies 'which are now grown to such a Height, as to threaten consequences fatal' to the empire. They therefore asked that the fighting 'be terminated without further Effusion of Blood'.[22] The resolution of the House of Commons went even further, calling on George III to champion 'conciliatory and healing Measures for the Removal of the Discontents which prevail in the Colonies' and to stop those men of 'mistaken Ambition' who 'continue to foment Disorders in that Country'.[23]

The Patriots were strong enough to carry the debate over Harcourt's address from the throne into a second day, but they lacked the numbers to prevail in passing their resolutions. Outvoted by a margin of nearly two to one in the lower house and by an even larger majority in the upper chamber, the Patriots were defeated and both the Lords and Commons gave their assent to Harcourt's address. Publicly, Harcourt left the impression that the outcome had never been in doubt. Justifying his actions to Whitehall, he privately reported that 'I saw the moment approaching' when the American question 'would have been pressed upon me by the Opposition to the King's Government in this Country, who were dayly gaining Strength upon this Ground'. With the convening of a new session he believed that the time had arrived when 'we should declare to the lower orders of People, through their Representatives in Parliament, the just Sense that we entertained of this unnatural

Rebellion'.[24] Given the satisfactory outcome, London was pleased and Harcourt was ecstatic. He saw this success as the greatest accomplishment of his political career. Parliament's decision the very next month to detach 4000 troops from the Irish military establishment for service in America only added to his sense of satisfaction. Patriots in both houses objected vehemently to sending soldiers, as George Ogle grumbled in the Commons, 'to cut the throats of their American brethren',[25] but to no avail. The Patriots were once again comfortably defeated by the Court side. This ended any attempt to align the Irish parliament with the American side.

Although Irish Patriots never abandoned their sympathy for the American cause, within a year of this defeat in parliament they recognized that the Americans were moving down a path they did not wish to take. The publication of Thomas Paine's *Common Sense* (1776) gave fair warning of what was to come. Irish supporters of American resistance had denied that armed resistance was the first step towards revolution – as, indeed, had the Americans themselves. When copies of *Common Sense* began to turn up in Ireland by the spring of 1776, the *Freeman's Journal* did not treat Paine's tract as a valid expression of American attitudes or ambitions. None the less, the Continental Congress eventually embraced the logic of revolution and agreed with the condemnation of crown and empire articulated so forcibly by Paine. The Declaration of Independence of 4 July 1776, which circulated in Ireland before the end of the summer, served official notice on Britain that rebellious Americans had at last been transformed into revolutionaries. The colonists now sought political independence rather than simply imperial reform. Moreover, they not only denounced George III as a bad king, they renounced monarchy altogether and embarked on an experiment in republicanism. Irish Patriots were not interested in following their lead.

Neither the Irish Patriots nor the American protesters before 1776 had made a sharp or consistent distinction between constitutional liberties and natural rights. They had conflated them in their polemics. For Americans, the difference only became clear after the Declaration of Independence, when they left behind their quest for guaranteed and secure rights in the empire. Irish Patriots, in contrast, continued to work within the British constitutional tradition.

24. PRO, State Papers (Ireland), 63,449, fos 87–8. Harcourt to the Earl of Rochford, 11 Oct. 1775.
25. Peter Force, ed., *American Archives* 9 vols (Washington, DC, 1937–53), 4th series, iii, p. 1645.

Nevertheless, when they failed to gain their rights, as they perceived them, they moved to higher notions of fundamental law – to what was intended under the constitution extended to them by Henry II, and to what all men were entitled to through divine ordination as well as natural rights. The line separating these various sources of liberty was indistinct, as was the understanding of what the unwritten British and Irish constitutions contained. Not only was the meaning and existence of fundamental law in doubt among British jurists and parliamentarians, but those who believed in its existence did not necessarily agree with the interpretations of it as offered by Irish constitutionalists who attempted to resurrect the proto-nationalist arguments of earlier writers such as William Molyneux.

Change over time had complicated the search for rights on both sides of the Atlantic. It was difficult for Molyneux and the constitutional advocates who followed him to argue persuasively that Henry II had extended to Irishmen the full rights of Englishmen, including the right to their own parliament, because those rights had not even been clearly extended to all Englishmen in the eighteenth century. American Patriots had read their colonial charters to mean that they too were entitled to the full and equal rights of Englishmen. But London's interpretation of what the rights encompassed clearly differed from theirs. Even when British imperialists could agree that colonial legislatures were an extension of the rights of legislation and representation, they could disagree violently over what those colonial legislatures had the authority to do. In both Ireland and America the questions of original intent and past practice as precedent were virtually impossible to answer. Consequently, instead of bringing greater clarity, the search for rights further muddied already murky questions. That search would ultimately take disgruntled Americans out of the empire. Nevertheless, even as late as 1776, most rebellious Americans wanted to believe that their disputes with Britain could be resolved within the empire. Thereafter, they could not sustain that belief, but Irish Patriots could. Irish Patriots were able to reconcile themselves to political existence within the empire, but American revolutionaries could not. For the moment, at least, difference proved more important than similarity; a reminder that political ideology is best studied within a social context. Though Irish Patriots could sympathize with their American cousins, they could not truly empathize with them. As the American War revealed, their circumstances had never really been the same.

Horace Walpole, like so many others in England, America and even Ireland, misread Irish affairs. Believing early on that the conflict begun in America would spread to Ireland, he repeated the rumour that Ireland was 'America mad'.[26] Later, after it became obvious that Irish Patriots would not seek independence, he expressed wonderment. Whereupon one of his correspondents, Lord Hertford, a former lord lieutenant, scoffed that too much had been made of any supposed similarities between Ireland and the American colonies. 'They appear to me from their constitution and formation to be very different', he told Walpole.[27] Hertford did not elaborate. That Ireland and America were different was to him a self-evident truth needing no further explanation. He evidently saw things that eluded contemporaries like Walpole, things that have even eluded some later historians.

Perhaps the most important difference between Ireland and the American colonies is also the most basic: sheer distance from Britain. Proximity and distance played crucial roles in how Ireland and the American colonies evolved, and in how they were treated by imperial authorities. America was several thousand miles and over a month away; Ireland, not even a full day's sail, was nearly visible from Wales. As a correspondent of the then lord lieutenant, the Duke of Rutland, would put it soon after the American War ended, 'Ireland is too great to be unconnected with us, and too near us to be dependant on a foreign state, and too little to be independant.'[28] For Rutland, as for Hertford, such sentiments were indisputable truths. These men also understood that distance alone was not the sole determining factor in the imperial relationship. Otherwise, by that logic all of Britain's overseas colonies should have revolted. No, what mattered was how proximity had helped shape Irish society.

The Ireland of the age of the American Revolution was dominated by a ruling elite dependent on Britain for its continuing power. Anglo-Norman lords from the reign of Henry II had been followed by successive waves of other adventurers who crossed St George's Channel. They never completely remade Ireland in their own image, but they did place their stamp on the island. Anglicized

---

26. W.S. Lewis, ed., *Horace Walpole's Correspondence* 48 vols (New Haven, CT, 1937–83), xxxii, p. 296. Walpole to Lady Ossory, 25 June 1776.
27. Ibid., xxxix, p. 396. Lord Hertford to Walpole, 6 Nov. 1782, replying to Walpole's letter of 30 Oct.
28. HMC, *Rutland MSS* 4 vols (1888–1905), iii, p. 155. C.T. Greville to Rutland, 3 Dec. 1784.

in fits and starts, Gaelic and Catholic Ireland had been brought to heel by the eighteenth century. The ruling elite – or the Anglo-Irish Protestant ascendancy, as it was coming to be called by the later eighteenth century – was drawn from a small segment of the island's 3 million or so inhabitants. The vast majority of the Irish – two thirds and more of the whole population – remained Catholic. The rest were Protestants, but a fair number of them – perhaps even half of the total number of Protestants – were Dissenters from the Church of Ireland. Catholics and Protestant Dissenters both suffered social liabilities because of their religious beliefs, as sectarianism continued to divide the peoples of the island. They could neither vote nor hold political office. Penal laws had kept practising Catholics out of the Irish House of Commons soon after the Glorious Revolution and unable to exercise the franchise for decades after 1728. But their differences with the ruling elite were as ethnic as they were religious; they were divided, if not literally by blood, then in their sense of cultural identity. Many Irish Catholics, especially those in the outlying districts of Connacht and Munster, still spoke Gaelic and resented the ruling elite as descendants of invaders and conquerors. Others had been more Anglicized, spoke English and even practised trades that in theory were closed to them by the penal laws, but they looked forward to the day when Catholic power would be restored. In the 1770s they sought no violent overthrow of their Protestant masters. Instead, they were willing enough to submit to Dublin Castle and London if by that token of good faith they could hope for an easing of the many legal restrictions that confined them.

None the less, Anglo-Irish leaders could never feel too secure. They might refer to themselves as the true 'Irish nation' and deny that they were only the heads of a garrison state, but they could not help looking over their shoulders at a politically disfranchised majority, especially as the Protestant Dissenters too, who were mainly located in Ulster, also resented their political ascendancy. Even parliamentary Patriots did not push their grievances against Dublin Castle or Whitehall and Westminster too far. They protested against the commercial restrictions on Ireland's trade and they resented the presence of troops in Ireland that they could scarcely call their own. And yet they understood that they might some day need those troops to preserve the Anglo-Irish Protestant ascendancy. This point was underscored in the American revolutionary era by violent disturbances in the countryside provoked by Whiteboys in the south and Oakboys and Steelboys in the north; disturbances that reflected deep social tensions as well as marked religious divisions. By the same token, the Anglo-Irish elite understood that the laws governing trade could stimulate as well as inhibit commercial activity: if woollens had suffered a decline because of them, linens had flourished.

An Irish lord lieutenant was placed in a much stronger political position than any royal governor on the North American mainland. Governors were often themselves colonists. Even when they were sent out from Britain, they were not drawn from the most important ranks of political society. A lord lieutenant, by contrast, was selected from the peerage and tried to act in concert with the British government in Whitehall. He did not move in the highest policy-making circles – his was not a cabinet-level post – but he was much closer to the political centre than any American governor. Once in Ireland he could wield considerable power. He had substantial crown patronage to dispense, in the form of places, pensions and peerages, that no American governor could hope to match. Moreover, the electoral system that supplied representatives to the Irish House of Commons, with its restricted franchise and a powerful role for aristocratic borough patrons, made it easier for him to secure majority support and to manipulate the legislative process, and also made him less dependent on public opinion. Members of the Irish parliament understood this all too well.

The Anglo-Irish, then, were tied to Britain in ways that Americans were not. But if Ireland stood as an example of how the reciprocal empire could work, it was not simply because the Anglo-Irish needed help from Britain. There was more involved than mere dependence. Members of the Anglo-Irish elite had much stronger filial ties with Britain. Some of them owned land in England; even more Englishmen were absentee landlords in Ireland. Some members of the Irish parliament also sat at Westminster and even more Englishmen held Irish titles. Still more Anglo-Irishmen had social connections with the English, either through marriage or holidays spent in Bath or the English countryside. Few Americans could boast such strong social ties. And while many American leaders before 1775 professed a great love for and attachment to the British constitutional tradition, perhaps it was not quite as real to them as it was for the Anglo-Irish. Only a handful of Americans studied at one of the Inns of Court in London. By contrast, all Irish barristers were supposed to spend at least one term there. Many of those barristers thereafter took seats in the Irish House of Commons.

Impact of the American War

These differences aside, there were some similarities and some tendencies that American revolutionaries and Irish Patriots shared. One was their concern with fundamental law and their couching of commercial and political protests in that language; the other, which to some extent flowed from their preoccupation with fundamental law, was their attempt to mobilize the public and use the violated rights of the people as the ultimate justification for their opposition to British involvement in their affairs. That Anglo-Irish Patriots did not advocate revolt or launch a war for independence does not mean that their pursuit of those political rights – at least for the ruling elite – was any less sincere than that of revolutionary Americans. The Irish parliament had claimed legislative autonomy as early as 1460 and Molyneux's *Case* essentially reaffirmed arguments that had been made periodically ever since. The American crisis gave them the opportunity and the excuse to resurrect those claims.

Hence the position taken in 1779 by Charles Francis Sheridan in his *Observations* on William Blackstone's *Commentaries*. Sheridan, an Irish MP, knew Molyneux's *Case* and agreed with what he read there. Even so, he turned more to political philosophy than to history, concluding that it would be better to discredit Blackstone's general views before turning to what the famous jurist had written about Ireland's place in the empire. Blackstone, charged Sheridan, was inconsistent, asserting that parliamentary power in Britain was irresistible and absolute in one part of his work and upholding the idea of immutable and inalienable rights derived from God and English history in another. All Englishmen, Sheridan countered, were entitled to certain inherent, inalienable rights; rights that were originally a gift from God, present in nature, and reinforced by positive law – witness Magna Carta and the 1689 Bill of Rights. Together these sustained England's sacred, inviolable constitution, a constitution based on fundamental law beyond the reach of any government. 'The King, Lords, and Commons, are *not* the constitution, they are only the *creatures* of the constitution', he insisted. To the extent that Blackstone had misled the public about that relationship, English liberty lay imperilled and the empire exposed. Such foolish ideas had already led to the American uprising:

> But as Great Britain has still remaining some *other* dependencies, *one* of which particularly suffers very severely from the narrow illiberal system of policy, which, with respect to that unfortunate country, has

long marked and disgraced the councils of this kingdom, for the sake of those dependencies alone, without in the least alluding to America, I think it highly requisite that juster notions concerning the nature of liberty; more accurate ideas respecting the principles of the constitution, and particularly with regard to the extent of the *power of parliament*, should prevail in Great Britain, than those, the artful propagation, and inconsiderate admission of which, have already cost us thirteen provinces.[29]

Sheridan was himself being 'artful', his American allusions intended as a warning to Whitehall and Westminster that they teetered on the edge of even greater disaster. Here again, he determined, the prevailing Blackstonian view was at fault. Parliament reigned supreme over the empire, Blackstone had contended, and Ireland was 'a dependant, subordinate kingdom'. Consequently, 'the king's majesty, with the consent of the lords and commons of Great Britain in parliament, hath power to make laws to bind the people of Ireland'.[30] Though the 1720 Declaratory Act, which Blackstone cited, gave credence to his assertion, Sheridan dismissed it as unconstitutional and unjust. To be just the empire had to be free, and to be free it had to be construed as a federation of equals united under the crown, each country within that federation entitled to its own independent legislature. By right, the Westminster parliament could only wield power entrusted to it by the people of Britain. It could not legitimately 'exercise any act of authority over the people of other communities, who have *not* entrusted [it] . . . with any power, but have on the contrary delegated their power to trustees of their *own chusing*' – namely, to Ireland's own parliament. This, concluded Sheridan, was Ireland's 'political creed'.[31]

Unlike Molyneux, Sheridan did not suffer official censure for putting his opinions in print. Times had changed, in both England and Ireland, and for that the Irish could thank the Americans. The rebellion in America that became a revolution had in turn become a great power conflict. Britain found itself almost alone, with France allied with the Americans, Spain about to enter the war alongside France, and the Dutch Republic drifting in the same direction. Anglo-Irish Patriots took heart and held fast, while politicians at

---

29. Charles Francis Sheridan, *Observations on the Doctrine Laid Down by Sir William Blackstone, respecting the Extent of the Power of the British Parliament, particularly with relation to Ireland* (Dublin, 1779), pp. 29–30.
30. William Blackstone, *Commentaries on the Laws of England* 4 vols (Oxford, 1765–9), i, pp. 98, 101.
31. Sheridan, *Observations*, pp. 61–2, 81.

Westminster relented. If the French entry into the conflict made it easier for Patriots to rally behind London, London's last-ditch attempt, through the Carlisle Commission, to woo Americans back into the imperial fold, while keeping the Irish Patriots at arm's length, proved infuriating. What began as a Patriot campaign to revise Poynings' Law escalated into a crusade to force a repeal of the 1720 Declaratory Act and formal recognition of Irish parliamentary independence.

Britain had shown a willingness to placate Ireland with commercial concessions even before France entered the fray. An embargo on trade with the rebellious colonies, proclaimed by Harcourt early in 1776, may have been a political necessity, but it further disrupted an already unsettled Irish economy. The linen business had suffered because of the fighting and the purveyors of other commodities, now restricted to certain ports within the empire, suffered a similar decline. Echoing complaints that the Americans had previously made about the Navigation Acts as applied to them before the shooting started, disgruntled Irishmen contended that they were paying too high a financial price for their place in the empire. 'As *England* and *Ireland* are one dominion, though two kingdoms,' complained one pamphleteer, 'it is the greatest absurdity imaginable to suppose, that what injures a part, can benefit the whole.'[32] He and others argued that restrictions on the provision trade in the previous century had driven up the price of beef in England, while depriving Irish landowners of their livelihood. The Wool Act had been no better; not only did it cost many law-abiding Irish their livelihood, it furthered an enclosure movement in England that pushed tenant farmers off the land and caused the less scrupulous in England and Ireland to become smugglers. When Irish protesters – including, interestingly, John Hely-Hutchinson – called for free trade, what they really wanted was an altering of the mercantilist system to allow more equitable Irish participation.[33]

Whitehall and Westminster eased some of the commercial restrictions, hoping that the Irish would be mollified. As these resolutions were working their way through the British House of Commons, Lord North begged the Earl of Buckinghamshire, Harcourt's successor as lord lieutenant, to keep the Irish Patriots in line. 'Unless the Irish appear satisfied, & willing to shew their regard for Gt Britain, I am undone', a worried North informed the earl. He feared

32. James Caldwell, *An Enquiry* (1779), p. 15.
33. [John Hely-Hutchinson,] *The Commercial Restraints of Ireland* (Dublin, 1779).

that 'a fatal quarrel will ensue, between the two countries'.[34] North exaggerated, but he was not being paranoid. Commercial complaints could lead into political minefields, as North well knew, and he had already been warned that leaders of the Irish parliamentary opposition intended to press forward and raise constitutional issues. An Irish barrister, Francis Dobbs, had in fact sent him a public letter that confirmed his apprehensions. Condemning North for treating commercial relief as a generous concession rather than a proper recognition of Irish rights, a matter of political expediency rather than of constitutional principle, he demanded repeal of the 1720 Declaratory Act. Ireland, he proclaimed, was a kingdom entitled to its own sovereign legislature. In the past Ireland's leaders may have acquiesced in Westminster's unconstitutional claims, but that did not justify these claims: precedent could not override first principles: 'I do not deceive you when I say, we are attached to England, and seek a connection with her, in preference to the rest of mankind.' Nevertheless, Dobbs cautioned, 'my Lord, our first attachment is to FREEDOM, and every other is a secondary consideration'.[35] Trying to nudge North's ministry into action, another pamphleteer urged that 'it would be singular enough if the same period which established American independence, shall be found to have destroyed the usurpation of the British Parliament over the legislative rights of Ireland'.[36]

Demands for an independent Irish parliament grew louder, inside Parliament House and out as both the Irish Patriots and the newly formed companies of Irish Volunteers pressed for constitutional reform. Administration men found it first difficult, then impossible, to stem the rising political tide. Resurgent Patriots, this time following the lead of Henry Grattan, increased their ranks, gradually cowed their opponents and eventually secured their greatest political triumph, with the backing of the Volunteers. Grattan, a protégé of the Earl of Charlemont, had taken his seat in the Irish Commons in 1776 as one of the MPs for Charlemont's home borough of Charlemont. Educated at Trinity College, Dublin, before passing on to the Inns of Court in London, he had never really intended to practise law. He spent less time at the Middle Temple than he did in the galleries of the House of Commons at Westminster. There he experienced a political epiphany. As he would later reminisce:

---

34. BL, Add MS 34,523, fo.329. North to Buckinghamshire, 9 Dec. 1779.
35. Francis Dobbs, *A Letter to the Right Honourable Lord North, on his Propositions in favour of Ireland* (Dublin, 1780), p. 13.
36. [Joseph Pollock,] *Letters of Owen Roe O'Nial* (Dublin, 1779), p. 19n.

When I went to London to the Temple, the first person I heard speak was George Grenville. He talked of American taxation, and of the indisputable law of the realm that gave that right; and he extended this to Ireland. It made a great impression upon me, and I felt very much at the time; and I recollect taking great pains to answer him. I wrote a reply, which I thought was very good, and with much care; but it touched every point, except the question: – it stood clear of that. However, this had great effect upon me, and was of much service. It impressed on my mind a horror of this doctrine; and I believe it was owing to this speech of George Grenville's, that I became afterwards so very active in my opposition to the principles of British Government in Ireland.[37]

Grattan may at that time have 'stood clear' of the question – Ireland's legislative subordination to Great Britain – but he would do so no longer. His passion outstripped that of most other Irish Patriots, who shared his opinions but none the less urged him to slow his pace and moderate his tone. He struck administration men with terror because they could sense that they were losing political control as the American War dragged on. North's weakened position in Britain carried over to Dublin Castle and, in the aftermath of the commercial crisis, firm government men began to dread the worst. By the spring of 1780 Grattan made it clear that he would no longer be restrained. Reading the draft of one of his proposed speeches, Sir John Blaquiere, an MP and one-time chief secretary under Harcourt, predicted that 'it is the signal for commencing hostilities'[38] – with the Irish Commons as the field of battle.

The Earl of Carlisle, who followed Buckinghamshire as lord lieutenant, managed to keep the opposition in check through to the end of 1781. Grattan and his colleagues did not prevail until after Cornwallis's defeat at Yorktown and the subsequent fall of North's ministry. Until that point Grattan's group was easily outvoted as the Irish Patriots themselves disagreed over what political course they should take. But Grattan could sense victory in the spring of 1782. Although the new Rockingham ministry, which came to power in March, wanted Grattan to desist, he would not be denied. When a new parliamentary session opened in Dublin the next month he finally succeeded as the Duke of Portland, sent over as the new lord lieutenant, looked on helplessly. At last the Patriots had closed

37. Henry Grattan, *Memoirs of the Life and Times of the Rt. Hon. Henry Grattan* 5 vols (1849), i, p. 136.

38. William Beresford, ed., *The Correspondence of the Right Hon. John Beresford* 2 vols (1854), i, p. 128. Blaquiere to Beresford, 11 Mar. 1780.

ranks, joined by some long-time administration men, all of them backed by the Protestant electorate. Virtually no one – publicly, at least – tried to stop Grattan's move.

In what many listeners considered an oratorical *tour de force*, Grattan reviewed the grievances of his generation of Irishmen and called for imperial reform, with Irish parliamentary independence the heart of his proposal. Westminster must, he proclaimed, repeal the 1720 Declaratory Act and restore the appellate rights of the Irish House of Lords. His own parliament, he added, must revise Poynings' Law to restore legislative initiative. Knowing that negotiations to end the American War had just begun, he chided that 'to acknowledge the independence of America, & not acknowledge the freedom of Ireland' would be 'the disgrace of England'. He intended no criticism of the Americans; rather, he wanted to shame Whitehall and Westminster into abandoning what he condemned as unconstitutional violations of Irish rights and liberties. Speaking in essentially religious language of the need for Ireland's 'redemption' as a 'nation', he simultaneously professed his love for Britain and his attachment to the empire. 'The two Nations naturally form a Constitutional Confederacy. The Crown is one great bond, but Magna Charta is a greater one.' Why? 'Because we could get a King any where, but England is the only Nation, that can communicate to us a Great Charter. This makes England your natural connexion. This makes the King of England your natural King.'[39] Revolutionary Americans had ceased to believe that Britain could preside over an empire of liberty; not so Henry Grattan.

Grattan's motion carried without opposition. Jubilant, Grattan and a procession from the Lords and Commons delivered their resolution to Portland at Dublin Castle. Portland dispatched it to London and within a matter of months Westminster had repealed the 1720 Declaratory Act. The Irish parliament put aside Poynings' Law and dropped the fiction of passing the 'heads' of bills. Henceforth it proposed to draft legislation that it passed along to the lord lieutenant, who in turn forwarded it to London 'without addition, diminution, or alteration'.[40] George III gave his assent to both of these changes and, seemingly, the Irish achieved what the Americans had at one time wanted but could not bring about: a federal empire

---

39. As taken from Grattan's speech of 16 April 1782, Library of Congress: Ireland. Parliament. House of Commons. Debates, 1776–1789, container 10, vol. 26, pp. 81–124; notes attributed to Sir Henry Cavendish, an Irish MP; perhaps the most accurate version of a much-cited speech.

40. [Ireland] *Statutes at Large, 22 George III, c.47.*

on the legislative level. In the middle of all of this, the American revolutionary, James Madison, observed wryly that 'Ireland is reaping a large share of the harvest produced by our labours'.[41] Irish Patriots would not have disagreed. 'It was on the plains of America, that Ireland obtained her freedom', wrote Francis Dobbs in his review of these eventful days.[42]

Dissatisfaction with Ireland's political gains

But how much, really, had changed? Henry Flood led those Irish Patriots who wanted the repeal of the Declaratory Act to be coupled with Westminster's formal renunciation of the constitutional right to pass any such law. Only thus, contended Flood, could Ireland be sure of its legislative and judicial autonomy. Westminster obliged the very next year. Grattan had not thought formal renunciation necessary. Feeling that it would hamper reconciliation between the two kingdoms, he successfully blocked Flood's campaign to make renunciation a formal demand by the Irish parliament. As this dispute made all too evident, the Patriots were a loose coalition at best. While they bickered and split, the administration men regrouped and regained their strength. What is now remembered, misleadingly, as 'Grattan's Parliament' was never really Grattan's to command.

What Irish Patriots had hoped would be a 'final adjustment' of the imperial relationship in 1782 actually resolved little. Parliament had more legislative initiative and gains had been made elsewhere – notably in securing, at long last, a habeas corpus act and judicial posts to be held during good behaviour rather than at pleasure – but the Dublin parliament was hardly 'independent'. The king in council still reviewed all acts coming out of Dublin and only those that received the royal seal became law. The crown still appointed the lord lieutenant and that choice had much more to do with political manoeuvring at Whitehall and Westminster than with the preferences of the Irish parliament. The lord lieutenant still appointed the chief officers of the Irish government and wielded power through the awarding of places and pensions and recommendations for advancements to or within the peerage. Together

41. William T. Hutchinson et al, eds, *The Papers of James Madison* 17 vols (Chicago and Charlottesville, VA, 1962–), iv, p. 432. Madison to Edmund Pendleton, 23 July 1782.

42. Francis Dobbs, *A History of Irish Affairs, from the 12th of October, 1779, to the 15th September 1782, the Day of Lord Temple's Arrival* (Dublin, 1782), pp. 7–8.

the lord lieutenant, the crown and the ministry in London could manipulate the opening and closing of parliamentary sessions, and intrigue to control the proceedings therein.

Events outside parliament proved even more unsettling to those who believed that the basic problems had been solved. Not surprisingly, the frustrations of Irish Patriots in the 1770s paled in comparison to the fears generated in the 1790s. Some of the same men who treated parliamentary independence as an elixir in 1782 therefore reversed themselves in 1800 and voted in favour of parliamentary union with Westminster. Their experience mimicked that of the American revolutionaries who decried strong central government in the 1770s and supported the Articles of Confederation, only to reconsider their views and support the Constitution of 1787. In both cases the quest for an institutionalized form of fundamental law proved elusive. Rights and liberties, many Irish as well as Americans found, could be difficult to define and even more difficult to defend.

Irish Patriots, like American revolutionaries, confronted something more basic still. Their battles to identify and secure fundamental law had been waged in a changing public arena. They had fought to mould and then mobilize 'the people'. In so doing they opened the Pandora's Box of democratic politics. A euphoric Grattan had rhapsodized in April 1782 that 'we are a united land, manifesting ourselves to the world' in 'glory'. Caught up in his rhetorical moment, he had even exclaimed, 'We are no longer a Protestant party oppressing the Catholick party' or 'a Catholick party without privileges, or the hope of privileges'. Celebrating those who had brought the 'nation' to that new, heightened sense of Irishness, he singled out the Irish Volunteers. He went so far as to liken their grand convention at Dungannon just two months before 'to the meeting of the English at Running Mead [Runnymede]', where Magna Carta had been secured.[43] It was an analogy that many of his colleagues in the Irish Commons would have preferred him not to make.

The Irish Volunteers had sprouted spontaneously in 1778, after France had entered the American War and rumours of a possible French invasion had begun to spread around the island. Ireland had no militia forces and nearly half of the regular troops who were usually garrisoned there had been dispatched to America. So

43. Library of Congress, House of Commons Debates, container 10, vol. 26, pp. 87–8, 96. Speech of 16 April 1782.

propertied men had come forward as Volunteers to defend their country. They had formed themselves into military companies and then regiments with their own colours and uniforms. Buckinghamshire, the lord lieutenant, had reluctantly embraced them and even allowed them some access to government armouries: he had little alternative. The rumoured French invasion never materialized and yet the Irish Volunteers did not disband. On the contrary, their numbers increased to well over 50,000 by 1780. What worried Buckinghamshire – and Carlisle, the lord lieutenant after him – was the political rather than the military side of the Volunteer movement as what had started as an armed defence force became an extra-parliamentary pressure group with a political reform programme of its own.

The Irish Volunteers championed the same political and constitutional causes as the parliamentary Patriots; indeed, leading Patriots such as Flood and Grattan and dozens of other members of the ruling elite, including the Duke of Leinster, Ireland's premier peer, became involved. The Volunteers also called for parliamentary independence, with a repeal of the Declaratory Act and a revision of Poynings' Law; they too talked of Ireland as a kingdom entitled to equal partnership, not subordination, in the empire; and they too referred to the Irish as a 'free' people entitled to fundamental rights. At the same time that Grattan had found it impossible to make any headway in parliament, Volunteer meetings had easily carried resolutions demanding all of these claims. Taking a page from the revolutionary American notebook, the Irish Volunteers had pushed for the non-importation of goods from Britain and the stimulation of local industry in order to secure commercial relief in 1779. From there they pressed on to larger issues. Grattan and his colleagues hoped to exploit this mass mobilization to carry their programme through the Irish parliament and to intimidate Dublin Castle and Whitehall and Westminster into meeting their constitutional demands. Their very success then later came back to haunt them.

Grattan may have come to regret his Runnymede allusion. The Volunteers, after all, were not his creation. They were the culmination of a form of popular politics going back at least to the 1740s and the days of Charles Lucas. Lucas, a Dublin apothecary, had spent more time practising politics than he did his trade. By the 1750s he was blending Irish concerns with larger imperial questions, and he was already drawing analogies between the Irish and American situations that anticipated those made later by others. It is quite likely that Isaac Barré, when referring to Americans as 'sons of liberty' during 1765 debates at Westminster on the Stamp Act, had borrowed a phrase that Lucas had used to try to inspire Irish voters.[44] Lucas's prose could be florid, his rhetoric dramatic. Turning to the Pauline epistles, he had admonished the readers of one of his pamphlets to '*Standfast in the* Liberty *wherewith* Christ *hath made you* Free, *and be not again intangled in the Yoke of Bondage*'.[45] Though an ally of the parliamentary Patriots of his own generation and eventually a member of the Irish House of Commons, his agenda had been more ambitious than theirs. True, he addressed many of the same issues, but in addition he had called for parliamentary reform and had characterized members of Commons as 'trustees' of the people, who should consider themselves bound by their electors' instructions. Patriot clubs that formed among middle-class Protestants in the 1750s echoed Lucas. Here was a notion of constituent power that members of the ruling elite rejected and an emphasis on extra-parliamentary politics that they feared.

Later Patriots such as Grattan, who thought that they could control the Irish Volunteers, were as wrong as those who had previously believed that they could keep Lucas in check. Both experienced first-hand the law of unintended consequences. They did not foresee that the populist strain in their own political rhetoric could be expropriated by others, and for more radical purposes. That, too, would eventually be something they shared in common with revolutionary Americans. The movement for rights in the empire in both Ireland and America had included – even depended upon – appeals to people traditionally on the fringes of political life. But talk of fundamental rights in general and of popular sovereignty in particular, combined with new opportunities for participation in public life, had legitimized a new level of popular politics. Thomas Hutchinson did not prove very astute in dealing with his political opponents in Massachusetts. And yet, as his 1772 letter to Hely-Hutchinson reveals, he had some sense of how protest movements could metamorphose into something altogether more radical and political demands could escalate.

For Americans, the transition from first-generation to second-generation leaders in the new nation – from the age of Washington to the age of Jackson – would be unsettling enough; for the Irish,

---

44. *Parliamentary History*, xvi, p. 39. For Lucas's allusion to the sons of liberty, see *The Political Constitution of Great-Britain and Ireland* 2 vols (1751), address iv, p. 26.
    45. Charles Lucas, *Seasonable Advice to the Electors of Members of Parliament at the ensuing General Election* (1760), cover page.

political changes were more unsettling still, and far more difficult to bring about. Grattan had willingly associated with the Volunteers so long as their ambitions complemented his. When they began insisting on parliamentary reform he drew away and was relieved when the movement peaked in 1783 and all but collapsed within two years. The Irish Volunteers themselves could not agree on how far or how hard they should push for political change. Their greatest strength had been among the Protestant Dissenters in Ulster and they could take satisfaction in the 1780 repeal of the Test Act that had kept the Dissenters from voting in elections or holding office under the crown. They divided over the question of advancing the rights of Catholics, however, some wanting to put that issue aside, others wanting to address it directly. A few had even welcomed Catholics within their ranks. None the less, the Irish Volunteer movement remained essentially Protestant and middle-class. Penal laws against the Catholics did begin to ease, though the Volunteers could not take direct credit for that development. Even the United Irishmen of the early 1790s, who regarded themselves as the Volunteers reborn, could not come up with a clear or consistent stand on the Catholic question or decide whether to champion universal manhood suffrage or attempt to bring down the ruling propertied and Protestant elite. Before their proscription in 1794, their republicanism was qualified and they were unwilling to make a clean break with the imperial past. Later, as revolutionaries, they failed utterly. The cause of Irish rights would have to be taken up by others, as the island continued to try to find its proper constitutional place in the British empire.

CHAPTER NINE

The Loss of America

JOHN CANNON

The effect of the loss of the thirteen American colonies upon Britain is one of those deceptively simple historical questions which fragments as soon as we try to think about it. There is the usual difficulty of distinguishing short-term from long-term consequences, the danger of flirting with counter-factual history, which had a brief vogue in the 1970s, or even of drifting into gentle speculation.[1] If Britain had won in 1783, could she have held America during the Revolutionary and Napoleonic wars, or would discontented colonists merely have seized their next opportunity? If a federal solution of some kind could have been found, would it have survived the changing balance of population between Britain and the USA in the nineteenth century, or the growing campaign against slavery, which, after all, brought the United States itself to the brink of disintegration in 1861?[2] If the Thirteen Colonies had remained part of the British empire, would their vast increase in population and wealth have taken place on the same scale? Such questions may help to identify certain factors in the overall situation, but it is unprofitable to pursue them far. The longer the perspective adopted,

1. The champion of counter-factual history in the 1960s was R.W. Fogel, whose views were expounded in 'The specification problem in economic history' *JEcH* 27 (1967), pp. 283–308. The technique was criticized by E.H. Hunt, 'The new economic history: Professor Fogel's study of American railways' *History* 53 (1968), pp. 3–18, and defended in a riposte by G.R. Hawke, 'Mr. Hunt's study of the Fogel thesis: a comment', ibid., pp. 18–23. An interesting comment on counter-factual history in this period of American history is in Robert W. Tucker and David C. Hendrickson, *The Fall of the First British Empire: Origins of the War of American Independence* (Baltimore, MD, 1982), p. 68, n.1.

2. The population of Britain (including Ireland) in 1776 was roughly 12 million: that of the Thirteen Colonies (including negroes) was 2.5 million. The population of the United States passed that of Britain just before the Civil War in 1861 when both were about 30 million.

the more likely it is that the original question will become contaminated or distorted by subsequent developments. This chapter will therefore be confined mainly to the more immediate consequences, while acknowledging that the rise of the United States to the position of perhaps the only superpower in the late twentieth century, together with the global spread of parliamentary institutions and the English language (albeit with an American accent) is one of the most important developments of the modern world.

For many Britons, the loss of the American colonies, after a long and expensive war, came as a devastating blow, heralding national doom. It is understandable that it should be felt painfully by George III, who from the beginning had identified himself with the struggle, had borne the brunt of American propaganda as 'a tyrant, unfit to be the ruler of a free people',[3] and had sought to the end to stiffen the resolve of his ministers. Should America achieve independence, he warned Lord North in June 1779, the West Indies and Ireland would soon follow: 'then this island would be a poor island indeed'. On 3 November 1781, with Cornwallis besieged at Yorktown, the king wrote: 'the die is now cast, whether this shall be a great empire or the least dignified of the European states'; even after Cornwallis's surrender he was unwilling to concede defeat, which must 'annihilate the rank in which this British empire stands among the European states'.[4] Many of his subjects agreed with him. Horace Walpole thought 'we shall be reduced to a miserable little island . . . I see little or no prospect of its ever being a great nation again' and Lord Sandwich was, if possible, even more dejected: 'we shall never again figure as a leading power in Europe, but think ourselves happy if we can drag on for some years a contemptible existence as a commercial state'.[5]

But the king had, after all, been in the eye of the storm, Horace Walpole had a taste for melodrama, and Sandwich was exhausted after years in charge of the navy during these shattering events. Prophets of doom can usually anticipate a good hearing, but there was another side to the picture. A minority of Britons, mainly Dissenters, had believed the war to have been unjust from the start and rejoiced in the success of the colonists: Sylas Neville, who

---

3. Declaration of Independence, 4 July 1776.
4. *Corr. George III*, iv, no. 2649; v, nos 3439, 3501. The king did not know that Cornwallis had already surrendered on 18 October.
5. W.S. Lewis, ed., *Correspondence of Horace Walpole* 30 vols (New Haven, CT, 1937–83), Walpole to H.S. Conway, 3 Jan. 1781; Walpole to Mann, 30 Aug. 1782; *Sandwich Papers*, iv, p. 26, quoted in H.M. Scott, *British Foreign Policy in the Age of the American Revolution* (Cambridge, 1990), p. 338, n.1.

claimed to be a republican, went down to Deptford in 1783 to see the Stars and Stripes flag flying on American ships.[6] Others were preoccupied with their own lives. William Cowper, in his snug retreat at Olney, though distressed at the terms of the peace, admitted that 'I find myself more interested in the success of my early cucumbers'. Parson Woodforde duly noted on 1 December 1781 the surrender at Yorktown, but Norfolk matters interested him more, and his entry continued: 'my people went a-coursing this morning and they brought home a brace of hares, a rabbit and a partridge, which they found in a trap. They saw a great many hares today and had fine sport.'[7]

Abroad, few commentators could conceal their delight at Britain's mortification and their satisfaction that a better balance of power had been restored after her great victories in the Seven Years War. Counting the League of Armed Neutrality, formed under Russian auspices in 1780, more than a dozen European states had been at odds with Britain by the end of the war. Joseph II, prone to disastrous misjudgements, thought that Britain 'had fallen completely and for ever', that she was in the ranks of second-rate powers like Denmark and Sweden, and would finish as a Russian satellite. Frederick the Great, a shrewder observer, believed that Britain had been laid low by corruption, and marvelled at her 'exhaustion and feebleness'.[8]

But it would be wrong to presume that the national mood – if such a thing ever exists – was one of utter despair. The American crisis had been a long time unfolding and many Britons had become exasperated with their colonial brethren. For many years, writers had argued that the separation of America was probable, if not inevitable, particularly after the expulsion of the French from Canada and the Spanish from Florida in 1763 had relieved the colonists from fear of foreign domination. Indeed Johnson, with his usual brutal candour, suggested in 1775 that the British government's best tactic would be to restore Canada to France in order to bring the colonists to heel.[9] The king was not the only one to comfort himself with the thought of 'good riddance' to America:

6. B. Cozens-Hardy, ed., *Diary of Sylas Neville, 1767–1788* (Oxford, 1950), pp. 309–10.

7. J. King and C. Kyskamp, eds, *Letters and Prose Writings of William Cowper* (Oxford, 1981), ii, p. 105, Cowper to J. Newton, 8 Feb. 1783; J. Beresford, ed., *The Diary of a Country Parson, 1758–1802* (Oxford, 1978), p. 175.

8. A. Sorel, *L'Europe et la Révolution Française* 8 vols (Paris, 1885–1904), i, p. 346, quoting A. von Arneth, *Joseph II und Leopold von Toscana* (Vienna, 1872); Scott, *British Foreign Policy*, p. 339.

9. *Taxation No Tyranny*, in D.J. Greene, ed., *Works of Samuel Johnson* (New Haven, CT, 1977), x, p. 451.

'knavery seems to be so far the striking feature of its inhabitants that it may not in the end be an evil that they become aliens to this kingdom'.[10] Nor had the conflict been inglorious. Against France and Spain, Britain had done well. Rodney won a great naval victory off the Saintes in April 1782, in which the French commander, de Grasse, was forced to surrender, and General Eliott, immortalized in Reynolds's painting, had held Gibraltar against a formidable and confident Spanish onslaught. And though Britons had suffered heavy taxation during the war, they had not seen the flower of their youth destroyed as in 1918, or their cities reduced to rubble, as did the Germans in 1945. The family links with America had been weakening for decades as more and more settlers arrived from Germany, France, Switzerland and other parts of Europe. The empire had been valued largely for commercial and military reasons and there was little of the sense of personal loss felt by many people at the collapse of the British empire in the twentieth century.[11]

Political and economic consequences: reform and recovery

The most immediate repercussions were political. Lord North, prime minister for more than twelve years, was forced out of office within three months of Yorktown. Two succeeding ministries, those of Rockingham and Shelburne, disintegrated within a few months, both over the American question; in March 1783 the Fox–North coalition stormed the closet, only to be ejected eight months later over the India Bill; Pitt's government which followed was defeated in the House of Commons time after time. For more than two years Britain was in a state of political crisis, and foreigners predicted civil war or revolution.[12]

The older Whig and liberal historians read far more into this than a mere clash of politicians: it marked, in their view, the end of a system of royal government and a crucial shift towards prime ministerial influence and the supremacy of parliament. Lecky, in his influential *History of England* in 1877 launched a slashing indictment

10. *Corr. of George III*, vi, no. 3978, George III to Shelburne, 10 Nov. 1782.
11. For patterns of settlement, see R.C. Simmons, *The American Colonies: From Settlement to Independence* (1976). John Ehrman, *The Younger Pitt: The Years of Acclaim* (1969), p. 161 suggests that there was little sentiment for empire as such.
12. J.A. Cannon, *Fox–North Coalition: Crisis of the Constitution, 1782–4* (Cambridge, 1969).

of George III: 'It may be said, without exaggeration, that he inflicted more profound and enduring injuries upon his country than any other modern English king. The root of his great errors lay in his determination to restore the royal power to a position wholly different from that which it occupied in the reign of his predecessor.'[13] Reginald Coupland, writing in *The American Revolution and the British Empire* in 1930 turned this into his main theme:

> The fact that the collapse of George III's system of government was due to the 'disgrace and failures' of the American War is one of the most certain facts in history... Not slight nor transient were the immediate effects of the American Revolution on British politics.... The parting gift of the colonists... was to give her a new birth of freedom.[14]

Though Lewis Namier, in the meantime, had destroyed much of the basis of the Whig interpretation, legends are a long time dying, and G.M. Trevelyan, Whig of Whigs, was maintaining the old position as late as 1937:

> It was a matter of great importance that owing to the catastrophe in America the attempt to gain political power for the crown came to an end when it did. If the personal government of George III and his children after him had been protracted into the next century, the democratic and reform movements of the new era, finding themselves opposed by the king as their chief source of conservative resistance, must have become anti-royalist and very probably republican.[15]

One wonders what Lecky could have said *had* he been exaggerating; Coupland's 'certain fact' was a very dubious hypothesis; and Trevelyan's assertion of a deliberate attempt at royal absolutism was derived largely from the credulous and partisan writings of Horace Walpole and Edmund Burke. It would not be easy today to find a single historian who still believed that George III supervised a royalist 'system'. Edmund S. Morgan, in an entertaining 'revision of revisions', commented on the transformation brought about by the Namierite interpretation: 'the righteousness of the Americans is somewhat diminished through the loss of the principal villain in the contest [George III] ... no longer the foe of liberty seeking to subvert the British constitution, but an earnest and responsible

13. W.E.H. Lecky, *History of England in the Eighteenth Century* 8 vols (1878–90), iii, pp. 14, 16.
14. Reginald Coupland, *The American Revolution and the British Empire* (1930), p. 32.
15. G.M. Trevelyan, *The History of England* 2nd edn (1939), p. 556.

monarch, doing his job to the best of his abilities'.[16] It is true that declining support in the House of Commons had forced Lord North to resign (though he was more than anxious to go), but Sir Robert Walpole had been forced out in similar circumstances in 1742 and the enhanced power with which Lecky credited the House of Commons did not enable the majority there to oust Pitt, armed with royal support, in the spring of 1784. The declining influence of the crown was more of a nineteenth-century than an eighteenth-century development, and the problem with George IV, regent 1810–20 and king 1820–30, was not that he hankered after personal monarchy but that he could scarcely be persuaded to exercise and defend those prerogatives that the crown still retained. If there was any diminution of royal interference after 1784, it was that in Pitt George III had found a minister who did not need the constant reassurance that North had sought, that the political waves were running less high, and that the king was older, in less robust health, and more preoccupied with his growing and troublesome family. It does not, however, follow that because the more lurid interpretation of the crisis may safely be ruled out, it was of no consequence at all. To many at the time, a great deal seemed at stake. The king contemplated abdication; Fox declared that it was his hope to stay in office long enough to give a good stout blow to the influence of the crown; and Burke, in the light of the coalition's rout in 1784, insisted that the authority of parliament had been fatally undermined. These were hysterical remarks in the excitement of the moment. The king did not abdicate; Fox did not manage to give the crown a stout blow, though he dealt one to his own career; and Burke had always been inclined to extreme opinions and did not change with the years. The constitution proved flexible enough to take the strain and the outcome was a modest shift in the parliamentary balance – a greater role for public opinion, tighter party organization, renewed emphasis on economical reform – all of them developments dating from before the American conflict. There was little evidence of any desire for fundamental change. Few Britons wished to act on Tom Paine's advice and set up a republic. Instead there was an evident rallying around the throne, which Linda Colley,

16. See articles 1 and 7 in I.R. Christie, *Myth and Reality in Late Eighteenth-century British Politics* (1970); E.S. Morgan, 'The American revolution: revisions in need of revising' *WMQ* 3rd series, 14 (1957), pp. 3–15. Very useful comments on the historiographical influence of Burke and Walpole are by John Brooke in L.B. Namier and John Brooke, eds, *The House of Commons, 1754–90*, 3 vols (1964), ii, pp. 145–53; iii, pp. 596–7.

in an important article, traced to the American War rather than, more conventionally, from the French Revolution.[17] Nor was there any perceptible discontent with aristocratic leadership such as that produced by the disasters of the Crimean War seventy years later. The heroes of the struggle against the Americans – Cornwallis, Eliott, Hood, Howe and Rodney – were given peerages or promotions, and their prestige used to bolster aristocracy, in much the same way as that of Nelson and Wellington was to do twenty years later.

The effect of the loss of America on the 'reform movement' is also hard to establish. It is always hazardous to attempt to isolate one factor in a complex situation. Reform, then and now, is a less clear-cut concept than is often imagined. But in the 1780s we may identify three main strands – the campaign for economical reform and for parliamentary reform; the movement by the Dissenters to widen the scope of religious toleration and secure the repeal of the Test and Corporation Acts; and the launch of the great anti-slavery campaign.

The campaign for economical reform – the abolition of sinecures and the pruning of pensions – undoubtedly received a great boost from the financial hardships of the American War, though it had started before, and in turn it sent the movement for parliamentary reform into orbit. Support for economical reform peaked in the spring of 1780 when Dunning's motion condemning the influence of the crown passed the Commons by 233 to 215 votes, and made an appearance on the statute book in the spring of 1782 when the Rockingham ministry carried three modest reform bills. The campaign for parliamentary reform had a longer life but Wyvill, organizer of the Yorkshire Association, admitted in 1783 that 'peace itself, so desirable, so absolutely necessary for this exhausted country, is more likely to add new obstructions to the work of reformation, than to remove those I have mentioned'. Even though the cause had been taken up by William Pitt, who presented a reform proposal as a government measure in 1785, it was heavily defeated. Ironically the success of Pitt's recovery programme damaged the prospects for his reform bill. In July 1787 Wyvill wrote to him that 'Peace had already lessened in some degree the pressure of calamity . . . as the benefits of your administration are more extensively experienced [the nation] seems more generally disinclined to any

17. Linda Colley, 'The apotheosis of George III: loyalty, royalty and the British nation, 1760–1820', *Past & Present* 102 (1984), pp. 94–129.

great parliamentary change.'[18] Economical reform was a different matter, partly because it did not touch on such profound political and constitutional issues, partly because it could be carried out gradually by administrative action, and it became one of the chief props of Pitt's recovery programme in the 1780s.[19]

It is not clear whether the victory in America did much service to the Dissenters. Soon after the accession of George III there had been indications that the attitude of the Dissenters was beginning to change and that they were becoming less willing to wait patiently for the redress of their grievances. Many of them were greatly encouraged by the example of their American brethren and were perhaps slow to realise how damaging the outbreak of hostilities might be to their cause. It was unfortunate for them that when they had, at last, shaken off their Civil War image as king-killers, they should once more be accused of disloyalty because of their American sympathies. Though they continued to bring forward America as a model after 1783,[20] few of their fellow-countrymen were in a mood to find inspiration in people who had spent seven years ruining their commerce and killing their sons and brothers. Even the mild Cowper confessed that he found it difficult to 'forgive the Americans as I ought. Perhaps I shall always think of them with some resentment as the Destroyers, intentionally the Destroyers of this country.'[21] There was a marked falling-off of interest in America after 1783. Far fewer books or pamphlets on American affairs were printed, and the new American ambassador, John Adams, reported that the United States was regarded with 'contempt' and that there was little willingness to learn from America's example.[22] Nevertheless, Dissenters were greatly encouraged by Jefferson's statute for religious

18. Christopher Wyvill, ed., *Political papers respecting the attempt of the County of York to effect a Reformation of the Parliament of Great Britain* 6 vols (York, 1794–1804), iv, pp. 289, 32–3, Wyvill to Samuel Shore, 27 June 1783; Wyvill to Pitt, 29 July 1787.

19. For economical reform, see 'Economical reform and "The influence of the crown"' in Christie, *Myth and Reality*, pp. 296–310; for parliamentary reform, see J.A. Cannon, *Parliamentary Reform 1640–1832* (Cambridge, 1972). E.C. Black, *The Association: British Extraparliamentary Political Organization, 1769–1793* (Cambridge, MA, 1963) is good on Wyvill's Yorkshire Association.

20. Richard Price, *Observations on the Importance of the American Revolution and the means of rendering it a benefit to the world* (1784). 'Next to the introduction of Christianity among mankind, the American revolution may prove the most important step in the progressive course of improvement . . . it is a conviction I cannot resist that the independence of the English colonies in America is one of the steps ordained by Providence to introduce these times.' A convenient text of Price's pamphlet is in D.O. Thomas, ed., *Richard Price: Political Writings* (Cambridge, 1991), pp. 116–51.

21. King and Kyskamp, eds, *Letters of Cowper*, ii, p. 109, 24 Feb. 1783.

22. Colin Bonwick, *English Radicals and the American Revolution* (Chapel Hill, NC, 1977), p. 171.

freedom, adopted by Virginia in 1786. Richard Price arranged for it to be printed in the *Gentleman's Magazine* for January 1787, with a characteristically sententious commentary. It was 'an example of legislative wisdom and liberality never before known. Had the principles which have dictated it been always acted upon . . . most of the evils which have disturbed the peace of the world and obstructed human improvement would have been prevented.' The following month, the joint committee of the Dissenters resolved to move to parliament for the repeal of the Test and Corporation Acts. Their spokesman, Henry Beaufoy, sensibly tried to demonstrate their loyalty by recalling their steadfast support for the House of Hanover during the Jacobite invasion of 1745, but there were more recent and less comforting examples to hand. Pitt, on whom they had relied, spoke against the motion and it was defeated by 176 votes to 98.[23] Though brought forward again in 1789 and 1790, the third time by Fox himself, the shadow of the French Revolution was beginning to fall across their aspirations. Some of them, Price in particular, were slow to learn from the American War, so strongly praising the French Revolution that new life was breathed into the old charges of disloyalty. Their third appeal was rejected more decisively than the previous two had been, by 294 votes to 105. When Fox urged the example of America, Pitt brushed it aside effortlessly: the circumstances were very different. Repeal had to wait nearly another forty years.[24]

In one respect, the loss of the American colonies did advance the cause of anti-slavery. By removing Virginia and the other southern colonies from the British Empire, it eradicated a group of lobbyists who were bound to offer powerful resistance to abolition. Clarkson himself wrote in 1788 that 'as long as America was our own, there was no chance that a minister would have attended to the groans of the sons and daughters of Africa', and marvelled at the 'wonderful concatenation of events'.[25] But it would be unwise to place too much emphasis on the importance of 1783 in the campaign as a whole, as Eric Williams, in his celebrated book of 1944, was inclined to do.[26] First, though the voice of the southern colonies was no longer heard at Westminster, that of the West Indian lobby remained strong and, supported by merchants in Liverpool, Bristol and London, had an enhanced voice in the diminished empire. Many regarded the West Indies as the last bastion of British

23. *Parliamentary History*, xxvi, pp. 780–832.   24. Ibid., xxviii, pp. 1–41, 387–452.
25. Thomas Clarkson, *An essay on the impolicy of the African slave trade* (1788), p. 30.
26. Eric Williams, *Capitalism and Slavery* (Chapel Hill, NC, 1944).

power, particularly her naval strength, and Lord Sheffield, returned in 1790 as the member for Bristol, argued forcibly in the House of Commons and in the press for retaining slavery. Second, the humanitarian case against slavery had been heard increasingly before the American troubles developed into war. Granville Sharp's *The injustice of tolerating slavery*, based on his chance encounter some years before with a negro slave in London, was issued in 1769; three years later Lord Mansfield's ruling in the Somerset case, in effect, declared slavery illegal in Britain; John Wesley's passionate and influential *Thoughts on the slave trade* was published in 1774, and Samuel Johnson in *Taxation No Tyranny* (1775) had twitted the Americans on their ambivalent attitude – 'how is it that we hear the loudest yelps for liberty among the drivers of negroes?' The period after the peace of 1783 certainly witnessed great strides in organization, but it would be wrong to underestimate the awakening of the public conscience beforehand, as the dreadful case of the Zong trader had shown in 1781.[27] Third, Williams assumed too readily that the secession of the Thirteen Colonies had dealt a mortal blow to the viability of the slave trade: indeed his main argument was that the British had abandoned the trade only after it had ceased to be of profit to them. This was not the case. In Bristol, the period of *maximum* investment in the slave trade was 1788 to 1792: there were fifteen slave voyages from Bristol in 1784, but forty-nine in 1792, based upon an investment in the latter year of £400,000.[28] While it seems unlikely that in Liverpool slavers were making a profit of 30 per cent from 1783 to 1793, it is clear that the trade was flourishing.[29] The best recent assessment of the trade as a whole suggests that more slaves were shipped between 1791 and 1800 than in any other decade – 393,000 and at the high rate of profit of 13 per cent.[30] However one strikes the balance between humanitarian endeavour

27. 132 slaves were thrown overboard from the Liverpool ship to conserve supplies. The matter became public when the insurers refused to pay and a legal action ensued.

28. David Richardson, ed., *Bristol, Africa and the Eighteenth-century Slave Trade to America* 4 vols (Bristol, 1986–96), iv, *The Final Years*.

29. The profit figure was suggested by an 'Eye witness' in 1795 and augmented by Gomer Williams, *History of the Liverpool Privateers and letters of marque with an account of the Liverpool Slave Trade* (1879). For a detailed and realistic estimate, see F.E. Hyde, B.B. Parkinson and S. Mariner, 'The nature and profitability of the Liverpool slave trade' *EcHR* 2nd series, 5 (1953), pp. 368–77.

30. J.A. Rawley, *The Transatlantic Slave Trade: A History* (New York, 1981), gives estimates for the total trade in Table 7.1 and for North America in Table 7.3. He offers some corrections to P.D. Curtin, *The Atlantic Slave Trade* (Madison, WI, 1979). See also Roger Anstey, *The Atlantic Slave Trade* (1975), pp. 38–57; Hugh Thomas, *The History of the Atlantic Slave Trade 1440–1870* (1997).

and economic self-interest, it seems improbable that the loss of the American colonies can have been decisive.

In addition to the usual post-war problems of demobilization, unemployment and crime, the new prime minister in January 1784 faced profound financial problems. He was helped however by the fact that the electoral result in March 1784 was decisive, and though Fox and the opposition remained capable of inflicting sharp defeats on particular issues, the government itself was not in danger. Pitt's first objective was the restoration of financial control and business confidence. The most immediate and daunting problem was the national debt, which had risen from £132 million in 1763 to £245 million in 1783: the mere servicing of the debt took more than half of the government's total revenue. In 1785 Pitt proposed a sinking fund of £1 million p.a. to reduce the debt: to meet the objection that a hard-pressed chancellor of the exchequer might raid the sinking fund, as Walpole had done, it was made inviolable, which created difficulties when war broke out in 1793 and the surplus disappeared. The increased revenue to create the surplus was to be raised by a variety of new taxes, by the reduction in army and navy estimates which peace allowed, and by a careful and sustained scrutiny of public expenditure. By 1793 revenue had risen by £3 million and Pitt had made some progress in debt redemption. Lower tariffs, particularly on tea, and fierce enforcement dealt a heavy blow at smuggling, and within five years the quantity of tea imported legally had doubled. Though there were good and bad years in the 1780s, the strength of the recovery may be gauged by comparing it with the post-war position in the 1760s or the 1810s: the distress of the decade after 1763 had fuelled riots and Wilkism; that after 1815 had contributed to Luddism, the Spa Fields riots and Peterloo. Pitt was also helped by the rise in population, which promoted purchasing power: a British population of 10 million in 1751 had reached 13 million by 1781 and nearly 16 million by 1801.[31] By the later years the outlines of a great industrial transformation were apparent – the achievement of self-sustaining economic growth which statesmen all over Europe had sought for so long. In this sense, the American Revolution and its consequences were swallowed up by the industrial revolution.[32]

31. P. Deane and W.A. Cole, *British Economic Growth, 1688–1959* 2nd edn (Cambridge, 1967); E.A. Wrigley and R.S. Schofield, *The Population History of England 1541–1871* (Cambridge, MA, 1981).

32. The historiographical controversy about the validity of the term 'industrial revolution' has grown tedious. For a succinct and sensible summary, see E.A. Wrigley,

Expansion in trade: 'a matter of astonishment'

These developments in the economic and commercial field confounded the pessimists. There was not merely a swift recovery from the difficulties of the war years but a rapid advance to a position of world dominance. True there had been voices raised in the past to suggest that Britain would be better off without any colonies, but they had not been much heeded. An old school of thought, represented by Samuel Johnson, maintained that they drained the mother country of men and money and consumed the trading advantage in the costs of administration and protection.[33] An emerging school argued the case for free trade. Josiah Tucker, dean of Bristol, had urged the advantage of a separation from the American colonies: their merchants were concerned not with loyalty but profit and would trade wherever it was in their interest to do so. He pointed to the amount of trade with the enemy – France and Spain – which had taken place during the Seven Years War and insisted that they would, under any circumstances, continue to trade with Britain. In 1783 he wrote: 'America ever was a millstone hanging round the neck of this country to weigh it down; and as we ourselves had not the wisdom to cut the rope, and to let the burden fall off, the Americans have kindly done it for us.'[34] Adam Smith, whose free-trade doctrine in *The Wealth of Nations* (1776) was making slow progress against traditional mercantilist and protectionist theories, wrote in December 1783 to William Eden that he had 'little anxiety about what becomes of the American commerce', because it could easily be made up in neighbouring Europe.[35] Nevertheless, negotiators between Britain and America before the treaty of Versailles devoted much time to their future trading relationship, which caused so much trouble that the question was, ultimately, postponed to a separate agreement. The fear of British diplomats was that the

---

Continuity, Chance and Change: The Character of the Industrial Revolution in England (Cambridge, 1988).

33. See J.A. Cannon, *Samuel Johnson and the Politics of Hanoverian England* (Oxford, 1984), pp. 49, 70, 93.

34. Preface to the 1783 edition entitled *Four Letters on Important National Subjects*. His argument had been developed in *A series of answers to certain popular objections, against separating from the rebellious colonies and discarding them entirely* (1776). For Josiah Tucker, see George Shelton, *Dean Tucker and Eighteenth-century Economic and Political Thought* (1981).

35. E.C. Mossner and I.S. Ross, eds, *Correspondence of Adam Smith* (Oxford, 1977), 15 Dec. 1783.

United States would afford favoured-nation status to its allies France and Spain, and that Britain would either find itself totally excluded from American markets or forced to resort to smuggling from Canada and the West Indies. They had some cause for concern. In 1780, when the American envoy Henry Laurens was captured, it had transpired that the Dutch were asking for favoured-nation status as the price for coming to the rebels' assistance.[36]

Before peace had been signed, William Pitt, then chancellor of the exchequer in the Shelburne ministry, introduced a bill proposing reciprocal commercial concessions between Britain and the United States. He is said to have assured parliament that the American plenipotentiaries in Paris had been shown the draft and were 'highly pleased at the generosity of Britain': if he did say that, he had still a good deal to learn.[37] It was too soon, either in domestic or colonial affairs, for handsome gestures. Hotly denounced by Lord Sheffield and others as a gross violation of the Navigation Acts, on which British security had always depended, the initiative foundered with the fall of Shelburne in March 1783.[38] Opinion in Britain hardened, with the Northites in the Fox–North coalition ministry favouring a protectionist approach. An order in council of December 1783 forbade American ships from trading directly with the West Indies, which led in turn to American retaliation and embargoes. Sheffield's hard line received considerable support within the ministry from Charles Jenkinson (Lord Hawkesbury 1796), one of the Northites who had joined Pitt, and who from 1786 to 1804 held the influential post of president of the Board of Trade.[39] Negotiations for some commercial settlement broke down repeatedly until the conclusion of Jay's treaty in 1794.

36. Scott, *British Foreign Policy*, pp. 305–6; Samuel F. Bemis, *The Diplomacy of the American Revolution* (Bloomington, IN, 1957). The Dutch approach was an unofficial initiative by the Amsterdam burgomasters.

37. J. Almon and J. Debrett, eds, *The Parliamentary Register*, ix, p. 501. Debate in committee of 17 Mar. 1783. Sheffield retorted: 'care ought to be taken that the active spirit of liberality, so conspicuous in this instance on the part of Great Britain, did not carry the House much too far'.

38. *Parliamentary History*, xxiii, pp. 602–15, 640–6, 724–8. Sheffield was more effective as a pamphleteer than in the House of Commons, and Edward Gibbon write in his *Memoirs* that his political writings had 'decided the public opinion on the great questions of our commercial intercourse with America and Ireland'. Sheffield's pamphlet on this issue, *Observations on the commerce of the American States* (1783) ran through several editions.

39. Charles R. Ritcheson, *Aftermath of Revolution: British Policy towards the United States, 1783–1795* (Dallas, TX, 1969), pp. 134–5.

Meanwhile, theory had been overtaken by practice, with results so dramatic that the disagreements and vicissitudes seemed of relatively little importance. France and Spain were in no position to challenge Britain's growing industrial power, and attempts by the Dutch and the Swiss to penetrate the American market ended in failure.[40] As early as 1784 British exports to America had recovered beyond the level of the last year of peace, and after that the expansion was extraordinary. By the 1790s the liberated Americans were buying twice as much from Britain as they had done as subjects of the empire in the 1760s. Britain was supplying 90 per cent of America's imports and in 1790 the inspector-general of imports and exports reported to Pitt that 'the vast increase of the Trade of this country since the termination of the last war must be a matter of astonishment'.[41] Even the slave trade to America continued, since South Carolina and Georgia had made it clear that they would not join the proposed union unless their right to import slaves was guaranteed. Not until 1807 – three weeks before the British – did the United States prohibit the trade completely.

In detail, the trading pattern between Britain and the United States is not easy to summarize, since it was affected by occasional diplomatic squalls, particularly over the treatment of the American loyalists, protectionist measures by some individual states, trade cycles, and warfare in other parts of the globe. The increase in trade to America was part of a general improvement in Britain's world trading position. In 1700 exports had been worth £4,303,000, had climbed slowly to £5,111,000 by 1740, risen to £9,503,000 on the eve of the American War, slumped during the war, recovered to £14,921,000 by 1790 and rose to £24,304,000 by 1800.[42] Even the war of 1812 between Britain and the United States hardly affected the pattern, since the New England states disapproved of the conflict and continued their time-honoured practice of trading with the enemy. What so many had predicted as decades of decline and eclipse turned out to be the start of that trading and manufacturing revolution that changed the face of the world. By 1815 the country whose position was said to have been lost for ever was the arbiter of Europe and the leading imperial power.

40. J.B. Williams, *British Commercial Policy and Trade Expansion, 1750–1850* (Oxford, 1972), p. 222, n.6.

41. Quoted by Ehrman, *The Younger Pitt*, p. 163. America had accounted for 5.7 per cent of British exports in 1700–1; 10.6 per cent by 1750–1; 26 per cent by 1772–3; 32.2 per cent in 1798–9. See Table 22 in Deane and Cole, *British Economic Growth*.

42. Dean and Cole, *British Economic Growth*, Appendix 1, pp. 319–21.

Restoring Britain's position in Europe

One of the first tasks of any British government after the war would
be to end the country's diplomatic isolation, since the array of
forces against her in 1783 had become overwhelming. The American
War was the first conflict since 1688 in which Britain had lacked a
major Continental ally to take some of the weight off her shoulders
and distract the enemy. The message was clear. But it would not be
easy to find a reliable ally until Britain could demonstrate some
recovery, since in 1783 she seemed too weak to defend her own
territories, much less give help to others. Fox had hoped to reach
an understanding with Russia and Prussia, but his overtures were
coolly received and he was not in office long enough to approach
any other country. Relief, in the end, came through the Dutch,
whose intervention against Britain in 1780 had been a marked de-
viation from their traditional policy and a disastrous mistake which
led to the decimation of their mercantile shipping and the loss
of the base at Negapatam on the Coromandel coast in south-east
India. The political situation in Holland was extremely volatile,
with a 'Patriot' party, supported by France and much influenced by
the American example, pitted against the Orange party, clustered
around William V. Frederick William II of Prussia, who succeeded
Frederick the Great in 1786, was the brother of the Princess of
Orange and eager to intervene on her behalf. When the crisis
erupted he joined forces with Britain, sent in troops, and the triumph of the Orange party led to the formation of a Triple Alliance
between Britain, Prussia and Holland. Though the objectives of the
alliance were limited and its strength moderate, it marked Britain's
escape from isolation. The crisis also revealed the damage done to
France's position by her over-exertions during the American War:
her military assistance and loans to the Americans, sorely needed in
1779 to prop up a flagging cause, led to financial disaster which, in
turn, brought about the political crisis of 1788. Paradoxically, French
victory in the war proved more debilitating than British defeat.
When in 1790 there was a very sharp confrontation between Spain
and Britain over Nootka Sound on the west coast of North America,
which could well have led to war and had important implications
both for Pacific trade and for Canada's future westwards expansion, France was in no position to fight and urged its Spanish ally to
be conciliatory. Britain's new allies, Prussia and Holland, supported
her, and Spain gave way. Pitt's mortification in 1791 when he challenged Catherine the Great over Ochakov had more to do with his

own over-confidence than any residual British weakness in the aftermath of the American conflict. The French Revolution completed the process of restoring Britain's links with Europe by giving her a central role in the coordination of resistance to French aggression and revolutionary ideology.[43]

The second British empire: India, Canada and Australia

The loss of America in 1783 is sometimes seen as the dividing line between the first and second British empires. But although the concept is a convenient shorthand, there was much greater continuity than it suggests.[44] The second British empire was built around India, but British influence in that country, through the East India Company, had been growing for decades. So had government interference, with Lord North's Regulating Act of 1773 setting the pattern of increasing political control. The dangers to which British possessions were exposed from the French during the course of the American War confirmed the need for further regulation. Fox's India Bill in 1783 did not make the statute book, but Pitt's India Act of 1784 took matters a stage further. The company was brought under a high-powered board of control, the position of the governor-general strengthened, and Dundas, the first president of the new Board, soon established himself as, in effect, secretary of state for India. Trade with India continued to expand and took an increasing share of British commerce, but it was a gradual process, partly because Indians lacked purchasing power, and the result was the persistent export of bullion to close the trade gap. Imports, largely of tea, cotton, indigo, pepper, sugar and silk increased from 13 per cent of total British imports at the beginning of the eighteenth century to almost 25 per cent by the end; exports of tin, woollens and other manufactured goods also took an increased share of Britain's trade, but grew slowly, rising from 2 per cent in 1700, to 8 per cent by 1772, and 9 per cent by 1798–9.[45] In economic terms

43. Jeremy Black, *British Foreign Policy in an Age of Revolutions, 1783–93* (Cambridge, 1994).

44. Vincent T. Harlow, *The Founding of the Second British Empire, 1763–93* 2 vols (1952–64), i, pp. 1–2; Peter Marshall, 'The first and second British Empires: a question of demarcation' *History* 49 (1964), pp. 13–23. The present position is summarized in A. McFarlane, *The British in the Americas, 1480–1815* (Harlow, 1994), pp. 284–5.

45. Deane and Cole, *British Economic Growth*, Table 22, 'Geographical distribution of eighteenth-century foreign trade'. For the product range, see E.B. Schumpeter, *English Overseas Trade Statistics, 1697–1808* (Oxford, 1960).

therefore that 'shift to the East', which some historians have identified, owed little to the result of the American conflict and, even by
the end of the century, was somewhat undramatic in character.

More remarkable was the effect of the war upon Canada, where
the arrival of some 40,000 loyalists, mainly settled in Nova Scotia,
changed the balance of the population, which until the outbreak of
hostilities had been overwhelmingly French. This reinforcement of
settlers devoted to the British crown and embittered at their shabby
treatment by the Americans was of critical importance in enabling
Canada to resist American attempts at conquest in the war of 1812.
The need to conciliate the Canadians in the hope that they would
be persuaded not to throw in their lot with the American rebels
had already shown itself in North's Quebec Act of 1773, which had
taken the unprecedented step of acknowledging the Catholic religion.[46] After the war, the loyalists could hardly be deprived of the
representative institutions they had enjoyed in the American colonies from which they had fled and the French Canadians, still in a
majority, had to be accorded the same privileges. The Canada Act
of 1791 therefore divided the province into Upper and Lower
Canada, each with an assembly and council.[47] Canada was therefore
in the vanguard of a more flexible system of imperial organization
and became in 1867 the first colony to be given dominion status. By
that time its population had reached more than 2.5 million.

Even more dramatic was the populating of a new subcontinent
in the southern Pacific. The circumstances, still debated by Australian historians, suggest how great developments can spring from
minor causes, and how limited the horizons of politicians can often
be. Cook's description of the potential of the region he had visited
in the 1770s, though strongly supported by Sir Joseph Banks, had
not been acted upon. The immediate trigger was an unexpected
by-product of the American War. Between 1718 and 1775 some
50,000 convicts had been transported to America – including Defoe's
fictitious Moll Flanders. There had been considerable resentment
of the practice by many Americans, some of the colonies had pro-
hibited the traffic, and Benjamin Franklin had suggested mordantly

46. Reginald Coupland, *The Quebec Act: A Study in Statesmanship* (Oxford, 1925).
North's concessions raised a storm of protest that he was favouring papists, but
General Carleton, governor of Quebec, gave evidence that there were only 360
Protestants to 150,000 Catholics. Motions to repeal in 1775 were defeated in the
Lords by 88 to 28 and in the Commons by 174 to 86. *Parliamentary History*, xvii,
pp. 1357–1407; xviii, pp. 655–84.

47. John Holland Rose et al., eds, *Cambridge History of the British Empire* 8 vols (Cambridge, 1929–63), vi, pp. 195–200.

that the Americans should send back rattlesnakes.[48] No sooner had transportation ceased after Lexington than British prisons began to fill up. The first reaction to this was to execute more felons and there was a marked increase in the number of death sentences. This caused some slight public concern and in 1777 a new expedient was found in the establishment of prison hulks on the Thames, which soon acquired a reputation for squalor, brutality and vice. One note of cheerfulness amid the gloom of 1783 was the hope of resuming transportation to America, and Lord North and the king sponsored two private enterprise cargoes of convicts. The Americans refused to accept them, the loyalists in Nova Scotia were no more keen than the rebels to take in Britain's unwanted malefactors, and the voyages ended in commercial disaster.[49] As the situation deteriorated and the prison population continued to rise, a committee of the House of Commons considered desperate alternatives. The wildest suggestion, examined with solemn care, was to use the island of Lemane, 'very fine with a great abundance of provisions', 400 miles up the Gambia river in equatorial Africa. The convicts were to be dumped, unsupervised and unvisited, with enough rations to see them through the first six months, and it was assumed that the surrounding natives and crocodiles would discourage attempts to escape. Though as a sociological experiment on the lines of William Golding's *Lord of the Flies* it would have been of interest, even the House of Commons perceived that there might be drawbacks: Sir George Younger remarked, rather sensibly, that 'if the convicts were armed they would probably kill and rob the natives, or if unarmed the natives would kill and rob them'. The Gambia proposal was abandoned in favour of a new scheme to use a strip of territory on the south-west coast of Africa, Das Voltas, sandwiched between Dutch territory at the Cape to the south and Portuguese territory to the north. First reports were most encouraging, 'the soil fertile, productive of the best herbage, abounding with great herds of wild cattle, and with a good and healthy climate'. It would prove an invaluable staging post on the way to India. HMS *Nautilus* was sent out in 1786 to reconnoitre, and duly reported that it had navigated between the 16th latitude and the

48. R.A. Ekrich, *Bound for America: The Transportation of British Convicts to the Colonies, 1718–1775* (Oxford, 1987), pp. 1, 139. A useful summary of the debate on Australian settlement is M. Gillen, 'The Botany Bay decision, 1786; convicts not Empire' *EHR* 97 (1982), pp. 740–66.

49. Ekrich, *Bound for America*, pp. 233–6. For the exchange between the king and Lord North, see *Corr. of George III*, vi, nos 4413, 4414, 4419, 4420.

32nd 'without finding a drop of water or seeing a tree'.[50] It was clear why neither the Dutch nor the Portuguese had troubled to claim it. The region was left unannexed, to acquire in due course the name of 'the skeleton coast' and to become later part of the short-lived German Empire. In desperation ministers remembered the enthusiasm of Cook and Banks, and the king's speech of January 1787 announced that the 'inconvenience' of crowded prisons would be met by transportation to Botany Bay. By the time transportation ceased in 1868, more than 160,000 convicts had been sent to Australia and Norfolk Island, and the total population had risen to well over one million. Australians still discuss to what extent the nature of the original settlement contributed to the national character.[51]

Federalism and free trade

It has been suggested that the experience of the loss of America produced in Britain a fundamental rethinking of possible imperial relationships and moved opinion towards federal solutions.[52] But federalism itself is by no means a simple concept and can take many forms. In essence, it is either a balanced sharing of power between two or more states of roughly equal strength, or a careful delegation of powers from a central authority to subordinate states or regions. The old colonial system was already federalist in this sense since the thirteen legislatures, though unrepresented at Westminster, had considerable powers of their own: had they not, their resistance would have been insurrection rather than a civil war. By 1783 they had already formed themselves into a confederation, though of a loose type, and it would have been exceptionally hard

50. *Commons Journals* 40 (1784/5), pp. 954–60, 1161–4; Gillen, 'The Botany Bay decision', p. 752.
51. A.G.L. Shaw, *The Story of Australia* (1955), pp. 110–11. See also C. Wilson, 'Convicts, commerce and sovereignty: the forces behind the early settlement of Australia', in Neil McKendrick and R.B. Outhwaite, eds, *Business Life and Public Policy: Essays in Honour of D.C. Coleman* (Cambridge, 1986), pp. 79–97. Wilson comments on counter-factual questions in *Australia: The Creation of a Nation, 1788–1988* (1987), p. 4, and on the controversy over convicts on pp. 127–42.
52. Harlow, *Second British Empire*, i, pp. 230–4, 251, 488–9. See also John Norris, *Shelburne and Reform* (1963), pp. 94, 163–7. Coupland, *The American Revolution and the British Empire*, traced the 1926 Commonwealth of Equal Dominions to the experience of losing America: 'the proceedings of 1926 are proof that we have learned the lessons of 1783: the second British Empire, born under black skies in 1783, had come of age in sunshine', pp. 268–9.

to reunite a federated state with a non-federated state. In any case, a more likely British reaction to the bitterness of defeat was that the colonists had been given too much autonomy and that a move towards a more integrated empire was desirable. It is true that Ireland had been granted additional powers under duress in 1782, but many people regretted this, and within eighteen years the Irish parliament had been abolished and Ireland incorporated into the Westminster system. Lord Shelburne, much influenced by Richard Price, talked during the peace negotiations of a 'federal union' as an alternative to independence, but he did not define it and was, perhaps, incapable of doing so; Vincent Harlow, who admired Shelburne, conceded that it was a 'somewhat vague scheme'.[53] Shelburne greatly overestimated enthusiasm for the idea among the Americans, who had scarcely waged war for seven long years in order to embrace re-union. They were however willing to amuse Oswald, Shelburne's negotiator, with amiable exchanges in the hope of winning further concessions, particularly possession of Canada. But the most recent study of the British tradition of federalism hardly glances at the situation in 1783.[54] It is true that the federal character of the United States, especially when strengthened by the new constitution of 1787, attracted some interest, but there was already the example of the Dutch Republic (officially the 'United Provinces'), and America's initial difficulties prompted considerable doubt how the new constitution would work in practice. Indeed, many Britons comforted themselves with the belief that the United States would soon fall to pieces, since at first the new federal government was so weak. The federal constitution for Canada was motivated less by theory than by the need to accommodate two distinct nationalities, British and French, and that of Australia was influenced mainly by the consequences of the distances involved.

If change in imperial policy and organization was slow and largely pragmatic, it is also true that the movement towards free trade was less vigorous than is often suggested. Older historians were so convinced of the superiority of free trade as a principle that they tended to regard it as an indication of human intellectual and even moral progress and to pour scorn on mercantilist and protectionist thinking as pitifully antiquated. Reginald Coupland in 1930 described the triumph of free trade as 'the future challenging the past' – ironically at just the moment that free trade was about to be abandoned during

53. Harlow, *Second British Empire*, ii, p. 784.
54. M. Burgess, *The British Tradition of Federalism* (Madison, NJ, 1995).

the great depression.[55] Free trade is one possible policy in certain circumstances. It suited Britain in the early nineteenth century because of its enormous lead in manufacturing; it did not necessarily suit other countries. The most cogent attack upon free trade as a theory was launched in 1841 by Friedrich List of Würtemberg, who saw it as a weapon of British domination. While not denying that free trade and competition between two countries at the same stage of development must be mutually advantageous, List argued that Britain's aim was 'to monopolize the manufacturing power of the whole world', eradicate German industry and leave her to supply Britain only with 'children's toys, wooden clocks and philological writings'.[56] Indeed, when Britain itself ran into increasing competition in the twentieth century, its belief in free trade faltered.

The effect of the American War upon free-trade theory was by no means decisive. Arguments for, not perhaps free trade but certainly freer trade, had been in circulation well before the American crisis developed: though Adam Smith's *The Wealth of Nations* appeared in 1776, it was based upon lectures delivered at Glasgow twenty years earlier. Shelburne and Pitt, as we have seen, were zealous advocates, but Shelburne was forced out of office before he could do much, and many of Pitt's efforts foundered in the face of protectionist opposition. War does not necessarily produce a generous spirit in the vanquished and many Britons believed that the Americans had been treated too leniently. Attacking Pitt's American Intercourse Bill in 1783, William Eden commented: 'He supposed that his national pride must sink into the sinking pride of the nation; but he was not yet brought so low as to be reconciled to the modern plan of gratuitous and endless concessions.'[57] Eden's friend and correspondent Lord Sheffield waged a lifelong campaign in defence of the Navigation Acts, and intervened in a later debate to protest: 'He had heard no satisfactory argument against considering the Americans at present as a foreign nation, the natural consequence of their asserting independence . . . the country expected the principle of the Navigation act should be kept entire.'[58] His pamphlet *Observations on the Commerce of the American States* attracted much support and Pitt abandoned his measure. A similar fate met Pitt's Irish commercial propositions in 1785, which were so mauled by protectionist lobbies that they could not be

---

55. Coupland, *The American Revolution and the British Empire*, p. 178.
56. Friedrich List, *The National System of Political Economy*, trans. S.S. Lloyd (1916), pp. xl, 297, 106.
57. *Parliamentary History*, xxiii, p. 607.   58. Ibid., pp. 762–4.

carried. The commercial treaty with France in 1786 (negotiated ironically by the same William Eden) is sometimes regarded as an example of free-trade progress. But it originated in France's hopes of breaking into the imperial system operated by the British and was not different in character from previous reciprocal treaties, particularly that between Britain and Portugal, signed as early as 1703. John Ehrman, surveying the whole range of commercial negotiations between 1783 and the onset of the French Revolution, gave a careful warning against interpreting the 1780s as 'the harbinger of a free trade summer: Britain was the great eclectic', each case was considered on its merits, and 'the familiar view of Pitt as a pertinacious advocate of free trade needs to be revised'.[59] The commercial understanding between Britain and the United States in 1794, known as Jay's treaty, has also been hailed as a step forward. It was, in fact, a rather desperate measure intended to prevent war between the two powers over the right of search, which the outbreak of the Revolutionary War between France and Britain had brought once more to the fore. It was limited in scope and Britain's main concession, the admission of small American vessels to direct trade with the British West Indies, was rejected by the American senate as unsatisfactory. American public opinion was extremely hostile to the treaty, complaining that their negotiators had acquiesced in British pretension in the realm of maritime law, and relations soon returned to prohibitions and embargoes. A recent comment describes the treaty as 'making a virtue out of necessity. It was a grudging modification to a system that remained resolutely protectionist in intent, rather than an early sign of a confident move towards free trade.'[60] The systematic dismantling of the British tariff system took place mainly between 1820 and 1849 under the auspices of Huskisson, Peel and Gladstone – rather too late to have been linked directly to the loss of the American colonies.[61]

59. John Ehrman, *The British Government and Commercial Negotiations with Europe, 1783–93* (Cambridge, 1962), pp. 8, 48, 177, 22.

60. P.J. Cain and A.G. Hopkins, *British Imperialism: Innovation and Expansion, 1688–1914* (Harlow, 1993), p. 97. See also Samuel F. Bemis, *Jay's Treaty: A Study in Commerce and Diplomacy* 2nd edn (New Haven, CT, 1962). In the fullest survey of Anglo-American relations after the war, Ritcheson, *Aftermath of Revolution*, p. 17 wrote that 'in judging British policy and the hardheaded empirical men who made it, it seems clear that they served their nation well. Their path was the old and tried one.'

61. Williams, *British Commercial Policy*, part iv, section 2, 'Trends and policies'. The Navigation Acts were not repealed until as late as 1849. See S. Palmer, *Politics, Shipping and the Repeal of the Navigation Laws* (Manchester, 1990), who makes the point that even then repeal was by no means inevitable. Abolition was carried in the House of Lords only by proxy votes, 173 to 163, and it was said that two insane peers voted, one with his keeper in attendance.

Conclusion

For the general British public, the experience of the American War was soon overshadowed by the French Revolution, nearer to hand, more protracted, and far more searching in the questions it posed. America remained longer in the minds of colonial policy-makers and administrators, though the message they drew from it differed greatly. Reginald Coupland, slightly intoxicated in 1930 by the apparent success of Balfour's definition of dominion status,[62] believed that from the disaster of 1783 British statesmen had learned the salutary lesson that British policy towards her remaining colonies must be liberal and generous.[63] Putting aside the question whether any such attitude ever applied in equal measure to the black and white populations involved, Coupland's views greatly overestimated the unanimity of response. There were, at least, two other possible reactions. One, held by many, was that the American colonists had bitten the hand that fed them – that, armed with legal and religious rights and practised in the arts of self-government, they had revolted while the French, Spanish, Portuguese and Dutch colonies, more autocratically ruled, had not: the liberality with which the Americans had been treated had been turned against their benefactors. This point of view was put with characteristic force by Lord Chancellor Thurlow in 1789 when he expressed mistrust of Grenville's proposal to provide Canada with a constitution assimilated as nearly as possible to that of Britain: 'It seems clear that if political liberty, which is the governing principle of our constitution, be established in a colony, the sovereignty which, following that principle, must be established in certain proportions among the people, must be established there; and the immediate effect of that will be an habitual independent attention to a separate interest.'[64]

Thurlow's views cannot be dismissed as either a lone voice or a typically legalistic attitude. The whole gist of C.A. Bayley's recent

62. Balfour's definition, offered to the Imperial Conference of 1926 after complaints from the Canadian prime minister, was that the dominions were 'autonomous communities within the British Empire, equal in status, in no way subordinate one to another in any aspect of their domestic or external affairs, though united by a common allegiance to the crown, and freely associated as members of the British Commonwealth of nations'. The word 'autonomous' avoided the difficult word 'independent'. The declaration was given the force of law by the Statute of Westminster of 1931, *22 Geo.V, c. 4.*

63. Coupland, *The American Revolution and the British Empire*, pp. 268–316.

64. 1/10 Sept. 1789, HMC, *Fortescue MSS,* i, p. 504. There are faint echoes of the controversy in the late twentieth-century debate whether devolution for Wales and Scotland is more likely to promote or retard independence.

survey is that British policy between 1783 and 1820 was authoritarian and heavy – indeed, he refers to the colonies in this period as
'overseas despotisms'.[65] Another reaction was that it did not matter
much either way – that colonies were a transient phase in human
development, and that whether the policy towards them was liberal
and devolutionary or firm and centralized would not greatly affect
the final outcome. If the colonies prospered, they would demand
self-government; if they did not, they were hardly worth keeping
and would be abandoned in a crisis. A surprising exposition of that
view is in Disraeli's letter of 1852 to Malmesbury when he declared
that 'these wretched colonies will all be independent, too, in a few
years, and are a millstone round our necks'. Disraeli's biographers,
clearly embarrassed at so unstatesmanlike an opinion and one at
variance with Disraeli's later imperialist reputation, dismissed it as a
'petulant outburst'.[66] But petulant outbursts can be revealing and,
as we have seen, there were thoughtful pedigrees for Disraeli's view
in those of Adam Smith and Josiah Tucker. In the light of the dismantling of the British empire after 1945, Coupland's confidence –
a mere fifteen years before – seems strange. The Commonwealth
which survives today, including as it does dictatorial regimes and
even countries that were never ruled by Britain, may have its own
meaning and validity, may even be a unique and admirable force in
the world, but it is not an empire in any sense that previous generations would have recognized.

The examples at the beginning of this chapter of falsified pre-
dictions were not intended to lampoon the people who made them.
Some soon perceived the truth. Horace Walpole, who had been
one of the most agitated pessimists, ringing the changes on meta-
phors of doom and eclipse, wrote in 1783 that 'I did not much
expect to live and see peace, without far more extensive ruin than
has fallen upon us'.[67] In any case, prediction is a precarious business; few in 1988 foretold the total collapse of communism a year
later. But they serve as a gentle reminder how difficult it is to read
the future, especially when standing in the middle of dramatic and
disturbing events. A second warning is not to hunt in history for
too many turning-points and watersheds, which often turn out to

65. C.A. Bayley, *Imperial Meridian: The British Empire and the World, 1780–1830*
(Harlow, 1989), particularly pp. 9–10. See also P.J. Marshall, 'Empire and authority
in the late eighteenth century' *JICH* 11 (1987), pp. 105–22.
66. 13 August 1852, W.F. Monypenny and G.E. Buckle, *Life of Benjamin Disraeli,
Earl of Beaconsfield* 6 vols (1910–20), ii, p. 385.
67. Lewis, ed., *Corr. of Horace Walpole*, xxxv, p. 371. Walpole to Lord Strafford,
24 June 1783.

be over-simplifications. Changes are often foreshadowed, causes are intricate and complex, currents have counter-currents, motives are mixed, patterns more varied than at first appears. If there is one conclusion from surveying the consequences of national defeat in 1783, it is perhaps a paradox. The loss of America has often been exhibited as an indictment of the eighteenth-century system, a political failure, and even in Namier's view a failure in the structure of government itself.[68] 'English statesmanship in the eighteenth century', declared the *Cambridge History of the British Empire* magisterially, 'had not been equal to the task of uniting her noblest colonies to the motherland.'[69] If this is fair comment, equity demands that we also place in the scales the remarkable recovery from the vale of despondency and the extent to which what appeared a crushing setback was shrugged off, testimony to the basic stability, resilience and vitality, politically and economically, of Hanoverian Britain.

68. L.B. Namier, *England in the Age of the American Revolution* 2nd edn (1961), pp. 37–41.

69. Rose et al., eds, *Cambridge History of the British Empire*, ii, p. 2. For one of the many later comments that, in the circumstances of the period, a solution acceptable to both sides would have been extremely difficult to find, see 'The spectrum of imperial possibilities: Henry Ellis and Thomas Pownall' in John Shy, *A People Numerous and Armed: Reflections on the Military Struggle for American Independence* (New York, 1976; rev. edn, Ann Arbor, MI, 1990), pp. 35–72.

Further Reading

Unless otherwise stated, the place of publication is London.

General works

Alden, John R., *A History of the American Revolution: Britain and the Loss of the Thirteen Colonies* (1969).

Christie, I.R., *Crisis of Empire: Great Britain and the American Colonies 1754–1783* (1966).

Christie, Ian R. and Labaree, Benjamin W., *Empire or Independence, 1760–1776: A British American Dialogue on the Coming of the American Revolution* (Oxford, 1976).

Cook, Don, *The Long Fuse: How England lost the American Colonies, 1760–1785* (New York, 1995).

Derry, John, *English Politics and the American Revolution* (1976).

Draper, Theodore, *A Struggle for Power: The American Revolution* (New York, 1996).

Gipson, L.H., *The Coming of Revolution 1763–1775* (New York, 1954).

Greene, Jack P. and Pole, J.R., eds, *The Blackwell Encyclopedia of the American Revolution* (Oxford, 1991).

Perry, Keith, *British Politics and the American Revolution* (1990).

Ritcheson, Charles R., *British Politics and the American Revolution* (Norman, OK, 1954).

Ritcheson, Charles R., *Aftermath of Revolution: British Policy towards the United States, 1783–1795* (Dallas, TX, 1969).

Speck, W.A., *British America 1607–1776* (Brighton, 1985).

Thomas, Peter D.G., *Revolution in America: Britain and the Colonies 1763–1776* (Cardiff, 1992).

Tucker, Robert W. and Hendrickson, David C., *The Fall of the First British Empire: Origins of the War of American Independence* (Baltimore, MD, 1982).

Britain and the American colonies

Barrow, Thomas C., *Trade and Empire: The British Customs Service in Colonial America 1660–1775* (Cambridge, MA, 1967).

Beer, George L., *British Colonial Policy 1754–1765* (New York, 1933).

Bellot, Leland J., *William Knox: The Life and Thought of an Eighteenth-Century Imperialist* (Austin, TX, 1977).

Clark, Dora Mae, *The Rise of the British Treasury: Colonial Administration in the Eighteenth Century* (New Haven, CT, 1960).

Dickerson, Oliver M., *The Navigation Acts and the American Revolution* (Philadelphia, 1951).

Greene, Jack P., *Peripheries and Center: Constitutional Development in the Extended Polities of the British Empire and the United States, 1607–1788* (Athens, GA, 1986).

Greene, Jack P. and Pole, J.R., eds, *Colonial British America* (Baltimore, MD, 1984).

Henretta, James A., *'Salutary Neglect': Colonial Administration under the Duke of Newcastle* (Princeton, NJ, 1972).

Hoffman, Ross, ed., *Edmund Burke: New York Agent* (Philadelphia, 1956).

Kammen, Michael G., *A Rope of Sand: The Colonial Agents, British Politics and the American Revolution* (Ithaca, NY, 1968).

Knollenberg, Bernhard, *Origin of the American Revolution, 1759–1766* (New York, 1960).

Koehn, Nancy F., *The Power of Commerce: Economy and Commerce in the First British Empire* (Ithaca, NY, 1994).

Labaree, Leonard W., *Royal Government in America: A Study of the British Colonial System before 1783* (New Haven, CT, 1930).

Leach, David Edward, *Roots of Conflict: British Armed Forces and Colonial Americans 1677–1763* (Chapel Hill, NC, 1968).

Olson, Alison G., *Anglo-American Politics, 1660–1775: The Relations between Parties in England and America* (Oxford, 1973).

Olson, Alison G., *Making the Empire Work: London and American Interest Groups, 1640–1790* (Cambridge, MA, 1992).

Rogers, Alan, *Empire and Liberty: American Resistance to British Authority, 1755–1763* (Berkeley, CA, 1974).

Shy, John W., *Towards Lexington: The Role of the British Army in the Coming of the American Revolution* (Princeton, NJ, 1965).

Sosin, Jack M., *Whitehall and the Wilderness: The Middle West in British Colonial Policy, 1760–1775* (Lincoln, NE, 1961).

Sosin, Jack M., *Agents and Merchants: British Colonial Policy and the Origins of the American Revolution, 1763–1775* (Lincoln, NE, 1965).

Spector, Margaret M., *The American Department of the British Government 1768–1782* (New York, 1940).

Stout, Neil R., *The Royal Navy in America, 1760–1775* (Annapolis, MD, 1973).

Ubbelohde, Carl, *The Vice-Admiralty Courts and the American Revolution* (Chapel Hill, NC, 1960).

Wickwire, Franklin B., *British Subministers and Colonial America 1763–1783* (Princeton, NJ, 1966).

Politicians and parliament

Ayling, Stanley, *George III* (1972).

Ayling, Stanley, *The Elder Pitt* (1976).

Ayling, Stanley, *Edmund Burke: His Life and Opinions* (1988).

Bargar, B.D., *Lord Dartmouth and the American Revolution* (Columbia, SC, 1965).

Brooke, John, *The Chatham Administration 1766–1768* (1956).

Brooke, John, *King George III* (1972).

Brown, Gerald S., *The American Secretary: The Colonial Policy of Lord George Germain,1775–1778* (Ann Arbor, MI, 1963).

Bullion, John L., *A Great and Necessary Measure: George Grenville and the Genesis of the Stamp Act* (Columbia, MO, 1982).

Christie, Ian R., *The End of Lord North's Ministry 1780–1782* (1958).

Christie, Ian R., *Myth and Reality in Late Eighteenth-Century British Politics* (1970).

Cone, Carl B., *Burke and the Nature of Politics: I, The Age of the American Revolution* (Lexington, KY, 1957).

Coupland, Reginald, *The American Revolution and the British Empire* (1930).

Donoughue, Bernard, *British Politics and the American Revolution: The Path to War, 1773–75* (1964).

Forster, Cornelius P., *The Uncontrolled Chancellor: Charles Townshend and His American Policy* (Providence, RI, 1978).

Guttridge, G.H., *English Whiggism and the American Revolution* (Berkeley, CA, 1966).

Hoffman, Ross J.S., *The Marquis: A Study of Lord Rockingham, 1730–1782* (New York, 1973).

Langford, Paul, *The First Rockingham Administration 1765–1766* (Oxford, 1973).

Lawson, Philip, *George Grenville: A Political Life* (Oxford, 1984).

Namier, L.B. and Brooke, John, *Charles Townshend* (1964).

Norris, John, *Shelburne and Reform* (1963).

O'Gorman, Frank, *The Rise of Party in England: The Rockingham Whigs 1760–82* (1975).

Pares, Richard, *King George III and the Politicians* (Oxford, 1953).

Peters, Marie, *The Elder Pitt* (1998).

Rodger, N.A.M., *The Insatiable Earl: A Life of John Montagu, 4th Earl of Sandwich* (1993).

Thomas, Peter D.G., *British Politics and the Stamp Act Crisis* (Oxford, 1975).

Thomas, Peter D.G., *Lord North* (1976).

Thomas, Peter D.G., *The Townshend Duties Crisis* (Oxford, 1987).

Thomas, Peter D.G., *Tea Party to Independence* (Oxford, 1991).

Valentine, Alan, *Lord George Germain* (Oxford, 1962).

Valentine, Alan, *Lord North* 2 vols (Norman, OK, 1967).

Whiteley, Philip, *Lord North: The Prime Minister Who Lost America* (1997).

Popular politics

Black, E.C., *The Association: British Extraparliamentary Political Organization, 1769–1793* (Cambridge, MA, 1963).

Bonwick, Colin, *English Radicals and the American Revolution* (Chapel Hill, NC, 1977).

Bradley, James E., *Popular Politics and the American Revolution in England: Petitions, the Crown and Public Opinion* (Macon, GA, 1986).

Bradley, James E., *Religion, Revolution and English Radicalism* (Cambridge, 1990).

Brewer, John, *Party Ideology and Popular Politics at the Accession of George III* (Cambridge, 1976).

Butterfield, Herbert, *George III, Lord North and the People* (1949).

Christie, Ian R., *Wilkes, Wyvill and Reform* (1962).

Dickinson, H.T., *The Politics of the People in Eighteenth-Century Britain* (1994).

Grant, Alfred, *Our American Brethren: A History of Letters in the British Press during the American Revolution 1775–1781* (Jefferson, NC, 1995).

Jacob, Margaret and Jacob, James, *The Origins of Anglo-American Radicalism* (1984).

Lutnick, Solomon, *The American Revolution and the British Press 1775–1783* (Columbia, MO, 1967).

Marshall, Peter, *Bristol and the American War of Independence* (Bristol, 1977).

Money, John, *Experience and Identity: Birmingham and the West Midlands, 1760–1800* (Manchester, 1977).

Pocock, J.G.A., ed., *Three British Revolutions: 1641, 1688 and 1776* (Princeton, NJ, 1980).

Reich, Jerome R., *British Friends of the American Revolution* (Armonk, NY, 1998).

Sainsbury, John, *Disaffected Patriots: London Supporters of Revolutionary America* (Kingston and Montreal, 1987).

Thomas, Peter D.G., *John Wilkes: A Friend to Liberty* (Oxford, 1996).

Wilson, Kathleen, *The Sense of the People: Politics, Culture and Imperialism, 1715–1785* (Cambridge, 1995).

Ideology and propaganda

Clark, J.C.D., *English Society 1688–1832: Ideology, Social Structure and Political Practice during the Ancien Regime* (Cambridge, 1985).

Clark, J.C.D., *The Language of Liberty 1660–1832: Political Discourse and Social Dynamics in the Anglo-American World* (Cambridge, 1994).

Dickinson, H.T., *Liberty and Property: Political Ideology in Eighteenth-Century Britain* (1977).

Gunn, J.A.W., *Beyond Liberty and Property: The Process of Self-Recognition in Eighteenth-Century Political Thought* (Kingston and Montreal, 1983).

Kramnick, Isaac, *Republicanism and Bourgeois Radicalism: Political Ideology in Late Eighteenth-Century England and America* (Ithaca, NY, 1990).

McIlwain, Charles H., *The American Revolution: A Constitutional Interpretation* (New York, 1923).

Miller, Peter N., *Defining the Common Good: Empire, Religion and Philosophy in Eighteenth-Century Britain* (Cambridge, 1994).

Osborne, John W., *John Cartwright* (Cambridge, 1972).

Pole, J.R., *Political Representation in England and the Origins of the American Republic* (1966).

Reid, John Phillip, *Constitutional History of the American Revolution* 4 vols (Madison, WI, 1986–93).

Robbins, Caroline, *The Eighteenth-Century Commonwealthman* (Cambridge, MA, 1959).

Schutz, John A., *Thomas Pownall: British Defender of American Liberty* (Glendale, CA, 1951).

Schuyler, Robert L., *Parliament and the British Empire* (New York, 1929).

Thomas, D.O., *Richard Price and America (1723–1791)* (Aberystwyth, 1975).

Thomas, D.O., *The Honest Mind: The Thought and Work of Richard Price* (Oxford, 1977).

Toohey, Robert E., *Liberty and Empire: British Radical Solutions to the American Problem, 1774–1776* (Lexington, KY, 1978).

The war for America

Alden, John R., *General Gage in America* (Baton Rouge, LA, 1948).

Anderson, Troy, *The Command of the Howe Brothers during the American Revolution* (1936).

Atwood, Rodney, *The Hessians* (Cambridge, 1980).

Baker, Norman, *Government and Contractors: The British Treasury and War Supplies 1775–1783* (1971).

Billias, George A., ed., *George Washington's Opponents* (New York, 1969).

Black, Jeremy, *The War for America* (Stroud, 1991).

Bowler, R. Arthur, *Logistics and the Failure of the British Army in America 1775–1783* (Princeton, NJ, 1975).

Brewer, John, *The Sinews of Power* (1989).

Calhoon, R.M., *The Loyalists in Revolutionary America* (New York, 1973).

Conway, Stephen, *The War of American Independence 1775–1783* (1995).

Curtis, Edward E., *The Organization of the British Army in the American Revolution* (New Haven, CT, 1926).

Gruber, Ira D., *The Howe Brothers and the American Revolution* (New York, 1972).

Hargrove, Richard J., *General John Burgoyne* (Newark, DE, 1983).

Hibbert, Christopher, *Redcoats and Rebels: The War for America, 1770–1781* (1990).

Higginbotham, Don, *The War of American Independence* (New York, 1971).

James, William M., *The British Navy in Adversity: A Study of the War of American Independence* (1926).

Ketchum, Richard M., *Saratoga: Turning Point of America's Revolutionary War* (New York, 1997).

Lanctot, Gustave, *Canada and the American Revolution 1774–1783* (1967).

Mackesy, Piers, *The War for America* (1964; rev. edn, 1993).

Mintz, Max M., *The Generals of Saratoga: John Burgoyne and Horatio Gates* (New Haven, CT, 1990).

Nelson, W.H., *The American Tory* (1961).

Onuf, Peter S., ed., *The New American Nation 1775–1820: II, Patriots, Redcoats, and Loyalists* (New York, 1991).

Paterson, A.T., *The Other Armada: The Franco-Spanish Attempt to Invade Britain in 1779* (Manchester, 1960).

Peckham, Howard H., *The War for Independence* (Chicago, 1958).

Reynolds, Paul R., *Guy Carleton: A Biography* (Toronto, 1980).

Robson, Eric, *The American Revolution in its Political and Military Aspects* (1955).

Seymour, William, *The Price of Folly: British Blunders in the War of American Independence* (1995).

Shy, John, *A People Numerous and Armed: Reflections on the Military Struggle for American Independence* (New York, 1976; rev. edn, Ann Arbor, MI, 1990).

Smith, Paul H., *Loyalists and Redcoats: A Study in British Revolutionary Policy* (Chapel Hill, NC, 1964).

Spinney, David, *Rodney* (1969).

Syrett, David, *Shipping and the American War 1775–1783* (1970).

Syrett, David, *The Royal Navy in American Waters 1775–1783* (Aldershot, 1989).

Tilly, John A., *The British Navy and the American Revolution* (Columbia, SC, 1987).

Tracy, Nicholas, *Navies, Deterrence and American Independence: Britain and Seapower in the 1760s and 1770s* (Vancouver, 1988).

Wallace, Willard M., *Appeal to Arms: A Military History of the American Revolution* (New York, 1951).

Ward, Christopher, *The War of the Revolution* 2 vols (New York, 1951).

Wickwire, Franklin and Wickwire, Mary, *Cornwallis: The American Adventure* (Boston, 1970).

Willcox, William B., *Portrait of a General: Sir Henry Clinton in the War of Independence* (New York, 1964).

Wood, W.J., *Battles of the Revolutionary War 1775–1781* (Chapel Hill, NC, 1990).

Diplomacy

Bemis, Samuel F., *The Diplomacy of the American Revolution* (Bloomington, IN, 1957).

Brown, Weldon A., *Empire or Independence: A Study in the Failure of Reconciliation 1774–1783* (Baton Rouge, LA, 1941).

Dull, Jonathan R., *A Diplomatic History of the American Revolution* (New Haven, CT, 1985).

Harlow, Vincent T., *The Founding of the Second British Empire*, vol. I (1952).

Hoffman, Ronald and Albert, Peter J., eds, *Peace and the Peacemakers: The Treaty of 1783* (Charlottesville, VA, 1986).

Madariaga, Isabel de, *Britain, Russia and the Armed Neutrality of 1780* (1962).

Morris, Richard B., *The Peacemakers: The Great Powers and American Independence* (New York, 1965).

Roberts, Michael, *Splendid Isolation 1763–1780* (Reading, 1970).

Scott, H.M., *British Foreign Policy in the Age of the American Revolution* (Cambridge, 1990).

Van Alstyne, R.W., *Empire and Independence: The International History of the American Revolution* (New York, 1965).

Ireland

Doyle, David Noel, *Ireland, Irishmen and Revolutionary America, 1760–1820* (Dublin, 1981).

Edwards, Owen Dudley, 'The Impact of the American Revolution on Ireland' in *The Impact of the American Revolution Abroad* (Washington, DC, 1976).

James, Francis G., *Ireland in the Empire 1688–1770* (Cambridge, MA, 1973).

McDowell, R.B., *Ireland in the Age of Imperialism and Revolution 1760–1801* (Oxford, 1979).

Moody, T.W. and Vaughan, W.E., eds, *A New History of Ireland: IV, Eighteenth-Century Ireland 1691–1800* (Oxford, 1986).

O'Connell, Maurice R., *Irish Politics and Social Conflict in the Age of the American Revolution* (Philadelphia, 1965).

York, Neil Longley, *Neither Kingdom Nor Nation: The Irish Quest for Constitutional Rights, 1698–1800* (Washington, DC, 1994).

Maps

Map 1   The American colonies
After Colin Bonwick, *The American Revolution* (London, 1991) and James L.
Stokesbury, *A Short History of the American Revolution* (New York, 1991)

Map 2   Europe 1775–83
After L.J. Cappon, B.B. Petchenik and J.H. Long, *Atlas of Early American History: The Revolutionary Era, 1760–1790* (Princeton, 1976)

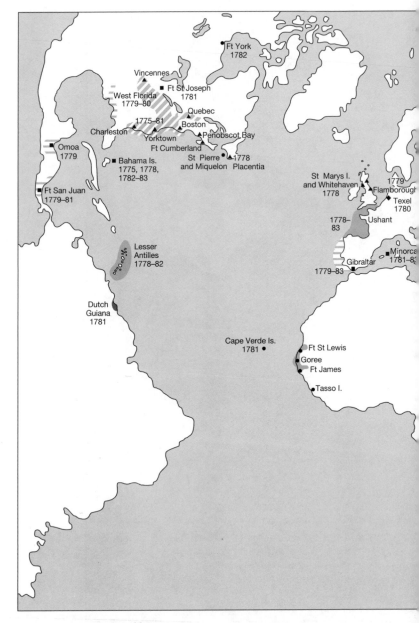

Map 3   Britain at war 1775–83
After L.J. Cappon, B.B. Petchenik and J.H. Long, *Atlas of Early American History: The Revolutionary Era, 1760–1790* (Princeton, 1976)

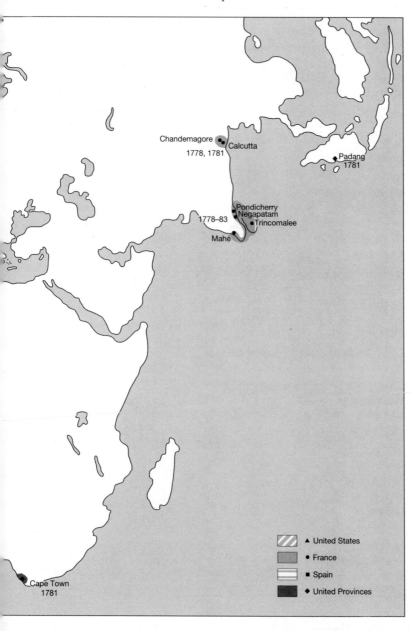

Map 4   The European theatre of the war
From Piers Mackesy, *The War for America* (London, 1993)

Index